CHESTER

CHESTER
A STUDY IN
CONSERVATION

Report to the Minister of Housing and Local
Government and the City and County of the
City of Chester by
Donald W. Insall and Associates

London   Her Majesty's Stationery Office   1968

Typography by HMSO : J. Saville, MSIA/D. M. Challis

Printed in England for Her Majesty's Stationery Office by
St Clements Fosh & Cross Limited, London

SBN 11 750045 3

Preface

This is one of four reports on the historic towns of Bath, Chester, Chichester and York. They were commissioned jointly by the Minister of Housing and Local Government and the City and County Councils concerned in 1966.

The purpose of the studies has been to discover how to reconcile our old towns with the twentieth century without actually knocking them down. They are a great cultural asset, and, with the growth of tourism, they are increasingly an economic asset as well.

The Civic Amenities Act 1967, sponsored by Mr Duncan Sandys, gave recognition for the first time to the importance of whole groups of architectural or historic value and required local planning authorities to designate 'conservation areas' and to pay special attention to enhancing their character or appearance. While the Act was in preparation, the Government decided that studies should be commissioned to examine how conservation policies might be sensibly implemented in these four historic towns. There were two objectives; to produce solutions for specific local problems, and to learn lessons of general application to all our historic towns.

At the same time my predecessor (Mr Crossman) asked Lord Kennet, the Joint Parliamentary Secretary to the Ministry, to convene a Preservation Policy Group. Its terms of reference are :

(i)   To co-ordinate the conservation studies and to consider the results.

(ii) To review experience of action to preserve the character of other historic towns.

(iii) To consider measures adopted in other countries for preserving the character of historic towns and villages, and their effects.

(iv) To consider what changes are desirable in current legal, financial and administrative arrangements for preservation, including the planning and development aspects, and to make recommendations.

Its membership is : J. S. Berry, BSc (Eng), AMICE, MIStructE, MIHE ; H. J. Buck, MTPI, FRICS ; Theo Crosby, ARIBA, FSIA ; A. Dale, FSA ; Prof. Alan Day, BA ; Miss J. Hope-Wallace, CBE ; R. H. McCall ; Prof. N. B. L. Pevsner, CBE, PhD, FSA, Hon FRIBA ; B. D. Ponsford ; H. A. Walton, B Arch, Dip CD (L'pool), ARIBA, MTPI ; S. G. G. Wilkinson (succeeded by V. D. Lipman) ; A. A. Wood, Dipl Arch, Dipl TP, FRIBA, MTPI ; and Lord Kennet as Chairman.

I should like to take this opportunity of thanking very warmly the members of the Group and particularly Lord Kennet. His deep knowledge of historic buildings and enthusiasm for their safety have greatly contributed to the Group's work. This has fallen into two parts.

The first, concluded in the Spring of 1967, consisted of indentifying those changes in the law which would improve our national system for the conservation of historic buildings and towns. The views of the Group were taken into account by the Government during the passage of the Civic Amenities Act 1967 and in devising Part V of the Town and Country Planning Bill. The latter provides a much improved system of controlling alteration or demolition of historic buildings, and makes other important amendments to the law.

The second part of the Group's work, that is considering the recommendations of the consultants, begins with the publication of these reports.

The recommendations the consultants make in these reports are numerous and diverse; with help from the Preservation Policy Group the Government and the local councils concerned will need to consider them carefully. The councils are not committed to adopt any recommendations of specifically local application, nor is the Government committed to adopt the various suggestions of more general application.

We shall now discuss the reports with the councils concerned and with the local authorities of other towns as well. The Preservation Policy Group will co-ordinate these discussions and study their results. Only then will the full value of these reports be seen.

Meanwhile I commend the reports to everyone concerned with the well-being of our old towns, and express the Government's warm thanks to the consultants who produced them.

Minister of Housing and Local Government

Contents

Notes

1 Date

Facts, conditions, ownership, and so on, are as noted during the period of survey, covering most of 1967. The Ordnance Survey base-map was correct to August 1967; our redrawn map is based on this, with further local amendments.

2 Costs, values and standards

All approximate estimates quoted in this report are based on prices ruling at the time of survey (1967), and should be adjusted accordingly. Professional fees are included in all cases. The costs quoted for redevelopment are approximate, based on the outline schemes, and include external works within the curtilage of the sites. The costs quoted for building conservation are totalled from individual cost assumptions by architects based on experience in repairing old buildings. Repair totals for groups of buildings (see also table, pages 232 and 233) are for all those recommended for the Ministry Lists, and exclude all others, and normal everyday repairs.

To arrive at an approximate capital cost, we have prepared approximate estimates of the value of properties in the area, as if for compulsory purchase. The figures are based largely on assumptions. They are on a vacant-possession basis and take no account of existing leases, or of any provisions of the Housing Acts. No allowance has been made for compensation, for instance on the disturbance of tenants, or for anything other than the cost of land.

In assessing budget figures for repair and conversion, we have assumed a good standard of conservative repair. This would set buildings in good manageable order, whilst maintaining their historic identity. Decorations and fittings have been included to a standard appropriate to their architectural status.

3 Responsibility for compilation

This is a pilot study to illustrate a method. The views expressed are the authors' own and are not necessarily those of the Ministry or of the City. While every care has been taken in compilation, no responsibility is accepted by the authors for error or omission either in fact or opinion.

4 Illustration numbering

In order to facilitate cross-referencing, the numbers of the illustrations correspond to the page on which those illustrations appear.

xvi   Abbey Square

Introduction: What should be saved?

Public interest in the conservation of historic places is today widespread and growing. The increasing pace of urban change has almost ironically focused public attention on the nation's architectural heritage. Perhaps, in a fast-moving world, there is some deep-felt social reassurance in the historical continuity of ancient towns. But these towns, the physical expression of much of our civilised history, are highly sensitive to change. Gone is the social and economic system which gave them birth; and without it they cannot always immediately adapt to the harsh pressures of new times. Many have perished forever in the process.

Here in microcosm, the whole problem of managing cities is in fact concentrated in dramatic and heightened form. These close-knit and ancient centres have a powerful vitality that even a persistent and gradual decay of buildings or whole areas cannot easily overlay. Both government and public are becoming increasingly uneasy, because the remarkable planning machine now worked out in Britain still provides so little opportunity for the public initiative needed to protect the past. Recent legislation like the Civic Amenities Act reflects a wide concern at these problems and their urgency, and a growing determination that new energies, new policies and techniques must now be applied in an active policy of town conservation.

Chester is a thriving commercial and tourist city, whose fabric is at once Roman and Medieval, Georgian, Victorian and modern. It exhibits all the pressures and problems of these accelerated 'growing pains'; and the Minister of Housing and Local Government and the Chester Corporation have therefore commissioned this study of the City, not only for the sake of Chester itself, but to help in achieving techniques and policies for the conservation of all historic towns.

Our *approach* has been to study the City in depth, whilst avoiding the temptation to reduce any complex, living place to the terms of a sterile equation. No science can be more exact than its data; and conservation, like all aspects of planning, must be based on a series of assumptions about the future, like a ranging shot on a rapidly moving and distant target. Each element has its own margin of error, and to over-complicate the matter is to make alchemy of planning. We have thus, for example, tried in our study to use clear English, even if sometimes this may over-simplify. If it does so, our survey data is available for reference. But we feel the dangers of simplicity are less than those of pseudo-science, and that simple language is more likely to produce clear-headed planning in a highly complex situation.

Aims and method. The aims of our survey are two: they are to pioneer a method of conservation, and to guide the future development of a particular city. To do this we first study Chester in its regional context, and then focus attention on the City itself, and the physical basis and historic development which led to its current form and townscape. We then examine the influences, destructive and otherwise, of traffic and 'piped' services that go to make up a City's infrastructure, and assess some major land-use trends in Chester. The

economic and financial implications of redevelopment are fundamental and vital, and these are examined in detail, as we believe that
conservation and the management of other assets cannot possibly be
priced separately; they are simply basic elements of all land-use
planning. Tourism is increasingly the life-blood of historic towns, and
to this we have given special attention.

In their terms of reference, the City Corporation has asked for an
assessment of the relative merits of individual buildings, over 400
of which we have now inspected and evaluated. The survey then
turns to selected Study Areas, examining their problems in detail, and
making recommendations for each. The focus of the study is finally
widened in the last few pages, so as to draw together the legal and
administrative problems of conservation on a national scale. This
section of the report tries to allocate responsibilities, and to define the
many authorities and people at all levels of society whose energies
and efforts will be needed to implement a national policy.

Nothing, either in Chester or nationally, will be achieved without
energy, application and incentive. This study tries to apply these
principles practically and constructively by asking: 'What do we
decide to save in Britain's ancient towns, and how do we set about it ?'

1 Chester in its region

1.1 The regional setting

Chester is both a regional, a shopping and a tourist centre, and is affected not only by local pressures but by change in the region as a whole. The growth of Liverpool and its employed population, and new towns planned in close proximity to Chester, will create development pressures in direct conflict to those of the City itself. These new urban environments will also have a built-in advantage: motor vehicles will be able to move around them with a freedom that the street pattern of Chester would never permit.

We must therefore consider whether Chester should try to retain its role as a regional centre, with any consequential damage to its environment; to what extent outside influences will compel the City to adopt this regional status; and whether planning growth in certain areas will enable the older central core to be preserved.

2 Regional transport network

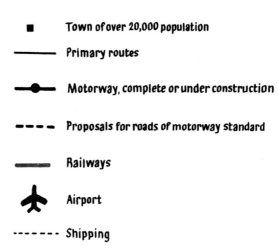

Large town

■ Town of over 20,000 population

Primary routes

Motorway, complete or under construction

Proposals for roads of motorway standard

Railways

✈ Airport

Shipping

2

1.2 Transport networks

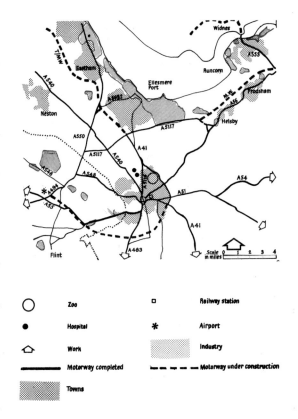

3 Local transport network

Legend:
- ○ Zoo
- ● Hospital
- ⬡ Work
- ▭ Railway station
- ✳ Airport
- ▓ Industry
- ▓ Towns
- ———— Motorway completed
- – – – – Motorway under construction

Chester lies on a crossroads between the exploding conurbations of Liverpool and Manchester and the less densely populated counties of North Wales. Eight 'A' roads meet there (Fig. 3); and six of these form part of the country's primary network (Fig. 2). Chester has always been a gateway to North Wales, and traffic used to pass through the City and across the Old Dee Bridge. The Grosvenor Bridge was opened in 1832 and still carries more traffic than any other road into the City.

A by-pass to divert Merseyside—Swansea traffic on the A41 was started before the war and its northern section is complete. There is a danger that the southern section, shown on the 1950 Development Plan with a Dee crossing to link east-west traffic with the A55 in Flint, might now be delayed in favour of the Queensferry Bridge route (Fig. 3). A further proposal for a possible crossing of the Dee, providing a direct link between North Wales and Liverpool, might well delay the completion of the by-pass which is so urgent for Chester.

As part of the 1967/8 Ministry of Transport road-building programme, some of the A56 traffic is re-routed on to a new motorway to Manchester; and the construction of another road of motorway standard linking the A5117 and running through the Wirral to Birkenhead is imminent. The A55 to Bangor and most of the A545 which runs along the Dee to Abergele are planned as dual carriageways. The effect of these improvements will tend to emphasise the northern access to Chester.

The City is also a railway centre. It is on the Euston to Holyhead line, which serves the North Wales coastal towns, and on the Manchester—Warrington—North Wales and the Paddington to Birkenhead lines. Since the closure of many stations in North and mid-Wales, a coach service, the 'Coastliner', from Caernarvon to Chester, has become very popular. Chester's nearest airports are Speke, near Liverpool (24 miles away) and Ringway, Manchester (33 miles away). Hawarden, only four miles away, is now a private airport and also operates regular passenger services.

The Land Use Transportation Study for Merseyside is expected to be completed in 1968 and will contain important forecasts up to 1991. Until this is available it is difficult to estimate with any accuracy the likely areas of population growth in the region; but it is already clear that the relationship between Chester, the Wirral and Liverpool will soon change radically. The pilot bore for a second Mersey Tunnel is completed and when this road connection is open, traffic capacity will increase by two-thirds, encouraging much more cross-river commuting during the next 15 years.

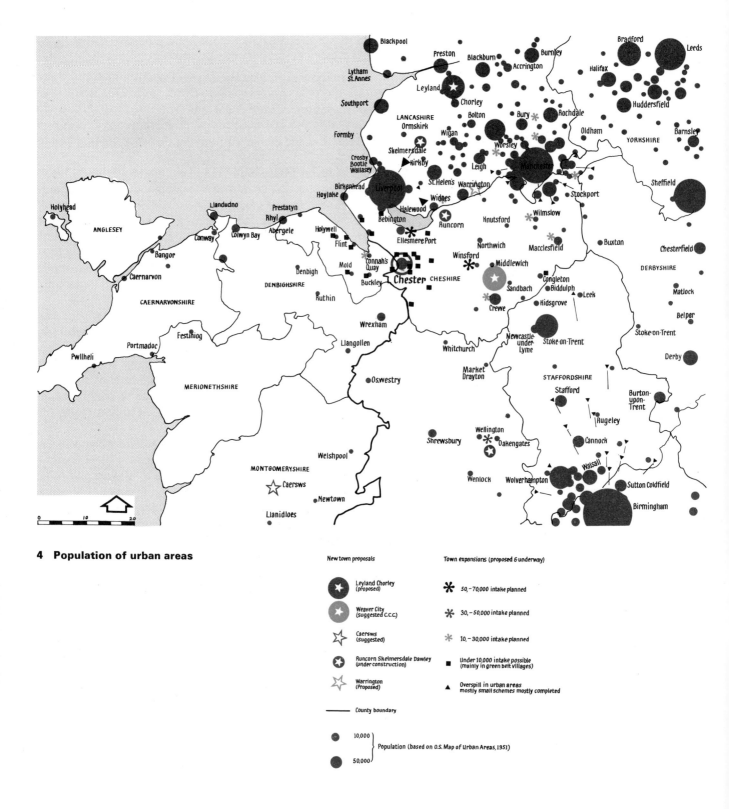

4 Population of urban areas

New town proposals

Leyland Chorley
(proposed)

Weaver City
(suggested C.C.C.)

Caersws
(suggested)

Runcorn Skelmersdale Dawley
(under construction)

Warrington
(Proposed)

——— County boundary

10,000
50,000
Population (based on O.S. Map of Urban Areas, 1951)

Town expansions (proposed & underway)

50, – 70,000 intake planned

30, – 50,000 intake planned

10, – 30,000 intake planned

Under 10,000 intake possible
(mainly in green belt villages)

Overspill in urban areas
mostly small schemes mostly completed

4

1.3 Population distribution

The statistical sources for this subject are legion and intensely difficult to collate. Although the basis for the statistics is constantly changing, it is clear that a huge increase in population is planned for the southern area of the North-west Economic Planning Region.

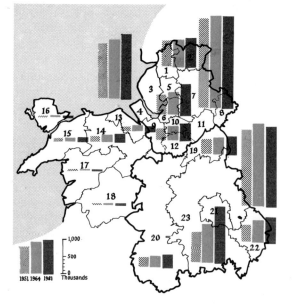

5 Regional population growth

1 Chorley—Preston
2 Blackburn, Burnley, Rossendale
3 North Merseyside
4 South Merseyside
5 Wigan
6 Warrington
7 Bolton, Bury, Rochdale, Oldham, Leigh, Nanch, Stockport, Stalybridge
8 Peak
9 Chester
10 Northwich
11 Macclesfield
12 Crewe
13 Flintshire
14 Denbighshire
15 Caernarvonshire
16 Anglesey
17 Merionethshire
18 Montgomeryshire
19 North Staffordshire Division
20 Rural West Division
21 Central conurbation
22 Coventry belt
23 The rest of the Central Division

Population distribution by Economic Planning Regions			Totals are non-additive		
NORTH-WEST			**1951**	**1964**	**1981**
	Ribble sub-division	1	270,100	288,800	
		2	493,500	475,200	
	Total		*763,600*	*764,000*	*857,610*
Mersey	Merseyside sub-division	3	1,207,800	1,277,100	
Division		4	337,100	419,700	
	Total		*1,584,900*	*1,696,800*	*1,892,750*
	Warrington, Wigan sub-division	5	380,000	390,500	
		6	215,400	233,900	
	South-east Lancashire sub-division	7	2,563,100	2,622,700	
		8	38,000	37,600	
	Total		*2,601,100*	*2,660,300*	*2,684,290*
Total			*4,781,400*	*4,981,500*	*5,479,580*
South	**Chester**	9	91,700	105,700	
Cheshire		10	74,800	81,200	
Division		11	89,200	102,000	
		12	103,500	112,500	
Total			*360,200*	*401,400*	*435,780*
WEST MIDLANDS					5,800,000—5,900,000+
North Staffordshire Division		19	455,400	477,000	
Rural West Division		20	297,100	319,000	
Central Division		21	2,230,900	2,384,000	
		22	494,800	612,000	
		23	904,600	1,121,000	
Total			*3,630,400*	*4,117,000*	
WALES			**1951**	**1966 (civil+)**	
		13	145,279	159,330	
		14	170,276	179,100	
		15	121,140	120,030	
		16	50,660	54,580	
		17	41,465	37,500	
		18	45,990	43,700	

The pattern of new development. Between 1951 and 1961 there was a considerable reduction in the populations of the county boroughs, but a steady growth in the overspill areas that are mainly grouped around the conurbations. Figure 5 shows the growth of population since 1951 and an estimate of the total population for the North-west and West Midlands up to 1981. These estimates are probably conservative, since the figures prepared for *A Regional Study: The North West* in 1965, for example, were based on the Government Actuary's 1962 forecast, and these had to be increased two years later by as much as 20 per cent.

In addition to the new towns that are planned in the vicinity, the 'urban area' of Chester, whose population was 59,500 in 1964, has a possible further capacity of 20,500-21,000 people. In the villages within a radius of 3½ miles of the City, there is an additional capacity of some 7,000. The ultimate population of Greater Chester may well be between 90,000 and 100,000.

It is probable that the planned growth of employment for Liverpool may attract large numbers of people to settle in the Wirral and commute to work. The County Planning Officer for Flint plans to accommodate another 14,000 in eight areas between Chester, Holywell and Mold by 1981, and to the west a further expansion of 8,600 is proposed by the same date in and around Rhyl. Salop County

Council has suggested that Shrewsbury's growth should be accelerated, and that there should be some limited expansion of places like Oswestry. The proposed new-town complex of Dawley and Wellington-Oakengates may tend to restrict even further the present limited catchment area that Chester enjoys to the south.

The shape of future development, which is already unclear due to the conflicting evidence of the available sources, could be even more radically altered by a number of factors. A decision on the location of the Dee crossing would make the chosen place attractive for development, while the Minister's approval, or otherwise, of the Cheshire and Lancashire Green Belt proposals would give administrative authority to the present position.

It is clear that any or all of these schemes would affect Chester radically. Both the new towns and Liverpool's redeveloped centre will eventually compete heavily with the City for the region's custom. On the other hand, however, it is possible that the smaller developments, in the Wirral especially, could turn to Chester as their shopping and social centre. Whether Chester can take advantage of this situation or not will largely depend on the facilities and degree of accessibility that Chester can offer.

Town centre redevelopment. Comprehensive schemes are already proposed for several towns and cities in the vicinity. Liverpool's £10 million precinct with shops, supermarkets, hotels, market and car-park is due to open in 1968; in Bootle, a giant scheme will replace the town centre; and in Birkenhead there is a £6 million scheme for precinct shopping and a market. Wrexham now also has another development project by Grosvenor Laing. It is in relation to, and in competition with these other schemes that Chester must assess the future of its £3 million shopping precinct. This is highly successful at the present time, but it will face considerable competition from the Birkenhead shops in the contest for the Wirral's custom.

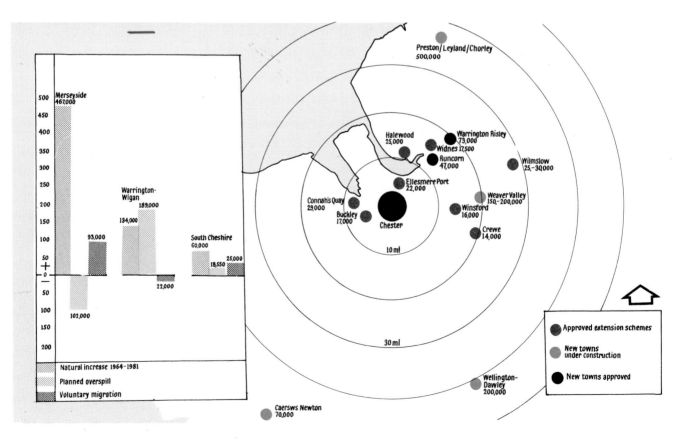

6 Future growth and redistribution of population

1.4 Employment growth in the region

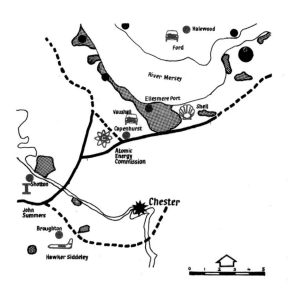

7a Major industrial sites

Figure 7a shows the location of the large-scale industrial sites near to Chester. Other smaller areas lie along the Flintshire side of the Dee estuary. Within the City's boundary, also along the estuary, a 50-acre industrial development is now more than two-thirds complete.

Wrexham's industrial employment is growing fast, and Liverpool has proved very attractive to large-scale growth. The Liverpool City Centre Plan of 1965 estimated that the demand for new office floor space would be about 3.5 million square feet by 1981, but since then a new scheme has been published for an office complex on the waterfront providing another 6 million square feet and bringing jobs for 40,000 people. This rapid growth in and around Liverpool is bound to create a great demand for the residential development of the Wirral. The Dee crossing could create a similar demand in North Wales. Meanwhile, Chester's role is likely to remain as a centre for shopping and the service industries.

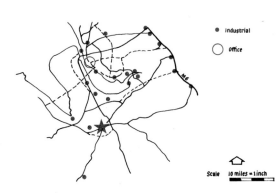

7b Developing employment areas

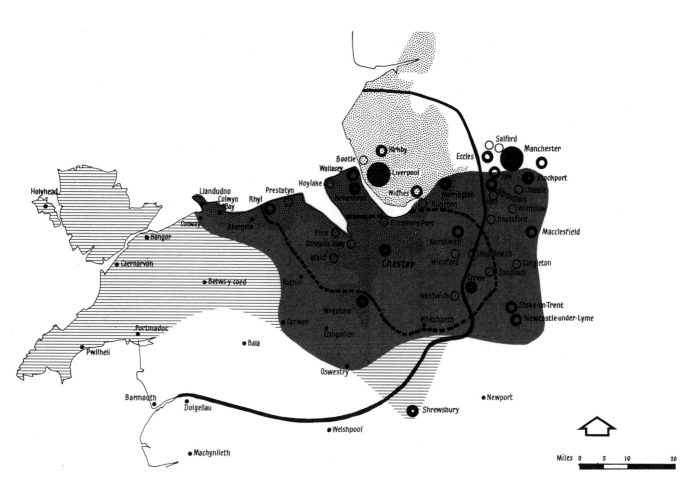

8   Chester's catchment area

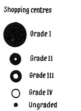

Shopping centres

- ● Grade I
- ◉ Grade II
- ◎ Grade III
- ○ Grade IV
- • Ungraded

Stores deliveries

Chester weekly

Chester 2–4 weekly

Liverpool area

Newspaper circulation

■ ■ ■ ■ Chester Chronicle

───── Liverpool Echo

Miles 0   5   10   20

8

1.5 The City's catchment area

Chester's catchment area for shopping is, of course, considerably smaller than the region just discussed. We have tried to determine this area by examining a number of urban activities that draw potential shoppers to the City and the facilities that Chester's shopkeepers provide for their customers.

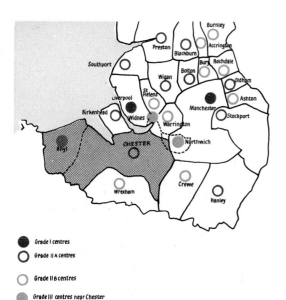

○ Grade I centres

○ Grade II A centres

○ Grade II B centres

● Grade III centres near Chester

9 Shopping hinterlands of Grade II centres

Deliveries (Fig. 8). The managers of three furniture and clothing stores told us that, on the basis of their deliveries, turnover was highest in the area close to Chester; next highest in North Wales and the Wirral; third in Runcorn, Winsford and Whitchurch; and fourth in Wrexham. Some trade reaches the south Manchester conurbation and even as far as the Potteries. These replies substantiated a survey of cars parked in Chester on 7th December 1963, which showed that shoppers came into the City from the same areas in roughly similar proportions.

Bus services obviously affect the shopping pattern closely. An hourly service runs along the North Wales coast to Chester, and there are half-hourly buses from Mold and Wrexham. Extra coaches run on the local village routes on market days. Most longer-distance services go through to Manchester and Liverpool, and this supports the conclusions of the 1961 Census of Distribution which emphasised the attraction of the Grade I centres on journeys of this length against Grade 2 centres such as Chester.

Newspaper circulation (Fig. 8). This shows delivery areas and news coverage of the *Liverpool Echo* and the *Chester Chronicle Series*. The *Chester Chronicle* itself carries advertisements for the Wirral, Crewe, Nantwich and Prestatyn.

The Livestock Market. The market is situated just outside the City walls to the north-east and is over 100 years old. The Tuesday and Thursday markets attract an average of 650 buyers and sellers a week, but a big sale can attract twice this number. Many shops report higher retail sales on market days, and although the local agents say that some buyers come from Anglesey, the Midlands and even Scotland, it is an essentially local occasion. Although it is planned to move the market to Sealand, buyers may continue to shop in Chester out of habit.

Education. Chester has no university, but it does have a new College of Further Education at Handbridge with courses on general academic and technical subjects. The City is also well provided with primary and secondary schools. Cheshire has elsewhere in its area seven colleges of further education and a school of agriculture, while Flint has a college at Connah's Quay. No polytechnics or colleges of advanced technology are planned for Cheshire. The C.A.T.s, like the nearest universities, are at Manchester and Liverpool.

Western Command. The headquarters of Western Command are in Chester on the left bank of the Dee. The Command has some 450 military and civilian personnel, while Saighton Camp has over 1,000 and the Dale 100. Families look to Chester shops for supplies, and the children attend civilian schools in the City.

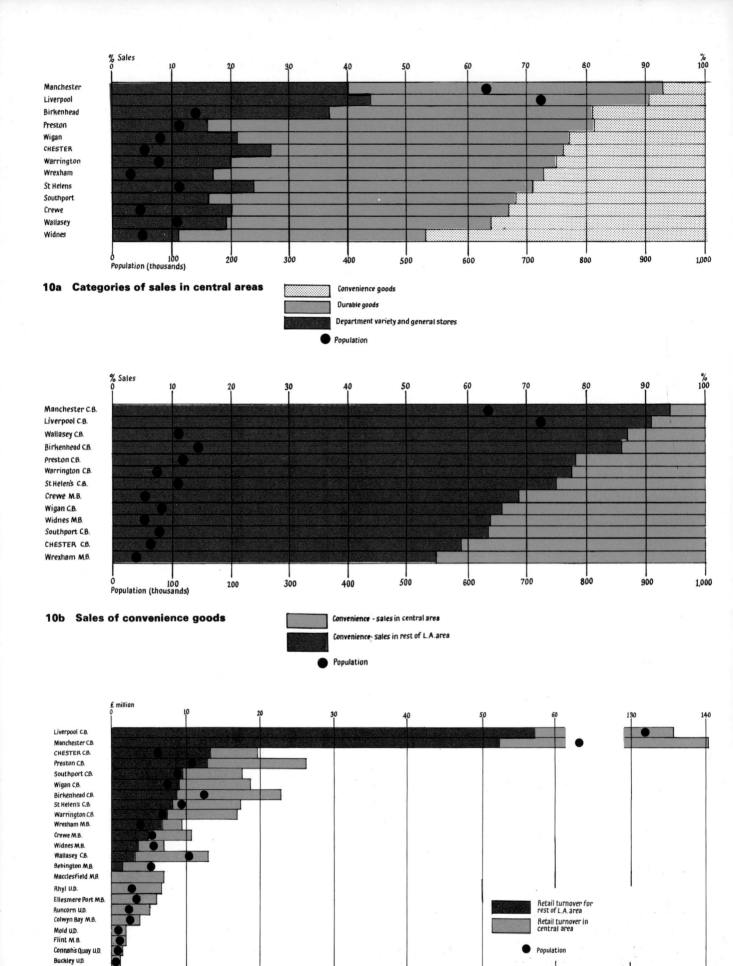

10a   Categories of sales in central areas

Convenience goods
Durable goods
Department variety and general stores
● Population

10b   Sales of convenience goods

Convenience - sales in central area
Convenience- sales in rest of L.A.area
● Population

10c   Central area shopping turnover in the region (1961)

Retail turnover for rest of L.A. area
Retail turnover in central area
● Population

1.6 Retailing structure of the region

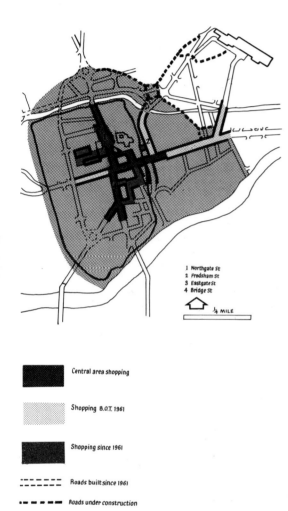

1 Northgate St
2 Frodsham St
3 Eastgate St
4 Bridge St

¼ MILE

■ Central area shopping

▓ Shopping B.O.T. 1961

■ Shopping since 1961

┈┈┈┈ Roads built since 1961

▬ ▬ ▬▬ Roads under construction

━━━ Shopping

11 Chester's central area shopping

In relation to its population, Chester has a very high sales turnover. This can be clearly seen in Figure 10c where towns in the area have been compared by the turnover of their central areas.

Categories of sales. Figure 10a shows a comparison of the same towns with the goods sold in the central area broken down into 'Stores', 'Durables' and 'Convenience' goods. A high turnover of stores and durables implies a regional catchment area, whereas a local centre tends to supply a higher percentage of foodstuffs and everyday supplies. It can be seen that Chester has a high percentage of stores and durables in relation to its population, expressing its regional retailing status.

Figure 10b shows where convenience goods were sold within the same towns in 1961, by the percentage of trade in their central areas. Here Chester ranked low, for it sold a high proportion of convenience goods centrally, as would be expected of a local centre. This is partly explained by the fact that the definition of 'Central Area' was that of the 1961 Census of Distribution. Since then the Shopping Precinct has been opened, which has accentuated Chester Cross as the centre. Shops in Upper Northgate Street, most of Foregate Street and much of Frodsham Street now have shops that serve mainly local residential needs. If sales are examined throughout the local authority area by categories, Chester again ranks high in its sales of stores and durables.

Future retailing structure. A study on *Regional Shopping Centres: A Planning Report in North-west England*, carried out in 1965 by Manchester University, has relevance for Chester's future shopping development. The study postulated the need for a large out-of-town centre in the region, perhaps at Haydock, and was based on the expected increase in retail trade; the possible increase in car ownership and the growth of regional shopping; the inability of Liverpool and Manchester to cope with the full regional demand; and the scarcity and high cost of land. Such a centre would present a great challenge to Chester which is bound to have much less retailing adaptability than Liverpool or Manchester. Chester's prosperity will depend ultimately on its ability to attract the region's custom, and this it can do not only by the variety of its goods but by making the best use of its environmental advantages.

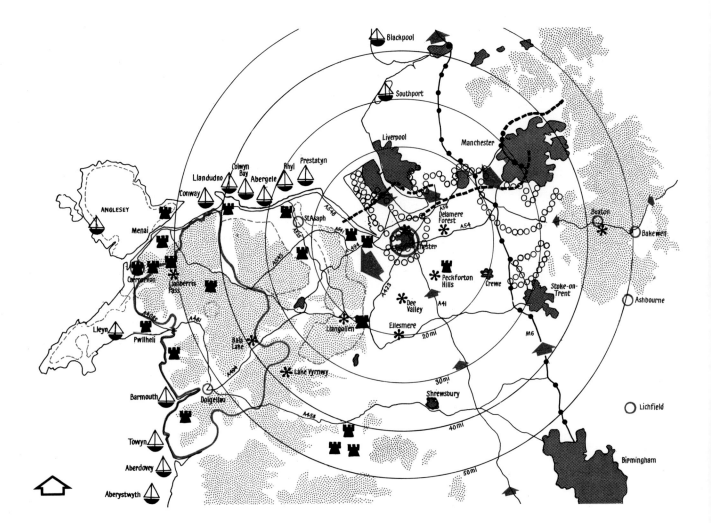

12 Regional tourist centres

1.7 Tourism in the region

Land over 800'
Direction of tourism
Beauty spot
Castle
Seaside resort
Green belt boundary
Areas of beauty and landscape value
Motorway
Snowdonia National Park
Incomplete road
Tourist centres

Chester is in an ideal position for tours to the beauty spots and coast-line of North Wales (Fig. 12). It is also a convenient stopping place for tourists by car who are visiting North Wales. Only some of the scheduled coach trips to these resorts pass through the City, but most of those that do so enter from the east on the A51. Many private hire coaches, mostly on day trips, include a stop at Chester, particularly when the weather does not permit lengthy stays at less protected places. Most tourists arrive by car and during the summer traffic in the area is heavy. A Land Use/Traffic Study for traffic with destinations at Conway, Llandudno and Colwyn Bay has been commissioned by these local authorities in conjunction with the Welsh Office, and this is likely to reveal interesting implications for Chester.

Chester Zoo. The zoo, which is three miles north of the City at Upton, attracts visitors from a wide area. An average of 10,000 people visit it on a summer weekday and 14,000 at weekends. A free coach park is able to take 147 coaches, and a car park 900 cars, but this has to be supplemented on Bank Holidays by the use of a nearby field. On Whit Monday 1966, 4,200 cars parked at the zoo. As the coaches often stay all day, visitors may well come into the town, and, indeed, a regular bus service operates from the market square, so that many people must visit the town *en route*.

C

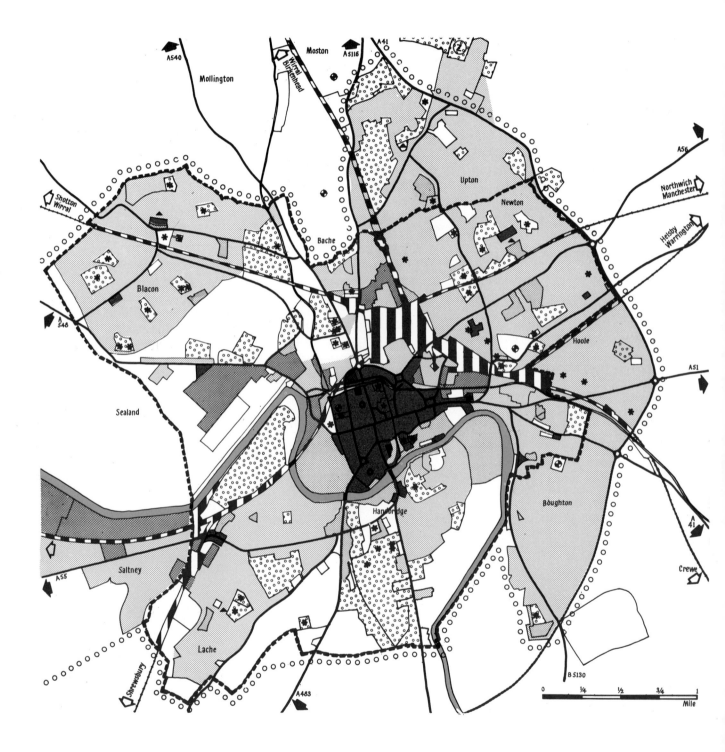

A540

Mollington

Moston

A5116

Wirral
Birkenhead

A41

Shotton
Wirral

Bache

Upton

Newton

A56

Northwich
Manchester

Helsby
Warrington

Blacon

A548

Hoole

A51

Sealand

Boughton

Handbridge

A55

Saltney

A41

Crewe

Lache

Shrewsbury

A483

B5130

0   ¼   ½   ¾   1
Mile

1.8 Land uses in outer Chester

14 Land use in outer Chester

Figure 14 shows a simplified version of the Town Map (Amendment No. 1, 1962) with recent minor alterations, and adjoining areas in the County now built up or planned for development. The map shows planned uses, although within the City boundaries most of the residential areas are already developed. It seems probable that those within the proposed outer ring road will eventually form part of the City. The Sealand area and that by the Dee to the south-east are considered unsuitable for development because of shifting-sand subsoil.

Public open space

Private open space

Industry

Central area uses and shopping areas

Residential

Green belt

Chester County Borough

Primary and Secondary schools

College

Cathedral

Community centre

Administration centre

Hospital

Upton Zoo

C*

FOREGATE STREET

¼ MILE

2 The City of Chester

2.1 Microgeology and climate

Geology.   Chester stands on an outcrop of Bunter Sandstone in the Cheshire Plain, some six miles from the present estuary. This keuper stone underlies the whole of the lower Dee Valley, and its soft, easily eroded quality and deep pink colour are characteristic of the area. Many of the City's landmarks are built of it—the walls, the Cathedral, several churches and the medieval cellars. Mineral deposits still exploited from the plain include coal, boulder clay, salt and iron.

Site.   Chester's rocky position has given rise to some peculiarities in its development. The first streets were built by the Romans on solid rock, and the surface today is in many cases only two or three feet above the Roman level. Cellars have often been carved out of the solid and have natural stone walls and floors. But, where the rock is near the surface, the provision of large underground storeys, car parks, subways or the like is today prohibitively expensive.

Land form.   The highest point in Chester, at the Northgate, is only 120 feet above sea level. Outside the walls the ground declines sharply to the river on the west and south, and the City commands the Cheshire Plain, with extensive and dramatic views to the Welsh Hills in the west. The hilly streets and views over the surrounding country-side give the town much of its shape and interest.

  The river Dee runs round two sides and has saved the City from sprawling uncontrollably in these directions. There are built-up areas beyond the Dee, but the break made by the river and its surrounding land, the Roodee and Earls Eye, both of which are frequently flooded, have kept the old town physically and psychologically separate, and the feeling of entering the centre at the gates is definite and clear.

  The slope to the east of the centre is very gentle, and it is in this direction that Chester has spread since the third century. In spite of this, the skyline and shape of the old City are very marked from as near as two miles away, and the landmarks of the Cathedral, churches and Town Hall stand out clearly.

Climate.   Due to the sharp decline of the land to the west, that part of the City is exposed to south-westerly winds. The climate is other-wise unexceptional. The average rainfall of 27.27 in. per year is naturally lower than in the surrounding high area of North Wales and the Pennines, and is considerably lower than the national average of 36.46 in.

18 Central Chester: geological features

20a   Drawing of the Roman Eastgate, discovered during the demolition of the medieval gate in 1768

20b   A house in Lower Bridge Street built around an outcrop of sandstone (left)

20c   Roman column base of the Principia, now 23 Northgate Street (right)

2.2 Historical background

The Chester of today has evolved from nearly 2,000 years of history. It is a city of contrasts, eloquent of its development; of strength and success on the one hand and vulnerability and failure on the other. The physical shape and characteristics of the Chester we see today are, equally, a synthesis of the architectural styles and social patterns of many ages.

2.2.1 Roman and Saxon Chester

The city owes its existence, its name and its plan to the Romans, who chose the location for a legionary fortress in A.D.76 (Fig. 21a). The site was commandingly positioned between the Welsh Mountains and the Pennines at the lowest practicable bridging point on the Dee. The river, which is tidal up to this point, gave added protection to the raised outcrop on which the City stands: here also there was ample sandstone available for building (Fig. 20b).

The basic grid pattern of the present City clearly demonstrates its origins as a Roman camp. A rectangle with rounded corners enclosed a camp of 59.3 acres, with the *Principia*, or garrison headquarters, on the site of the present St. Peter's Church. Recent excavations have shown that a Roman military hospital existed on the site of the old market. The camp was centred on the *Via Principalis*, the *Via Praetoria* and the *Via Decumana*, the uncompromisingly offset main roads that still form the heart of the City. These principal streets had a width of nearly 70 ft., and contained covered drains beneath metalled carriageways and stone footpaths. The Walls had 26 towers, the bases of some of which are still clearly visible on the north-east and east sides.

As Chester's military importance declined, trading and residential quarters grew up outside the walls, chiefly around Foregate Street, and even today the more random layout of this area contrasts sharply with the straight streets and abrupt right-angled junctions of central Chester. At this time the City developed as a river port, serving such industries as the lead mines of Flintshire, and the axial spine running down to the river crossing is also Roman.

When the Romans left Chester, almost three centuries after the first legionary settlement, the City rapidly fell into decay. The Danes came in the ninth century A.D., but it was the Saxons who rebuilt the City early in the tenth century. Under Queen Ethelflaeda, the walls were restored and enlarged on their present line, giving Chester its sense of enclosure and tight-knit character. The central area was in fact increased to three times the size it had been in Roman days. Until the Conquest, Chester grew in importance as a port and trading centre, laying the foundations of its present-day success.

2.2.2 Medieval and post-Reformation Chester

The last town in England to fall to the Conqueror, Chester was granted the status of a County Palatine in 1070 and was governed by a series of Earls, independent of the King. In 1237, however, the Earldom was annexed to the Crown, and the City used as a valuable base in the wars against the Welsh.

Due mainly to her port, which was the most important in the north-west, the thirteenth and fourteenth centuries became the time of the City's greatest influence and prosperity. Trade flourished with many European countries including Ireland, and raw hides, grain and wine were among the most significant imports. The first of these gave birth to a leather industry in the area, including tanning, and the

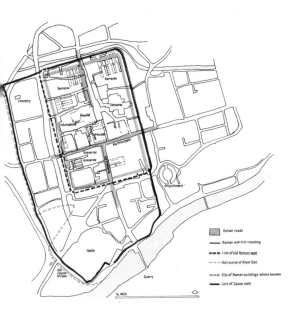

21a   Roman Chester

Roman roads
Roman wall still standing
Line of old Roman wall
Old course of River Dee
Site of Roman buildings where known
Line of Saxon wall

21b   Masonry in the amphitheatre

22a The City Walls

22c Thirteenth-century vaulted cellars in
Watergate Street

22d King-post room in 65 Northgate Street:
the best of Chester's few examples of medieval
timbering

22b Late fifteenth-century Lamb Row, in
Lower Bridge Street, from an etching by Cuitt
(1814). This Row collapsed in 1821

manufacture of gloves and shoes, a tradition that is still carried on today. The arms of a few of the many original Guilds can still be seen at the old meeting place in King Charles' Tower, among them the Cordwainers, Saddlers, Painters, Stationers and Brewers.

The most interesting and intriguing legacy of this productive era is undoubtedly the Rows. Centuries of research have produced no certain explanation for their origins, but P. H. Lawson's theory of a gradual development from early structures built over and against Roman debris is persuasive. The Roman building-line coincides in most cases with the present frontage of the upper Row-level shops, and supports the idea that the ruins on the four main streets were too great to be moved, making it simpler to build on top and in front than to remove them. Gradually the area at street level was rebuilt, perhaps after some of the many fires in the thirteenth century, giving Chester the stone–vaulted cellars at this level that are such an important architectural feature of the City (Fig. 22c). The two oldest churches, St. Peter's and St. Michael's, provide further evidence for this theory, as both have floors 5 ft. above street level. A Saxon tiled floor has been discovered above Roman masonry in Eastgate Street within 3 ft. of Row level.

Within the strict Roman lines, the winding later frontages and some buildings are medieval. The only surviving examples of medieval timber framing we have found are in Lower Bridge Street. Here two plain houses (numbers 30 and 32) seem from their construction to be fifteenth century, and 65 Northgate Street has an excellent kingpost roof (Fig. 22d). Several other houses date from the mid-sixteenth to mid-seventeenth century. The earliest is probably Leche House, in Watergate Street, which retains its original great hall and gallery.

23 Braun's map of Chester, 1581

**24a   Chester Cathedral, before its extensive
Victorian restoration**

24b   St Peter's Church

Although the house has seventeenth and eighteenth century additions, it is one of the least restored of Chester's older 'black and white' buildings. Bishop Lloyd's House, Stanley Palace, the Falcon, Tudor House, the Old King's Head and the Bear and Billet all illustrate the ensuing period of local architecture, medieval in spirit but with Jacobean and Renaissance detailing and decoration.

The only truly medieval architecture remaining today in Chester, apart from the stone cellars and parts of the Walls, is in the churches. Chester Cathedral (Fig. 24a) was founded on its present site in the early tenth century as a shrine for St. Werburgh. It became a Benedictine Abbey in 1093 under Hugh Lupus, first Earl of Chester. The Abbey held great influence and power in Chester, and even today the Cathedral owns a considerable part of the City centre. After the Dissolution in 1539, the foundation was fortunate in being made a cathedral.

The south transept has a curious history of its own. From the foundation of the Abbey it was a parish church, dedicated to St. Oswald, but it lost its parochial role in 1280 to a church in St. Werburgh Street, dedicated to St. Nicholas. The arrangement was unpopular with the laity, and after 50 years the south transept became once again a parish church, and remained so until 1880. St. Nicholas' church has since served as a Wool Hall, a Common Hall, a theatre, music hall and one of the first cinemas in Chester. It is now less appropriately a supermarket.

Of the seven medieval parish churches in Chester only three now remain, and these are very much restored, due partly to the quality of their pink sandstone which easily decays. The oldest of the three is St. Peter's, at the Cross, which dates from A.D.907. St. John's became a collegiate church during the Middle Ages, after having lost its cathedral status when the See was moved to Lichfield. The third is St. Mary's-on-the-Hill.

The characteristic pattern of tightly-packed, tall and narrow facades set endwise along Chester's principal streets is the legacy of the Middle Ages that survives today. Later buildings have largely conformed to it, adding the architectural characteristics of their period to the inherent vigour of the City's main streets. The height of the buildings flanking narrow ways makes it impossible to 'stand back and look', and consequently the view is always oblique and the attention directed to detail. The scale is human, and the pace pedestrian. The spectator moves through a series of immediate and highly localised cameos that are all packed with incident. Most of the buildings are actually of considerable size and their skyline is immensely varied and lively, a fact that reads best from Row level and from the windows opposite (Fig. 24b). In some cities it is said that the 'eye never strays above fascia level': in Chester every level attracts the eye, and every building makes its contribution to the overall street scene.

The City's ancient churches themselves contribute more than the sum of their architectural merit. St. Peter's Church pinpoints the Cross (Fig. 24b), St. Michael's the entry to Bridge Street, and Holy Trinity, the inland half of Watergate Street. All three buildings terminate long views with architectural distinction. The view to the Castle area from the Old Dee is crowned by The Tower of St. Mary's Church. The former cathedral of St. John, which lies outside the walls to the east, is the key element in an area otherwise lacking in focus. The Cathedral itself presides over the north-east quarter of the City centre, and in spite of its size is comparatively unassertive. The squatness of the central tower gives this impression, but principally it is due to the way the City has clustered around it in a manner rather more French than English. In fact, the Cathedral can only be seen as a single composition from the east: this is typical of central Chester where the grand setting is notably absent, and wide open spaces are nearly always damaging.

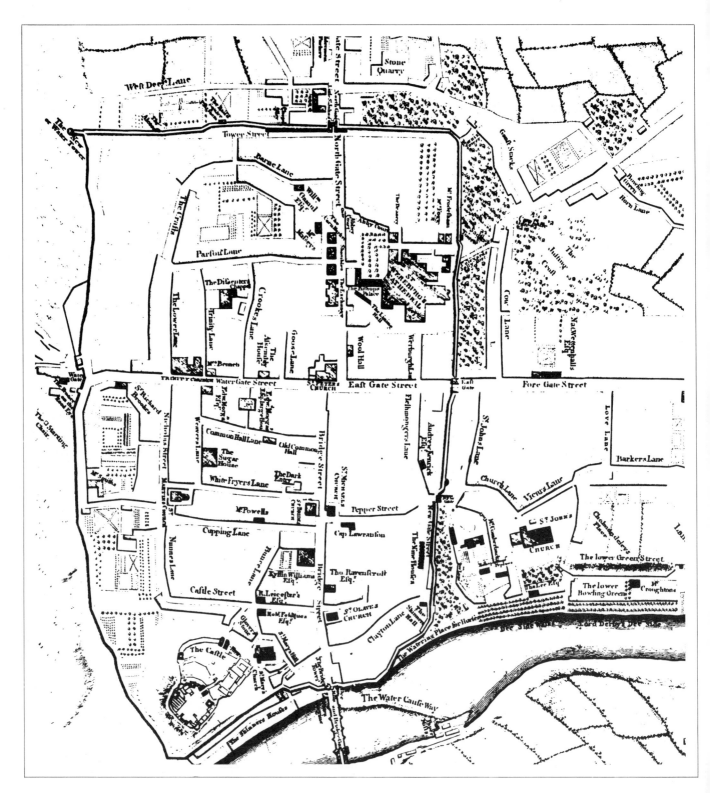

2.2.3 Georgian Chester

In spite of Chester's reputation as a medieval city, much of its character is in reality Georgian. Before 1850, when the Victorian rebuilding started, Batenham's etchings show that most of the houses in the four main streets had been rebuilt or refaced in brick. Whole new developments took place in the eighteenth century, notably in the Cathedral precincts and west of Nicholas Street.

Inevitably, the visitors first sight of Chester is of eighteenth-century buildings. Each of the four main entrance gates was rebuilt between 1769 and 1808 with elegant classical arches and posterns. The Northgate, by Thomas Harrison (1744-1829), built in 1808, is particularly fine, and Harrison's buildings also dominate the Grosvenor Street entry to the City. To reach the Castle, the visitor will have crossed the splendid arch of the Grosvenor Bridge (Fig. 27) which, in 1832 when it was built, had the longest single masonry span in the world. The pure classical style did not reach Chester until almost the end of the seventeenth century, as the medieval tradition of timber framing continued into the middle of the century, with a few mostly internal details from the Renaissance (Fig. 28a). The earliest classical houses in Chester were of a good red brick, usually with stone quoins and keystones, for example some of the houses in Whitefriars, Upper Northgate Street and notably, the Bluecoat School.

Chester's unfortunate history during the late sixteenth and early seventeenth centuries explains why so much redevelopment was necessary in Georgian times. The Dee silted up rapidly after the fifteenth century, and various attempts by the City authorities to improve navigation met with only temporary success. The commercial life of the City suffered a sharp decline in consequence, and throughout the sixteenth century there were severe attacks of plague. Official functions such as the Assizes were moved to other towns, and the City was so badly neglected that grass was reported to be a foot high at the Cross. Recovery from these disasters was delayed by the Civil War, for in 1643 Chester entered a state of siege which lasted for almost two years, reduced the population to starvation and caused damage to almost every building. Several serious fires added to the City's troubles.

26 From a map of the *City and Castle of Chester*: by Lavaux, 1740

27 Grosvenor Bridge, 1832, by Thomas Harrison

28a Early Classical detailing in the courtyard of Leche House, Watergate Street

The Georgian reconstruction of parts of the City was made possible principally by the traditional trade in Irish linen. Abbey Square (Fig. 28b), which was built in the 1760s, was the best of the Georgian developments, and is today one of the town's greater assets. The area originally housed the old monastic brewery, bakehouses and kitchens, and although it was owned entirely by the Cathedral, two or three developers were granted leases and individually and simultaneously built houses different in detail but with an overall uniformity. This typical eighteenth-century practice was common in Chester, and Stanley Place, the terrace in Nicholas Street and King's Buildings were all developed in this way. The Abbey Square houses are a microcosm of Georgian Chester, with all the features that seem peculiar to the City.

One of Chester's greatest attractions, the walk on the City Walls, only became possible after sections had been reconstructed between 1701 and 1708. Many of the medieval towers were adopted as lookouts and resting places, and the whole became not so much an archaeological monument as a pleasant amenity.

After designing the Castle, Thomas Harrison decided to spend the rest of his life in Chester and gave the City its finest Georgian buildings. All his work, from the Commercial News Room in Northgate Street, the Castle and the Grosvenor Bridge to the Northgate itself, was designed with a consistency of detail, scale and thought that placed his buildings above every other of the period in Chester.

The Georgian legacy is twofold. The formality of the larger developments, such as Abbey Square and Stanley Place, fits in well with the Roman 'grid' plan, and the contribution of individual buildings is strong and distinguished, while many are of splendid quality. The Georgian refacing of a number of older buildings in the central streets retained their scale while adding new contrasts. The Canal, which was formed partly from the Roman moat, provides drama by its gorge outside Northgate and evokes a peculiar and compelling interest that this kind of construction always seems to possess.

28b Abbey Square: a mid eighteenth-century development

2.2.4 Victorian and Edwardian Chester

The fervour of the eighteenth-century rebuilding was equalled if not surpassed by the Victorians. After the economic instability of the sixteenth and seventeenth centuries, the City became prosperous again, not as a port or industrial town, but as a county town, business and tourist centre. It is on these same foundations that Chester's prosperity depends today. A few of the traditional industries continued, such as paint, furniture-making, leather work and tobacco, and indeed many still do, but after the nineteenth century 70 per cent of the population worked in non-manufacturing occupations.

Chester's easy communications with the rest of the country was an important factor in her Victorian prosperity. Telford's canal, a branch of the Shropshire Union, built in 1771, linked the City with Liverpool, and in 1848 Francis Thompson designed the railway station as a terminus for six different lines.

In common with many other cities, Chester benefited from the Victorian's delight in expressing their new wealth in building. Happily, the reconstruction fell largely into the hands of four very competent local architects, and it is from them that the City has inherited a legacy of unique Victorian buildings. The earliest of the four was T. M. Penson. His most important extant work is the Crypt House of Brown's in Eastgate Street, designed to be in the same manner as the medieval cellars beneath. Here in about 1858, Penson built the first Victorian 'black and white' building in Chester (26 Eastgate Street). In this building, the timbers were purely decorative and not structural as in later examples.

This revival of the local traditions brought many fine buildings from the mid-nineteenth until well into the twentieth century, and these have successfully deceived generations of tourists. The east side of St. Werburgh Street, by John Douglas, is particularly good. So are the buildings on the west side of Northgate Street, and many individual examples in the Rows and Foregate Street, also by Douglas. T. M. Lockwood, a contemporary of lesser calibre, was responsible for the building on the corner of Eastgate Street and Bridge Street, and for many others.

The greatest exposition of the Victorian attitude is the Town Hall (1869) by W. H. Lynn of Belfast (Fig. 29a), which is monumental in scale and commands everything around it, including the Cathedral. Its neighbour, the recently demolished Market Hall, built in 1862 by W. Hay (Fig. 29a), was a splendid and unique building with a jolly baroque facade whose passing is to be regretted.

30 The Georgian character of Chester before the Victorian restoration work began (from a mid nineteenth-century etching by Gahey)

Victorian building traditions survived for a long time in Chester, and timber–framed buildings were still appearing as late as 1920 (for example, the Old Royal Oak in Foregate Street). Thereafter until the war, there was very little building of note. The pretty neo-Georgian House of Bewlay in Eastgate Street is of the 1920s, and St. Werburgh Row dates from 1935. The realignment and improvement of Pepper Street (1938) involved a rebuilding of the Newgate, designed by Sir Walter Tapper, unhappily with none of the quality or sensitivity of scale of the other four gates.

Although Chester can be grateful to its nineteenth–century City Fathers for continuing its architectural traditions with skill and assurance, it must be conceded that the Victorian legacy is both good and bad. Grosvenor Street, perversely diagonal in a rectilinear City,

seems like a sword slash across the City's face. Streets of mean little tenements push unsuccessful cul-de-sacs into the spare spaces. The tower of the Town Hall overbears the Cathedral. But the Victorian part of St. Werburgh Street, whose diagonal alignment brought it perilously close to repeating the disaster of Grosvenor Street, is justified by the erratic curves and right-angled entries of its medieval footway pattern, and by the quality of its buildings.

Outside the City Walls, the attractive Victorian and Edwardian developments of the Riverside Groves and Grosvenor Park add much to Chester's charm (Fig. 78b). Their sensitivity is a reproach to the pomposity of much commercial and public building of the period, and to the more recent speculative housing of the inter-war years.

32

32   Aerial view of Chester today (pages 32/33)

34a   Sympathetic modern 'infill' need not be 'pseudo' (Lower Bridge Street)

34b   Broken frontage lines and architectural diversity in Bridge Street

2.3 Chester and new building

2.3.1 Definition and clarity

Since the war, Chester has entered an age of rapid change and widespread redevelopment. But the City's historic centre has been firmly restrained from spreading by the encircling girdle of the river Dee, the Walls and the canal. In this way, its definition and clarity have by good luck been saved. Proposals were advanced after the war for still further clearance from the immediate setting of the Walls: even St. John's Street was to have been cleared and laid down to grass. But it seems unlikely and perhaps unnecessary that the walled City will ever be displayed with the nakedness of a Carcassonne.

2.3.2 Imageability

One of the most successful and satisfying features about Chester is its imageability. It is easily understood, and one can find one's way in and around it with ease. This is largely due to the survival of the Roman camp plan, divided into four quarters, each of which now has its own focus. The north-east and south-east quarters are dominated by the Cathedral and the shopping precinct, and the north-west and south-west quarters respectively by the Town Hall (Fig. 32) and by the Castle (and possibly soon, the new Law Courts). The dominant effect of these key buildings must be maintained and reinforced by every possible means. It is vital to maintain and underline in future development the feeling of the rectangular 'City within the Walls', especially within the line of the inner ring road. At the same time, new streets and buildings within the inner ring road should reinforce the north-south grid which is such a marked characteristic of the City.

2.3.3 Street alignment and building lines

The City's ancient layout was once a reticulated pattern of building blocks, subdivided by narrow roadways. Today this is being opened up not only by sweeping modern traffic routes, but by the new structural independence that comes with modern architecture. The visual impact of continuous access ways, tightly walled by tall and narrow buildings, is giving way to wider spaces, less directional and enclosed, and set with buildings at once taller and less related to the city street. One of the most exciting qualities of Chester's central streets is their stepped and broken frontage line. This is accentuated by the varied height of buildings and by exposed flank walls which, in perspective, reinforce the verticality and contrasted individualities within the group effect (Fig. 34b). The enclosure is strengthened by the stopped vistas from north and south to the crossroads.

36a Architectural detailing needs particular care

36b The new Police Headquarters is in scale with the area

36c The skyline of Abbey Square is spoilt by a new office block

2.3.4 Double levels and viewpoints

The City's system of separated pedestrian levels brings a valuable additional dimension. The Rows, with their open pedestrian balconies continued in all the central streets, provide twin levels of circulation and use, and add an entirely new system of internal dimensions, vistas and detail. Visually, they are dramatic, exciting and delightful. Socially, they are the perfect framework for segregated movement and purposeful use. They cater for outdoor living, for the Cestrians liking and talent for impromptu conversation, and for simply leaning on the balcony rails and watching the world go by. Within the Rows, a special effect is the apparent widening of the street (as by a nave and aisles), and these are in turn reduced and enclosed above by the jettied upper floors.

2.3.5 New buildings

The best of Chester's new buildings combine a real efficiency and attractiveness with a respectful sensitivity to their surroundings. Others show some of the difficulties of new design in an historic city.

The contrast of past styles has brought variety, vitality and interest. But the builders of each period were working within a comparatively limited stylistic palette, based largely on natural materials. The result was a basic sympathy, afterwards reinforced by the passage of time.

Certain modern materials call for special care and restraint. Exposed aggregate and shutter-faced concrete suit Chester's face: coloured glass and plastic panels do not. Restraint is needed to prevent the anarchy of some of the latest commercial and medical buildings (Fig. 36a). New vernacular materials can be acceptable, but the gimmick and the architectural cliché are a constant danger.

Other new buildings in Chester have opted out of the problem by their design in 'pseudo' styles. The City's nineteenth—century Revival buildings had a robustness and decisiveness which was all their own, and was specific to Chester, but later semi-modern examples are a disappointment.

2.3.6 Height and skyline

Height and skyline dominance in earlier days were an index of social importance in buildings. Today they are often merely a marker for the highest site values, and a symbol of high-return property investment. The problem is a universal one. But the inward views of the City within its Walls derive much of their present character from the punctuation of its skyline by civic and public buildings. Any change in these in turn brings a specific change in character, sometimes for the better and sometimes for the worse, as two examples may show. The new *County Police Headquarters* (Fig. 36b) is one of the tallest buildings in the City to date, yet by its siting in relation to the Castle and the inner ring road, it marks and distinguishes a formerly somewhat weak approach over Grosvenor Bridge, and avoids all violence to the City centre.

By contrast, the tall and self-righteous block of Commerce House in Hunter Street stands as an unrelated dominant in an otherwise low and clinging roof silhouette (Fig. 36c). Granted that the tower of the Town Hall once did the same, this was at least a mark of status for the civic and administrative centre, which had every public right to assert itself. Between these two, the restrained height and horizontality of the new Market Hall shows how successfully large new buildings can still be introduced into the City's very heart with good manners and integrity.

38 New buildings of rectilinear design with unscreened flank walls (Nicholas Street)

2.3.7 Scale

Essentially, Chester has always been a close-knit City with few powerful dominants and a strong corporate spirit. Its architectural attractions arise largely from domestic scale and intimate visual incident. Framed and prefabricated structures are by no means new to the City. Most medieval buildings were, in fact, just this. But their modern counterparts are not only larger and taller but less varied in their articulation. The result is a bulkier apparent unit size which produces an entirely different rhythm in the street independent of what we normally think of as architectural scale.

In fact, contrasts between the scale of buildings are one of the principal attractions of historic cities. There is nothing more dampening to the interest of a romantic street (as distinct from a classical one) than a uniform facade height, and a universal lining-up with everything. Central Chester has successfully avoided this error.

2.3.8 Individuality

The City's central streets are not only romantic (in the sense that they create their impact emotionally rather than by order) but are made up of strongly individualistic units. There is no form more individual than the pointed gable, and a glance at the street elevations (Fig. 34b) will show how characteristic this feature is in central Chester. The straight parapets and flattened frontages of newer buildings (Fig. 38), while suited to a through route such as this, may help to make the point. Many of the City's most successful new buildings (Fig. 34a) are intensely individualistic.

2.3.9 Integration

A less tangible and more insidious indignity is any building that ignores the street, and by inference the people who use it. Before the days of lifts and concentrated vertical circulation, few buildings could have offered to the footway some 50 yards of continuous and entryless wall, as does a new building in Hamilton Place. In this case, its side-road siting makes it less damaging, but a repetition anywhere within the central shopping area would be disastrous. Interest at eye level meets a simple human need.

Chester's new shopping precinct (1966, architects, Sir Percy Thomas & Partners) is a brilliant achievement in urban revitalisation. Without disturbing the characteristic perimeter facades, it decisively unifies an entire island of city property and provides 72 new shopping units, linked from street to Row level by a beguilingly imperceptible ramp, and bringing new life into the heart of the City's unique covered shopping area. Psychologically, the precinct exploits the 'already indoors' quality that exemplifies so much modern shopfront design. It achieves this with consummate ease and has at the same time a feeling of 'belonging' which makes it perfectly at home with its neighbours. The rear facade to Pepper Street is less happy, being symmetrical and entirely in pink concrete, but in its planning and inside, the precinct is a well-mannered achievement and in every way an asset to the City.

2.4 Traffic and movement

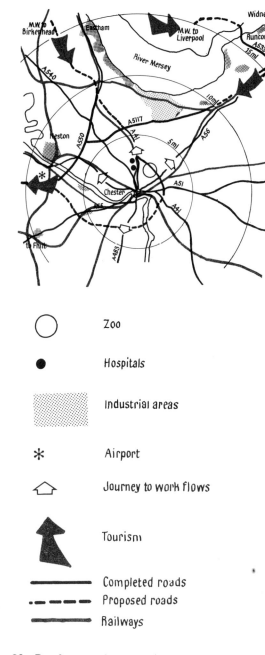

Zoo

Hospitals

Industrial areas

Airport

Journey to work flows

Tourism

——————— Completed roads
-- - —— - Proposed roads
——————— Railways

39 Road networks around Chester

2.4.1 Historic towns and traffic: a paradox

A city is the physical result of civilised pressures towards a concentrated business and social life. This is partly due to the value placed on time and therefore on rapid accessibility, a value which increases with a rising standard of living. But modern methods of communication, like the telephone and teleprinter, have been making centralisation for business purposes less essential. A rising population and increasing car ownership now bring intense congestion and accelerate the trend to decentralise, and even outside the large conurbations, people commute to work over increasing distances. This trend is producing a paradox. The cities which grew over centuries are suddenly beginning to disperse: they remain, however, a focus of routes. Once they were developed for easy communication on foot, but now roads and railways concentrate the daily labour-force and bring commerce to them. Thus in cities with strong human ties and loyalties, the functions change, but the forms remain.

Car ownership and the dispersal of cities. The national economy favours the motor industry. Hire-purchase and concealed subsidies like business tax—remissions bring car ownership within the reach of millions. At the same time, mobility is becoming so important socially that many people spend more on a car than they do on their home. In the United States social pressures have already made the car a necessity, even for teenagers, and have produced a growing pattern of 'out-of-town' shopping.

Car travel in towns demands major highway works financed with public funds. To qualify for grant, road schemes must conform to a rigid standard layout. But in town centres these standards are often inappropriate. They call for the successive setback and straightening of frontages, the splaying of corners, and the dispersal of buildings. This destroys character and penalises the pedestrian.

Car ownership: some limitations. Financial limitations aside, it is impossible for reasons of age, health and eligibility for more than two in three of the population ever to be car drivers. These form a higher proportion of those who travel regularly, but there must always be some 12- to 14-million town dwellers in the United Kingdom who cannot drive.

Striking a balance. If we are to provide a car for every person and a town-centre space to use and park it, the dispersal of towns must follow as night follows day. For the sake of both towns and people, we must stop to ask whether our city centres can survive. In each of them, we must analyse the pattern of movement and match it with every available resource. Research is needed in new techniques, if adequate overhead and underground routes, moving pavements, miniature shopping vehicles and the like are ever to be available. The cost of essential research will be fully justified by the lengthened useful life of our older city centres.

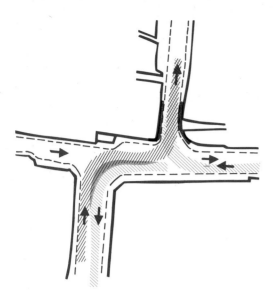

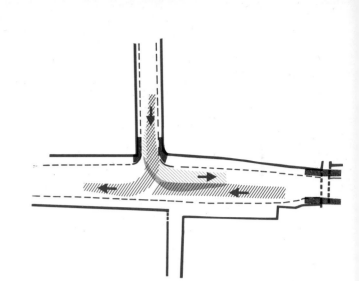

40a Conflicting paths of traffic and pedestrians

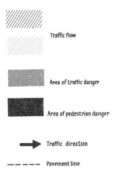

(diagonal hatch)	Traffic flow
(light stipple)	
(grey)	Area of traffic danger
(dark)	Area of pedestrian danger
→	Traffic direction
– – –	Pavement line

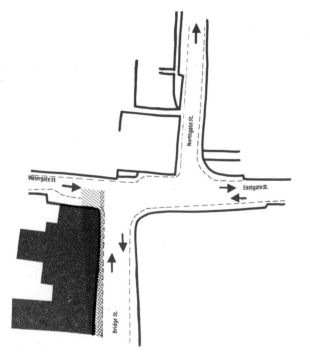

Watergate St.   Northgate St.   Eastgate St.   Bridge St.

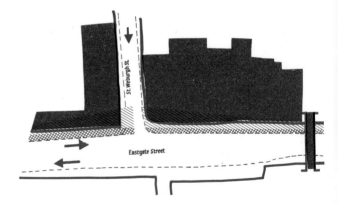

St Werburgh St.   Eastgate Street

40b The demolition of buildings required to achieve adequate vision for traffic

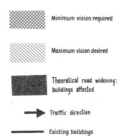

(cross hatch)	Minimum vision required
(diagonal hatch)	Maximum vision desired
(dark)	Theoretical road widening: buildings affected
→	Traffic direction
——	Existing buildings
– – –	Pavement line

41 Shoppers overflow into busy Eastgate Street

Traffic and conservation areas. In conservation areas it is not only the available money which will limit traffic capacity but also the built environment itself. This is the kernel of the problem. Should we for instance, remove the Cathedral to ease traffic movement? Few would permit the actual destruction of what people come to see, merely to make accessible the place where it used to be; yet there are more subtle forms of destruction. The modern road to hell is paved with tarmac and lined by buildings, all financed by conscientious building societies. The most insidious enemy is lack of thought: the next is planning by rule-of-thumb.

To apply standard design criteria to Chester's central streets would be disastrous. The sketch of junctions near 'the Cross' (Fig. 40b) shows which buildings would be demolished if we designed by regular criteria, only for traffic. The other sketch (Fig. 40a) shows the dangers and restrictions to pedestrian and highway traffic which result from Chester's historic buildings today. It can be seen how stringent the demands of the motor vehicles are. Turning circles and sight-lines need immense elbow-room, and the tightly built fabric of our old centres simply cannot meet these demands.

The capacity of cities. The logical course in congested urban areas, if they are not to be rebuilt, is clear. It is:

a. to decide, after survey, what buildings and environmental elements we can and what we cannot afford to lose;

b. to provide the best possible pavement and carriageway systems, within the limits so defined; and then

c. to organise for maximum efficiency of vehicle and pedestrian circulation within this allocated space.

All extra traffic must be directed to other routes, which in turn must not overpower the areas through which they pass. The touchstone is to plan for maximum efficiency and attractiveness, consistent with capacity.

Within a town centre the solution is thus to control capacity. Roads which narrow to points of constriction cause chaos; widening elsewhere merely makes the problem worse. The carriageway width between kerbs should be constant and laid out to give a distinct pattern of traffic lanes. The only logical answer is first to decide which points cannot be widened, then to design the remaining system to match, and to keep these lanes clear in the same way as a pipeline. Away from these lanes in the space remaining, lay-bys and service bays can then be provided and clearly defined by different surfacing. On some of them, limited stopping might be allowed; others may have to be allocated, for example, to specific shops with a regular van-service. No bus stop should ever be in such a position that it succeeds in halting traffic for a quarter of a mile. A clearly marked lay-by is safer, even if over its short length it has to borrow space from pedestrians. Where this is impossible, there is no place for a bus stop (Fig. 41).

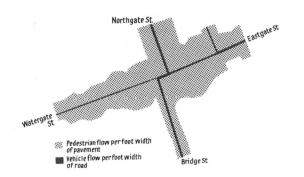

42a The utilisation of space by pedestrians

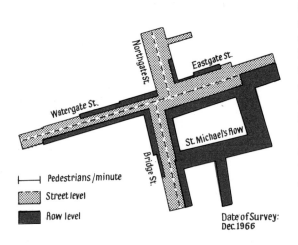

42b Pedestrian flow in the Rows area

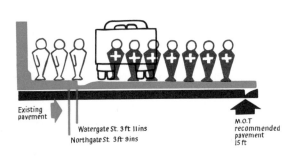

42c Actual and recommended pavement widths

2.4.2 Movement patterns in Chester: the pedestrian

Our terms of reference exclude the full movement survey which will eventually be needed. But if Chester is to retain its attraction as a shopping and tourist centre, travel to the shops must always be stimulating and never a chore. And shopping itself should be a pleasure, not a running battle with traffic queues, noise, fumes and danger. Chester will increasingly have to 'sell' itself, if its prosperity is to continue.

In our survey, we have set first in importance Chester's most important visitor—the shopping pedestrian. All shoppers, however they travel to a centre, shop on their own two feet. Chester owes her success to her concentrated attractiveness to the pedestrian. How can this be reinforced for the future? The answer is again to organise for *'maximum efficiency and attractiveness, consistent with capacity'*.

Figure 42a shows how much more intensively pedestrians use town space than vehicles do. Demand for the precious space in a city centre comes from both vehicle users and pedestrians alike. But our counts of pedestrian and vehicle flows on a normal Saturday morning showed that vehicle users make very inefficient use of this space: in addition, the densely used pavement system alongside busy traffic routes brings dangers. Principal accident points are shown on Fold out Map 1 which analyses the pedestrian system in the study area, and the main hazards and 'pinch' points on it, such as those where there is insufficient room for two mothers to pass with prams. On the principal streets, some crowded routes (as shown) have pavements too narrow for safety. The Ministry of Transport recommends for central shopping areas 1 ft. of pavement width for every 10 to 15 pedestrians per minute, plus 3 ft. of 'window shopping' space. The minimum pavement width recommended is 15 ft. In Chester, the narrowest pavement in Northgate Street is 3 ft. 9 in. and in Watergate Street 3 ft. 11 in. Figure 42c shows the recommended widths and the present footway widths for the purposes of comparison.

Most ancient towns were basically pedestrian. Through the centuries, their footways have been paved and raised. When this happens the kerb-lines are usually parallel with the buildings, leaving between an irregular space for vehicles. Since then, carriageway improvements have frequently been made at the expense of the footway. In Chester, as in many historic towns, the town-centre carriageway pattern needs careful redesign. Every foot of space, however irregular, which can be paved and given back to the pedestrian, will carry more shoppers in safety. Pedestrians circulate naturally on pavements of varied widths, and do not need parallel 'lanes' so much as space in which to circulate, and this is especially so in front of shops.

The system of pedestrian routes in the Chester conservation area is the product of centuries. The original Roman 'grid' of streets followed the standard plan of a legionary camp, but later growth reflects nature's rules for footways—sensitivity to barriers, to levels and to hazards such as flights of steps.

The Rows. While cities elsewhere strive for shopping segregated from traffic by levels, Chester has enjoyed this facility for centuries. Our survey brings out strongly that accessibility and prosperity go hand-in-hand. The new Row-level shopping precinct is exemplary in segregating pedestrians, private cars and service vehicles. It is approached by ramps and lifts and is a successful, convenient and attractive place for housewives with prams, and for shoppers. An upper-level link across the inner ring road (Pepper Street) would complete the system of safe pedestrian ways to complement the unique advantages of the Rows.

43a   Steps into Eastgate/Bridge Street Rows are low, wide and inviting

43b   Those at the opposite corner are dark, steep and little used

We recommend the following further pedestrian improvements:

a. easier and more inviting access points to an improved upper Row in Eastgate (north) and to Bridge Street (west) at the Cross (Fig. 43b);

b. a new stepped approach to the Row at the south end of Bridge Street (west side);

c. bridged links between individual Rows on the west side of Bridge Street together with the closure of the roads beneath them; and also

d. on the north side of Watergate Street at Goss Street, linked directly with the new market;

e. when Watergate Street becomes pedestrian, as is planned, two bridges from Row to Row would greatly help the prosperity of these upper shops; and

f. a pedestrian way to join the severed ends of Watergate Street, under the dangerous Nicholas Street.

The City Walls form a continuous, raised pedestrian circuit, away from the street traffic—a two-mile perimeter promenade. The best access points are where the land form provides natural ramps: elsewhere, approach steps are a deterrent. The new footbridge from the shopping precinct is a valuable addition at the east.

The pedestrian routes. In the town centre the routes evolved when the whole population lived in that area. Today most people have to travel to the town centre, and arrive through the bus stations, the railway station or a car park. Frequently the pedestrian routes from these places into the town centre are poor. More attention is needed to these vital connecting links.

In connection with the Bus Station proposals (page 52) for example it would be possible to provide a highly attractive approach into Chester past the Cathedral towards Town Hall Square. The route from the car parks to the shops must be especially clear.

Filling stations

Car parking

Multi-storey car park

Garages and car showrooms

Limited waiting

¼ MILE   JULY 1967

44a   Car parking in Chester

44b   Hypothetical parking area to accommodate all Chester's cars

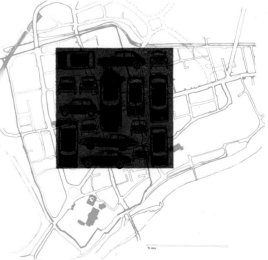

44

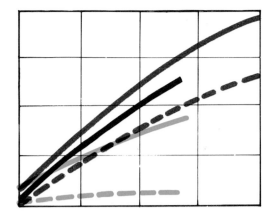

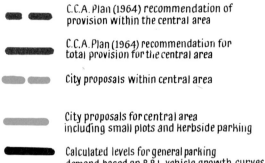

- - - C.C.A. Plan (1964) recommendation of provision within the central area

——— C.C.A. Plan (1964) recommendation for total provision for the central area

- - - City proposals within central area

——— City proposals for central area including small plots and kerbside parking

━━━ Calculated levels for general parking demand based on R.R.L. vehicle growth curves

45a Car parking provision

2.4.3 Car parking

Parking is the link by which the private motorist becomes a pedestrian. The parking principle adopted in Chester has been to reduce kerbside stopping and to concentrate empty vehicles in large multi-decked parks. Based on the 1960 figures, these are planned to provide spaces for about 9,000 vehicles within the central area, and 3,500 outside. Already the cars owned by the population of Chester, if parked together, would fill a space nearly half a mile square (Fig. 44b), and yet car ownership is expected to double in 10 years.

In the City plan there will be 10 car parks with good access to the ring road. For the motorist, they will be easy to find and use, but once he becomes a pedestrian, the route to the shops must be easy and clear.

The first car park buildings are of concrete construction and probably more permanent than the changing vehicle types they will have to serve. In view of the constant evolution in vehicle sizes and types, it may be more logical to build and finance parking structures which are more easily demountable, for instance in steel rather than in concrete. This would enable them to be adapted more easily to future vehicles. Meanwhile preference could be given in allocating space to encouraging the smaller types of 'city' cars. So far, most new car parks have been architecturally bleak, and some in Chester are exposed to viewpoints higher than themselves. A notable exception will be the car park beneath the market hall. Modern parking buildings have perimeter screening: in overlooked situations a top screen is needed too. Many car park constructions are as unsightly from inside as they are from outside.

The clarity of Chester's route system is a basic ingredient of the historic centre, but it is less good in some modern development. Clarity for motorists, both in and out of their cars, deserves considerable attention. In multi-decked structures for example, the sense of direction could be strengthened by strong numerical and colour coding.

Under normal conditions, the car parks so far constructed can cope with a total of about 600 entering and leaving vehicles per hour. But the present system is often inadequate, especially on Saturdays when queues for entry interfere with the main roads. Longer service links, careful junction design and more rapid handling would help.

45b Fully used street-level car park

45c Some parking structures are not well patronised

46a Traffic volumes

2.4.4 New roads: Chester in change

An increasing proportion of central area users arrive by car (Fig. 46a). In Chester, since 1960, a bold traffic plan has been adopted and is now half constructed. It entails a new inner route to carry cross-town traffic from over the Dee by a circuit northwards through the City Walls, with roundabout junctions north and east of the old City.

Physically the new traffic route is a barrier to free circulation within the walls, and this has brought problems. But the traffic congestion is eased, and the blood-letting has perhaps paid off. At peak hours the traffic flows already approach the designed capacity figures, and as soon as the road is completed, more detailed studies will become urgent. The completion of the outer ring road is of the first urgency for Chester.

The future capacity of cities for cars has too often in recent years been confused with estimates of future demand, based upon projections from a short period of increase in post-war car travel. There might well be many people who could theoretically be tempted into the town. But is there room for everyone to come by car? The urban environment has a limited capacity, and road building is like feeding the pigeons: the more you give, the more will come.

The inner ring road. The completed *north-west section* of the new inner ring road covers approximately 1,000 yards between the Castle and Northgate Street (Fig. 46b). Outside the City Walls, it is elevated over the canal and railway, and is designed to M.O.T. standards as a primary distributor road. Roads of this standard carry a flow of over 2,000 vehicles per hour each way with ease. Within the Walls, the road has junctions at intervals of approximately 100 yards, which

46b The new Inner Ring Road

Miles per hour

| 0 | 10 | 20 | 30 | 40 | 50 |

47a Driving speeds in central Chester

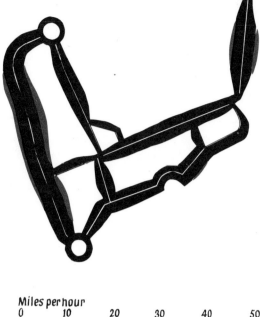

47b Pedestrians are crowded by a bus negotiating the Cross

reduce its capacity to about 1,200 vehicles per hour each way. Already, traffic counts show average flows at weekday peak hours of about 900 vehicles per hour each way on this road, and full capacity will surely be reached as soon as the inner ring is complete. The *north-east section* is designed to carry similar flows of traffic, and plans show side turnings as on the north-west section.

The southern section (from the Bars to the Castle). This is some 1,000 yards long, and although it incorporates older winding streets with many junctions, it is a visually attractive route along which to drive. Its capacity as now upgraded is approximately 750 vehicles per hour in each direction.

The inner ring takes the only possible line, and until the outer by-pass (planned since 1923) is completed, it must serve the interim dual function both of by-pass and of inner distributor road. It has been designed as a 'free-flow' route with roundabouts at major junctions.

On this kind of road it is smoothness of flow and constancy of speed which enables maximum volumes to be achieved. Overloaded round-abouts with fast connecting links intersected by access roads provide neither for rapid journeys nor for safety. Figure 47a shows typical vehicle speeds on the major roads at the time of survey. The system rapidly deteriorates when it is overloaded, and traffic control systems then have to be introduced.

Free-flow or 'green wave'. The capacity of the inner ring and the speeds at which the motorist is tempted to drive vary considerably from one section to another. The north-western section of the inner ring is already interrupted by a set of traffic signals at Watergate Street, partly to enable pedestrians to cross. It is almost certain that as congestion increases, the most efficient use of the inner ring will be achieved by controlling it with phased signals, electronically linked for the best use of all available road space. A system could be developed to refuse entry to the central area inside the inner ring road, whenever the central area space is being used to its acceptable limit. The signals could also be used to monitor the approaches to car parks, directing motorists to the nearest available spaces.

Central area traffic. Within the inner ring, the plan so far adopted provides for unrestricted access to the Cross by public service and delivery vehicles, with the aim of reducing private through-traffic by one-way systems and breaks. Watergate Street is to become pedestrian, and Town Hall Square will be largely pedestrian but also open to buses.

The proposal for one-way use of the Bridge Street to Foregate Street route, complementing Union Street to Pepper Street, was aimed to achieve maximum vehicle flow. It would immediately produce an increase of up to 50 per cent in the volume of traffic through the town centre. Rather than this, it seems better that, as at present, the southern section of the inner ring road should be retained as a two-way 'weak' link. This could be done partly by controlling the development along it. For instance, in the present city plan, 1,750 car parking spaces have access from it, and this could well be reduced, with compensations elsewhere. Traffic entering the town centre itself could then be strictly controlled by traffic management measures, for example, prohibition of the turns from Grosvenor Street and Pepper Street into Bridge Street would reduce congestion at the Cross.

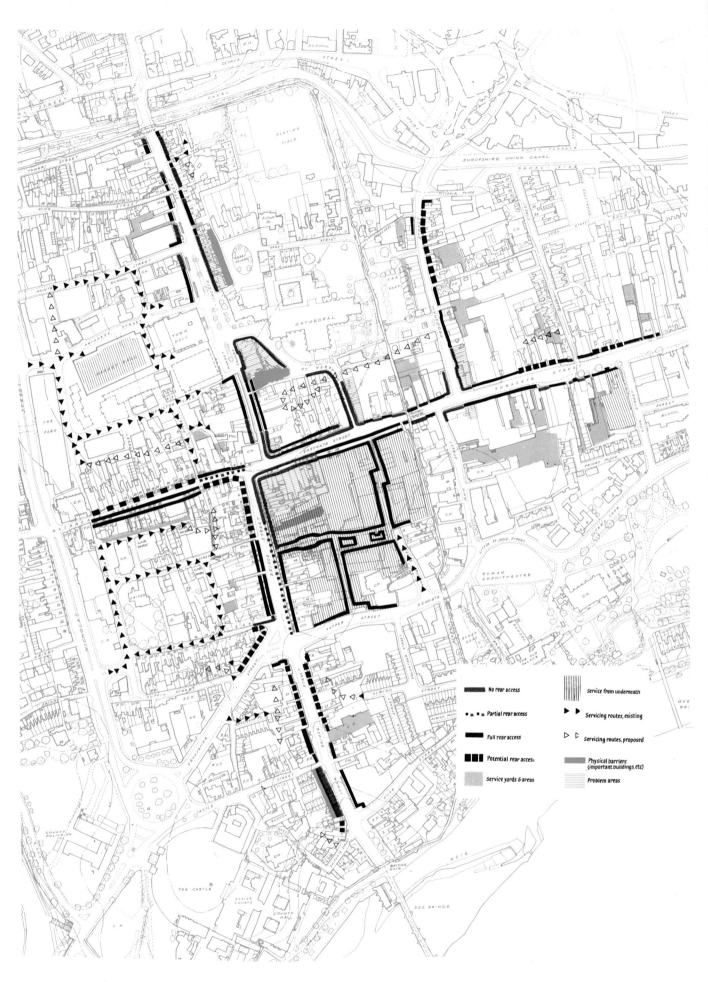

▬▬	No rear access	▥	Service from underneath
▪▪▪	Partial rear access	▶ ▶	Servicing routes, existing
▬▬	Full rear access	▷ ▷	Servicing routes, proposed
▮▮▮	Potential rear access	▨	Physical barriers (important buildings, etc)
▦	Service yards & areas	▤	Problem areas

48 Goods deliveries

2.4.5 Goods deliveries

We carried out a sample survey of shops within the area of the Cross. Service access for goods in Chester's central area is most restricted in the areas shown in Figure 48. Service traffic consists mostly of regional deliveries by large vehicles, local regular services, and continuous work like grocery deliveries, or waiting during service calls by the driver. The trend is constantly towards much larger delivery vehicles and increasing numbers of servicing vans.

These shops receive about 20 deliveries per week. Four-fifths of them need goods service daily; 15 receive over three deliveries an hour. In addition, there is daily refuse collection. At present, some 18 to 20 vehicles are often present at any one time within the area of the Cross. This is a most serious traffic consideration in these narrow streets (Fig. 49).

Deliveries to the new shopping precinct, with its excellent upwards servicing from a lower deck, have been made possible by taking advantage of the slope of the land. But provision is still needed for perimeter shops without any rear access. If this proves impossible, preference may have to be given in planning control to users with minimal servicing requirements.

To prevent abuse by short-term parking, rear service roads in town centres may have to be open only to commercial vehicles and closed to private cars. Distinctive surfacing and possibly 'gateways' or snap-down bollards may help. Service routes should be reasonably direct but should prevent through-travel. Where in Chester roads serve more than one purpose, patrolling will be necessary. Service roads should be planned with easy access from the inner ring road. Direct goods loading is undesirable from the ring road itself. These service roads need careful detailing and take much space. It seems likely that, for example around Goss Street, any new housing (earlier suggested by the City Plan) would be difficult to accommodate.

Giant vehicles such as car delivery transporters have no place in the centre of cities. They should be banned from passing through the historic centre. Lorries delivering locally cause enough confusion of themselves (Figs. 50a/b/c).

Between Eastgate Street and St. Werburgh Street, the Chester Central Area Plan suggests that segregation by levels might again be followed, but headroom for access will be difficult. An alternative is to establish a central delivery point, possibly in Goss Street, with local delivery by electric trolleys, similar to those used on railway stations.

Good rear access roads are not only imperative but increasingly urgent. Ideally, they need unrestricted access; clear 'through' lanes, planned for lorries with the largest of turning-circles; and well-defined standing bays, especially if long waiting times are likely to be needed.

50a Lorries parked in Bridge Street (right)

50b Trucks dominate pedestrians in Northgate Street (below)

50c Lorries negotiate parked vehicles with difficulty in Foregate Street (bottom right)

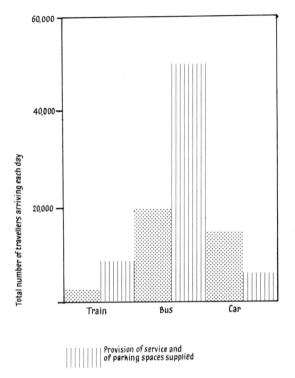

51a Modes of daily travel

||||| Provision of service and of parking spaces supplied

Actual utilisation of passenger seats and of parking spaces

51b Chester bus routes

2.4.6 Public transport in Chester

Other than by car, people arrive in Chester's centre by rail, coach and bus (corporation or private) (Fig. 51a).

Rail. The rail service is being simplified, and Northgate Station is to be closed. Good services connect with Liverpool (35 minutes) and Crewe (20 minutes) from where the line is now electrified to London. The railway station is not particularly convenient or well-equipped and needs improvement. The link to the town centre, at present through City Road and Foregate Street, is by taxi, by bus every 15 minutes (2 hours on Sunday) or by a 15-minute walk. From the other end of the line, in Liverpool, the routes and services to Chester are by no means clear or easy to find. Chester's shops need to sell themselves better than this. A direct rail service between the two cities is also desirable.

Coach. Private touring coaches visiting the City are at present allowed to park at the Zoo, the Riverside or the Roodee. On wet days, they are sometimes diverted from scenic countryside tours for a day in Chester, but the City lacks a well-equipped centre to cater for these visitors. For people leaving on tours, the coaches stand in Hunter Street. Better provision for this means of travel is clearly needed.

Bus. There are two bus undertakings with separate stations. The corporation buses operate from the Town Hall Square, and a public company (Crosville) from Lower Bridge Street, Delamere Street and the Town Hall Square. The latter has regional services over the whole area from Liverpool to Wales, and runs express buses from Liverpool, Chester, Cardiff and London. In the Central Area Plan (1961), new termini are proposed behind the Town Hall and beyond the Northgate, across the canal at Delamere Street, but this means most present services would still traverse the town centre. In fact, over 1,000 buses already depart daily from the Town Hall Square, an astounding total (Fig. 53b).

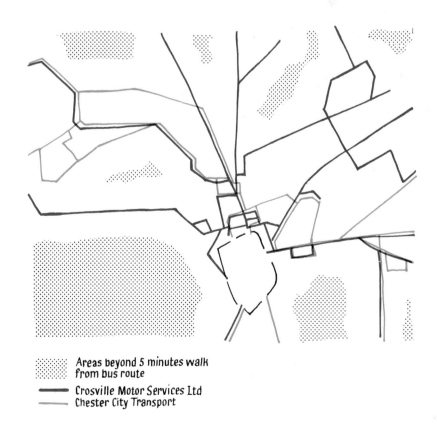

Areas beyond 5 minutes walk from bus route

━━━ Crosville Motor Services Ltd
─── Chester City Transport

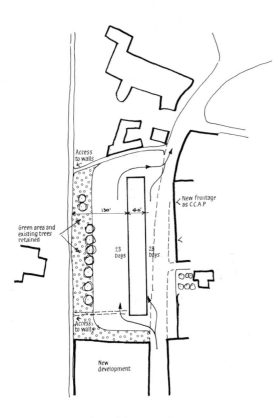

52a Proposed new bus station in Frodsham Street: alternative scheme 1

Suburban bus routes are quite good, and outer Chester has few places which are more than ten minutes from a bus stop. Only improvements on the actual frequency of services can combat increasing competition from the private car. The City Plan suggests two new bus stations, both of which would be a considerable distance from the focus of shopping activity and the major stores in Eastgate and Foregate Streets. Present proposals for car parks would then give private motorised travel a fatal advantage over public transport.

2.4.7 A new central bus station for Chester

A new bus station is currently projected by the City Corporation. But in the face of competition with other new shopping centres, Chester can afford to lose no trade, and the best possible access for both regional and local shoppers is vital for the City's continued success.

We therefore suggest a more *central position* for the new bus station, with immediate access to the principal shops. Part of the land is by good fortune already available outside the City Walls in Frodsham Street, hard by the old Hop Pole Paddock: certain adjoining shops may have to be displaced and rebuilt as suggested.

Any new central bus station in Chester must be a well-appointed and efficient centre, with every facility, like indoor waiting rooms, luggage, toilet and rest rooms, and a well-run information desk for timetable (bus, coach and rail) and tourist enquiries. It must segregate passengers from vehicles, their noise and fumes, and may require two-level planning with escalator service. (Liverpool has already set the lead in its new Pier Head bus station.) The upper deck can be directly linked by a footbridge to the City Walls, taking pedestrians to the shopping precinct, or past the Cathedral into Town Hall Square.

The sketches (Figs. 52a/b and 53a) show alternative ideas. Scheme 1 is the more conservative but provides less facilities. We recommend Scheme 2, which could be built in two stages, and incorporates integral space for shopping.

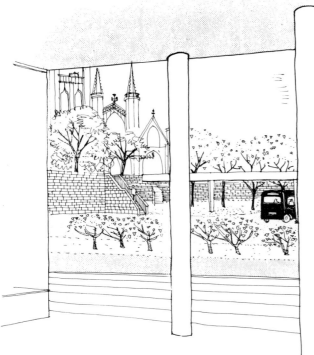

52b Perspective from Frodsham Street of the proposed new bus station (scheme 1)

53a   The new bus station: scheme 2

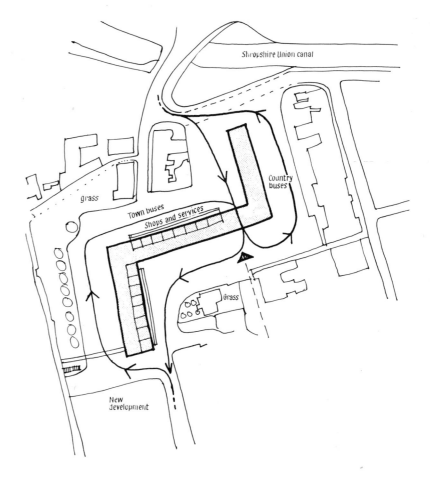

The bus routes approaching the new bus station are shown in Figure 53a, which also shows the service links with the New Market. All routes are shown in the map; and the new station would clear empty buses from Chester's crowded central streets and allow a better service. It could also cater for the coach traffic which is at present so neglected.

To reduce peak-hour congestion at the centre, 'commuter' services only could operate from peripheral sites such as Delamere Street outside the ring road. Otherwise this should, we suggest, be used only for a temporary service and later for coach parking, limiting any expenditure on permanent buildings. In this way advantage could be taken of new national policies which may in turn financially favour this more advantageous new proposal for Chester.

A Highway Use Authority.   All movement systems in a city must be integrated and planned with their land-use activities. Bus services, for example, should connect with all major train services. The new bus centre should make possible an entirely new level of efficiency in the economic use of all available facilities. Efficiency, and not subsidy or raised costs, can alone succeed. A policy is needed, based on the provisions of the White Paper on Transport Policy (1966), to improve, develop and integrate all public transport on the widest economic basis in the public interest, and with the primary aim of maximum service. A new Highway Use Authority could advantageously be formed, to operate from the new bus centre. Its duty would be to co-ordinate all the modes of transport best suited to Chester's needs. The executive officer should have the backing of the Ministries of Transport and Housing and Local Government, and would be in a position to pioneer the implementation of the new Whitehall policy, as an example to other cities, both old and new.

53b   Buses parade past the Town Hall

54a Competing modes of transport

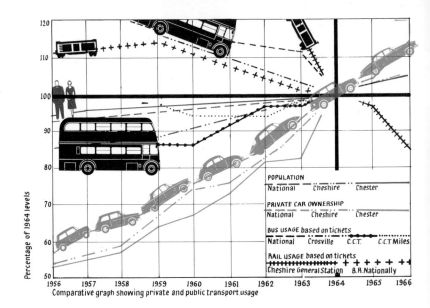

Comparative graph showing private and public transport usage

POPULATION
National   Cheshire   Chester

PRIVATE CAR OWNERSHIP
National   Cheshire   Chester

BUS USAGE based on tickets
National   Crosville   C.C.T.   C.C.T.Miles

RAIL USAGE based on tickets
Cheshire General Station   B.R.Nationally

Percentage of 1964 levels

54b Traffic danger to pedestrians in The Groves

54c Delivery vehicles disrupt the passage of buses in Eastgate Street

55a Traffic noise levels

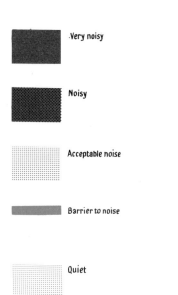

- Very noisy
- Noisy
- Acceptable noise
- Barrier to noise
- Quiet

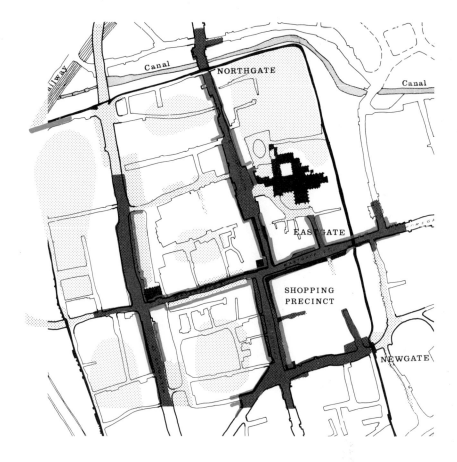

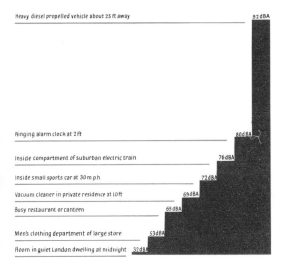

Heavy diesel propelled vehicle about 25 ft away — 92 dBA

Ringing alarm clock at 2 ft — 80 dBA

Inside compartment of suburban electric train — 76 dBA

Inside small sports car at 30 m.p.h. — 72 dBA

Vacuum cleaner in private residence at 10 ft — 69 dBA

Busy restaurant or canteen — 65 dBA

Men's clothing department of large store — 53 dBA

Room in quiet London dwelling at midnight — 32 dBA

55b Comparative noise levels

2.4.8 Environmental standards and transport

Traffic noise. Excessive traffic noise is unpleasant, especially in shopping areas, and is detrimental to urban living. We examined the traffic noise in Chester on a typical weekday. The results are shown in Figure 55a, and lead us to recommend that noise surveys are carried out in all historic town centres.

The meter we used records levels of noise over a range of frequencies matching the response of the human ear. The main points brought out in the survey map are:

a. The high average reading over much of the central area of Chester;

b. The extent to which noise is increased when trapped between high buildings. The worst situation is in Northgate Street, where levels reached 83 decibels. This street is plainly unsuitable for pedestrian shopping with heavy vehicles noisily accelerating and climbing from the Cross. In narrow domestic streets like Castle Street, the noise of a bus is a major nuisance. Office users on wider roads like Nicholas Street are much less seriously affected;

c. The improvement given by screening is remarkably effective. On the upper deck of Nicholas Street car park, noise from the street drops away rapidly when screened by the structure;

d. Tall buildings are less successful in escaping from town and traffic noise than screened enclosures like Abbey Green. Within the Green non-reflecting surfaces also help to silence the area, rather like towels in a bathroom.

A curious feature is that the high noise level in St. Michael's Row, the older part of the shopping precinct, almost equals that in Northgate Street, although in practice it seems less annoying. By contrast in the new shopping precinct with built-in sound absorbents, the background noise is much reduced. Noises that one subjectively associates

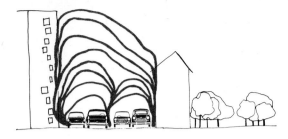

with dangers (buses, lorries, and so on) are more annoying than others. Urban noise control is worth careful research, perhaps by the new Centre for Environmental Studies.

Reducing noise-irritation for occupants receives more attention than external noise in vehicle design. Sometimes the external noise is sought after, rather as a kind of virility symbol. The law exists, but it needs to be enforced.

56a   Echo in narrow streets

56b   Noise screening

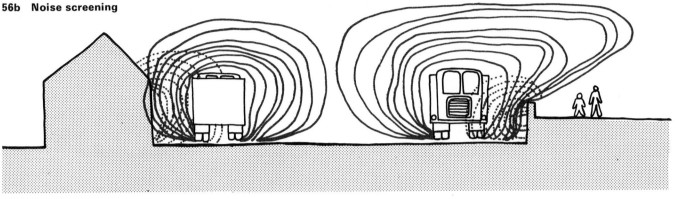

Other environmental studies.   Noise is only one aspect of the conflict of traffic and pedestrians. Standards for the safety, comfort and convenience of the pedestrian lag painfully behind those of the highway user. Chester has started to remedy this in implementing some of the *Chester Central Area Plan* recommendations of 1964. But in smaller places, the nettle has yet to be grasped. Some authorities have completely pedestrianised town centres, and it has been found that a real cash return results from this new preoccupation with shopping comfort and convenience.

Conservation areas call for more flexibility, and for layout standards more sympathetic to the scale of the environment. Even modest roundabouts occupy just over an acre, and smaller free-flow junctions are likely to be ineffective. Multi-level intersections may absorb 5 acres or more of valuable town centre land. Here the trouble is often the excessive minimum headroom requirement of 16 ft. 6 in., allied to the gradients and ramps needed in interweaving levels, and now that cities are increasingly 'double-decked', this figure should be reconsidered. In restricted spaces, much can be done by signals, which can handle and direct motorists and pedestrians, and deal with awkward manoeuvres, for instance turning buses.

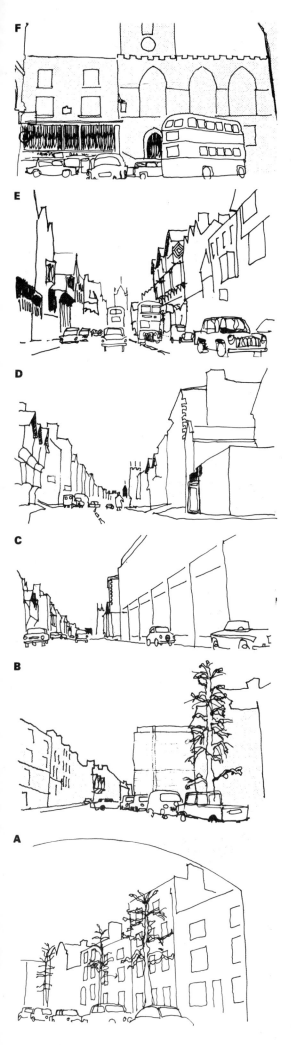

2.4.9 New roads and Chester's historic character

The biggest single component of the urban scene is the road. The appearance of the highway is an important element in urban design. Jarring road signs and visual clutter proliferate because too many people have responsibility for the organisation of highways: the result is visual chaos, and confusion for road users.

To demonstrate the different aspects of the environment in the city centre, we compared the route from Bridgegate to the Cross with the route along the ring road between the Northgate and Grosvenor roundabouts. Two completely different environments emerge. The first is an old and delightful street, with much visual activity and interest, which has grown slowly and naturally over the centuries. It is this that people come from many countries to see. The scale is suited to the pedestrian. Figure 57 shows changing views in a journey up Bridge Street to the Cross. Its best elements are: the variation of buildings, unified by the clarity of the overall form; the element of 'surprise', the buildings leading on to what one cannot see; and the importance of 'landmarks' like church spires, which enable the motorist to gauge his progress and give a sense of orientation.

Figure 58 shows a journey along the new ring road. The environment here is for the motorist rather than the pedestrian. The most noticeable points are: (a) clear 'route form' and landscape views of the mountains at the north end; (b) through the footbridge, a loss of clarity, among confused surroundings (confusion makes for danger both for the motorist and the pedestrian); and (c) at the south end, grouped trees and the formal Castle approach, restoring the definition and identity of the route, which swings away to cross the Grosvenor Bridge.

In our speeds survey, a distinct drop is noticeable at points of surrounding visual muddle. The relationship between road safety and the driver's freedom of vision is clear, especially where the 'scale' of the route is an incentive to high speeds. The motorist reacts strongly to his environment.

As important as the effect of the road upon the driver is its appearance in the whole fabric of the town. Road design and construction is one of the country's biggest investments. Yet unlike individual buildings, which fall within detailed town planning control, urban roads receive little co-ordinated environmental design. In conservation areas, the scale and character of roads must be handled with the utmost care to relate successfully the new and the old.

The integration of the new inner ring road into Chester has been greatly helped by using indigenous materials. But such considerations do not necessarily deal with the essential forms and design components of the highway. The art and science of kinetics needs more thorough study than it yet receives, and here again is a subject for the new Centre for Environmental Studies.

57 Sequence of changing views along Bridge Street to the Cross
A. framed view of terrace at the entrance to Bridgegate; B. semi-enclosed space formed by new buildings, but which entices the eye beyond to the next scene; C. the church tower is the target point, and the new building is out of scale with the varied small-scale architecture of the street; D. a new view opens with a target of the Town Hall beyond; E. the church tower replaces the Town Hall spire; F. the target, the Cross, is reached, and the distinctive terminal building in a different material emphasises the obvious need to change the direction of travel as the linear enclosure of Eastgate and Watergate Streets emerges

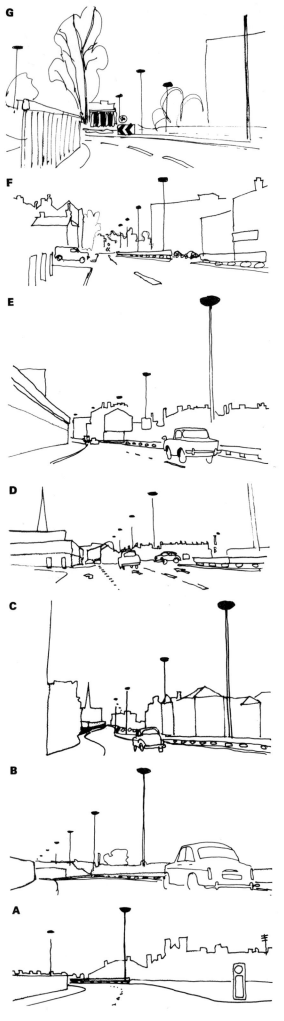

New traffic in old cities can only be resolved by providing:

a. defined routes for through traffic;

b. proper facilities for essential service vehicles;

c. easily accessible and efficient car parks;

d. a first-class public transport service; and

e. safety and comfort for the pedestrian.

In this, the sequence must be:

a. to assess the traffic and generation demand;

b. to arrive at appropriate environmental standards; and

c. to design road patterns, traffic management measures and pedestrian systems to complement the environment.

A summary of our detailed proposals for dealing with Chester's traffic is shown in diagrammatic form in Figure 59. To implement them satisfactorily, not only in this city but in other historic towns, involves not only more expense, but also a more ingenious investment of available resources, and better co-ordination between all the various authorities concerned.

2.4.10 Transport proposals: a clarified system of priorities

Primary distributor roads (inner ring): southern section. Two-way traffic returned along the Pepper Street route with signals at the two main junctions, limited right turns and no left turns into Bridge Street.

Western section. Capacity improved by limiting right turns between Grosvenor Street and Northgate roundabouts to two light-controlled junctions and closing end of roads not required for service access.

Access and service roads. Access improved by completing service roads north of Watergate Street and west of Bridge Street; linking the west ends of Princess Street and Hunter Street; and by widening Grosvenor Park Terrace north of The Groves.

Public transport. A single new central bus station in Frodsham Street giving direct pedestrian access to the central shopping area at street and City Wall levels. St. John Street is made one-way from south to north to give bus access from the southern section of the inner ring.

Private transport. Main car parks are close to the inner ring road and follow previous proposals; but their size especially on the south side is limited to the capacity of the primary distributor.

58 Sequence of changing views along Nicholas Street
A. deflection from roundabout, with a clear route ahead; *B.* the target is the bridge, and the wall and entrance signify a distinct place; *C.* within the City Wall, the scarred ends of buildings can be seen, and on the long downward slope the only punctuation is the church spire; *D.* mixture of scale on all sides, and little target on the road; *E.* car park on the left and a gap and muddled backscape on the right; *F.* the end of the route in sight with trees and distinctive signing at the termination; *G.* motorists deflected on to a new route

Pedestrian improvements. Priority is given to pedestrians within the central area. Watergate Street is pedestrianised with its western end linked by an underpass below Nicholas Street. The ends of lanes into Watergate Street and Bridge Street are closed with new footbridges linking the Rows at these places. The narrow western and eastern sections of The Groves are also pedestrianised.

59   Transport proposals for Chester

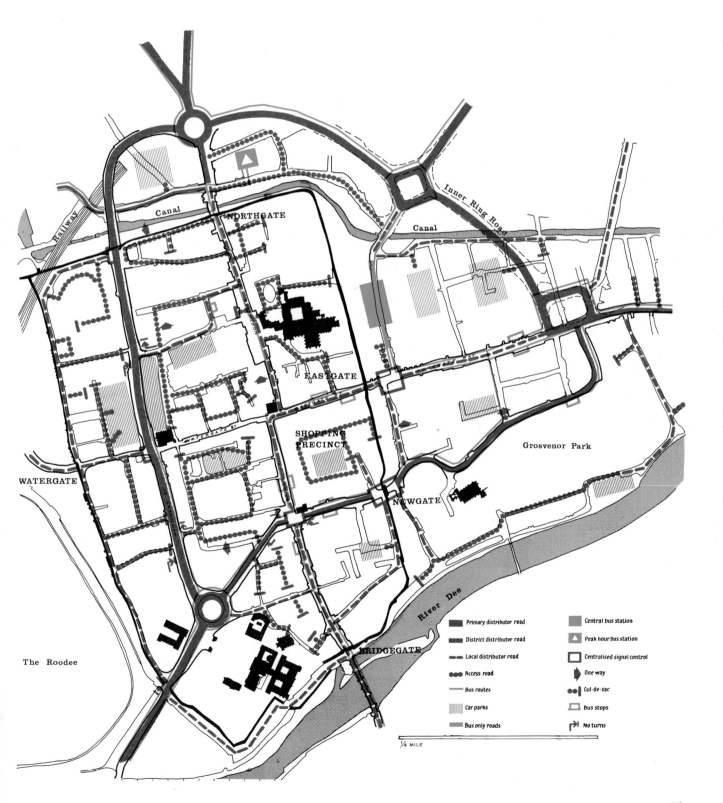

Primary distributor road	Central bus station
District distributor road	Peak hour bus station
Local distributor road	Centralised signal control
Access road	One way
Bus routes	Cul-de-sac
Car parks	Bus stops
Bus only roads	No turns

¼ MILE

2.5 Chester's services

2.5.1 Water

Chester has a good supply of soft water. Fragments of Roman lead pipes, medieval earthenware and hollowed wooden ones have been recovered. In 1600 a water tower was built on Bridgegate. Today's supply is chiefly from the Dee. Some 4½ million gallons are filtered daily, sterilised and pumped to water towers supplying taps up to 174 ft. above Ordnance Datum. Water is pumped through 256 miles of mains in a multi-directional network of pipes.

60a   Water services

2.5.2 Drainage

Main sewers in central Chester are under the streets at depths from 8 to 16 ft. The oldest are of brick, and some are large (up to 48 in. diameter). Some have channels cut in solid rock. The main outfall is along the right hand bank of the Dee, supplied by major branches at Bridgegate, Souter's Lane, Dee Lane and Watergate Street. Some of the old brick culverts have collapsed under modern traffic, and newer sections are in stoneware or concrete, while many older ones are lined with plastic tubing. The occasional manhole still occurs in busy roadways, but to facilitate inspection, television cameras can now be sent along inside.

Large-bore gravity sewerage, like old-fashioned heating systems, might in future give place to localised processing with disposal into pressurised circuits in small-bore tubing. Immovable underground pipework, as a barrier to roadworks and underpasses, may then be a thing of the past. The River Dee at Chester is polluted by sewerage, but steps are being taken to overcome this as soon as possible.

60b   Drainage services

2.5.3 Gas

The gas service in Chester is apparently well organised, and only the unsightly gasholder brings the comment it deserves. High-pressure storage is promised within a very few years, and this should create a better local 'image' for gas.

2.5.4 Electricity

Electrical services are of necessity relatively modern: most cables in Chester run underground. The use of electrical power in Chester has increased between 1963 and 1966 by 50 per cent. To spread the load, cheap rate electricity is now offered during afternoons and overnight on a series of off-peak tariffs for storage space and water heating. Greatly increased use is likely to be made of the facility. Night store heaters are very suitable in older buildings, because they can be installed with so little structural disturbance.

2.5.5 Heating

Many buildings in central Chester are heated by oil. Deliveries are at present made by tanker separately to individual premises, and it seems possible that by arrangement with the oil companies, combined tanks could be sited for groups of buildings, with a metered supply to private service pipes. This could well at one time ease the traffic problem and produce economies in supply, giving to oil the advantage of a more competitive price.

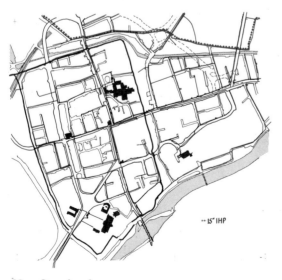

60c   Supply of gas

61a Electrical services

61b Telephone facilities

61c G.P.O. permanent underground walkways for services.
Although the G.P.O. adopts this system in certain urban areas, underlying rock would make it impractical in Chester

2.5.6 Postal services

Postal delivery services in Chester are complicated by the separate numbering of the Rows; and the numbers themselves are often very difficult to find. In Chester as elsewhere, efficiency could readily be improved if the G.P.O. were to insist upon clear numbering as a condition of prompt delivery.

2.5.7 Telephones

The telephone service is the voice of the city. Chester's exchange serves a large area, although in practice its own lines seem inadequate. Within the walled City there are only ten call boxes. None are within the Rows area, none in the Castle area and none in the neighbourhood beyond Nicholas Street. Space is hard to find, but call boxes are essential in an area of over 300 busy shops.

The Rows, with double the shopping facilities of a normal street, make a customary spacing of call boxes ($\frac{1}{4}$-mile apart) irrelevant. The provision of new boxes is based on the profit made by existing ones. The two latest are wall kiosks in the shopping precinct (the only ones at Row level), but they are difficult to find. The stainless steel booths cost £250 apiece (against £110 for a standard kiosk) and attract little custom. Chester's Planning Committee rightly objects to too many free-standing red boxes. Red is the traditional colour, and is easy to find, but it is important to allocate attractive positions for well placed wall-boxes, both in new developments and among older buildings.

Telephone service lines in Chester are mostly underground. They were first in cast iron, then in steel. Now they are in fireclay with access trapdoors well placed clear of roadways. The only exception is at Newgate, where the roadway has been realigned, and the manhole left behind.

2.5.8 Building maintenance

Facades in the narrow central streets are remarkably well maintained. If as traffic increases it becomes any more difficult to stand ladders in the street, it may be worthwhile to set aside holidays or occasional Sundays (as with the railways) entirely free of through traffic for maintenance work.

2.5.9 Road maintenance

Stone setts are disliked by maintenance engineers. They are expensive to lay and clean and can become slippery when wet. But their craftsmanship is a joy, and their texture varies the dominating effect of road surfaces so near to eye level (Fig. 62a). In Chester, except for special locations, stone setts as elsewhere are gradually being submerged in cold asphalt and tar. St. Mary's Hill has some setts covered with asphalt, so that 'no parking' could be written on the road!

Stone paving is mostly being renewed in concrete, except in gardens or special areas. At the time of reporting, the cost when new is £7 per yard for stone, and 25s. for concrete. Concrete does not stand up well to wear and needs expensive maintenance. Old stone paving in our older towns is valuable and deserves grant aid. Its repair in areas like the Cathedral precinct should qualify for help from the Historic Buildings Council (Fig. 62b).

Decorative cobbling as at St. Martin's Gate is becoming popular but can look 'contrived', if used without logical reason. It is, however, better than thoughtless, universal tarmac.

62a Attractive 'floorscape' in Abbey Square

62b Careful maintenance is necessary

62c/d Two examples of graffiti

63a Converted lamps in Abbey Square

63B Town lighting: a check list

1 The chief failing in most town lighting is that rules are often adopted without thought from techniques of carriageway lighting in open country.

2 There must be an individual decision on the placing and type of each light source. On what principles has their spacing been designed?

3 Upon what surfaces has the light from each fitting been designed to fall? Vertical wall surfaces are as significant from motorist and pedestrian level as the road surface.

4 What buildings or features will receive the most light, and which the least? Will this be related to (a) their architectural, and (b) their townscape importance?

5 Will the brightness of lamps be standardised, or varied with the importance of their placing?

6 At what bracket length will wall lamps be mounted in each case, and has the relative lighting of wall surfaces been foreseen?

7 What will be the light emission pattern of each lamp type, and will each be screened to avoid glare?

8 Of what colour range will lighting be? Will it be tungsten or fluorescent, and if the latter, within what spectral range?

9 Will provision be made for floodlighting principal buildings?

10 Lastly, what will the bracket or post design look like in the daytime?

2.5.10 Cleaning an historic city

It is important to realise the scope of public cleaning in a city like Chester. Main streets are sprayed, disinfected and brushed down daily. One man is employed full-time on the walk around the Walls. From Chester as a whole, 5,600 bins of rubbish are collected every week; and 25 tons of fibreboard and 50 tons of mixed paper are salvaged annually. The congested yard on Canal Street will soon be replaced by another, a mile and half from the Cross.

The Cathedral grounds, Police Headquarters, Racecourse, Hospital and Queen's School are cleaned privately. The canal sometimes seems neglected.

Street gulleys are topped up, snow cleared (1,000 tons of pure salt are stored), and rude words scrubbed away nightly. The result is an exceptionally clean town centre.

2.5.11 Town lighting

Like many ancient towns, Chester has a variety of lighting. The back streets have widely spaced lamp standards. The central shopping area is brilliantly lit and gives 'shape' to the city by night.

The two newest lighting schemes are on the inner ring road and in Eastgate Street. In Nicholas Street, it was hoped to light carriageways from the central reservation at guard-rail level, but this was too expensive for Ministry grants. So a remorseless line of tall poles with heavy tops now marches through the city, regardless of the City Walls or of anything but its own destiny. As techniques improve, it should be possible to vary the intensity and colour of lighting to express the identity of the walled City, with the new road sweeping in and through it. In Eastgate Street, lamp standards have been removed, and light sources wall-mounted to floodlight the opposite sides of the street. The result is charming and effective, and gives something of a 'moonlight' glow. Lighting the Rows is a special problem. The best light is from shop displays which could readily be given synchronous switching. The Walls are dark and dangerous, and deserve low-level pavement light—especially at flights of steps.

Town lighting must be designed for the *town*, not only on standard traffic rules, regardless of environment. Lighting is not a matter of designing poles, but an art of presenting cities by night. Reasoned technical advice is needed on individual town lighting. Figure 63b gives a sample checklist of some primary questions.

2.5.12 Floodlighting

In Britain in winter, up to half our working hours are spent in artificial light. Many visitors come to Chester all the year round. Only recently has major floodlighting been installed and then mostly for the Town Hall—a building which scarcely merits the honour. The following is a summary of the suggestions of floodlighting specialists.

Viewpoint. Most tourists, it is assumed, would view the lighting from the main attraction for visitors—the City Walls.

Cathedral. This should become the focus of floodlighting, lit to the highest intensity. We support the proposal to light the stained glass of the west window from inside, leaving this facade otherwise in darkness as a foil. The most attractive view is from the north-east and this could be beautifully floodlit. The south elevation, with its flying buttresses, and backed by the central Tower, makes an important view up St. Werburgh Street. The colour of the stonework here determines the type of light, and tungsten fittings are suggested.

64a The tower of St Peter's is illuminated

64b The floodlit Town Hall

St. Peter's Church tower. Again, its focal position makes this tower ideal for floodlighting, and this has been already undertaken (Fig. 64a).

Holy Trinity spire. A key landmark from most points in Chester, could well be lit from two directions.

St. Michael's Church. The church is already floodlit experimentally, and this idea might be developed. Tungsten halogen (horizontal linear) sources are less suitable than a symmetrical floodlight, giving sharper vertical shadows. The porch under the tower—the terminal point of the Rows—could also be strongly lit.

The City Walls. The east side would be left dark in contrast to the floodlit Cathedral. The Water Tower and King Charles Tower are admirably suited to floodlighting. The best length of wall is at the north—a superb subject for lighting from among the trees over the canal.

Bluecoat School. This could be floodlit quite simply from behind pavement bollards; and the *Canal Bridge* and the *Bridge of Sighs* could be wonderfully lit from under the bridge.

St. Mary's Church. Its tower is mostly seen from across the River Dee; this and the clerestory should be floodlit.

The Castle. A dark building, difficult to floodlight. The north flank could be strongly lit by mercury vapour, and the east side less brightly in tungsten halogen. The portico would be more effective strongly lit from one side to give shadow and 'shape'.

The Agricola Tower. On the other hand, this could be floodlit beautifully. Oblique lighting from a flagstaff, and the removal of one external drainpipe, would bring out its texture and form to the full.

River Bridges: the Old Dee Bridge: This is a good subject and could be lit from both sides, keeping sources low to avoid all traffic glare.

Grosvenor Bridge. The soaring soffit of the single arch could be floodlit to great effect from below.

St. John's Church and ruins. The church has a fine west and a good east window for back-lighting. Some tree pruning might be necessary if the church were floodlit. This would give a fine night view from across the river.

City Gates: Newgate and Roman ruins. An attractive possibility would be to light these from lamps behind one of the buildings in Little St. John's Street.

Bridgegate, Eastgate, Watergate and Northgate. These could be floodlit to emphasise the entrances to the City.

The Groves. Lastly, the Groves seem to lend themselves not so much to floodlighting as such, but to an 'umbrella of light' from some of the trees.

65 'Planning approval for office use'

2.6 Economic pressures on land use

The economics of urban living bring many threats to historic towns and their old buildings that other cities do not have to face. We here examine the general principles determining the viability of historic areas and then apply them to Chester as it is today, assessing the possible future development that the City can expect and must plan for.

2.6.1 Historic towns and property values

Changing social patterns and increases and decreases in demand lead more frequently to the destruction of old buildings than does their structural decay. Two market conditions may endanger these old structures:

Where there is a very high demand for property. Often a site cannot be fully utilised while an existing building remains. Where its development value exceeds the value of the present building, the temptation is to demolish and to rebuild.

Where demand declines, it may be economically unwise for the owner to invest more capital in his property. It is, therefore, allowed to deteriorate and fall into decay. It is clear from our survey that this has happened in many areas in Chester. The aim must be to guide market value in such a way that buildings of historic merit will be fully used and maintained in good condition.

2.6.2 The value of property

The market value of an interest in land and buildings is the price at which it can be sold by a willing vendor to a willing and able purchaser. Except in special circumstances, the value is governed by supply and demand. The following are the more important considerations which govern market values, and we have examined these points in some detail:

The permitted use of land and buildings;

Location and environment;

Design of buildings, suitability for function and their aesthetic qualities;

Existing interest vested in the property;

Security; and

Structural condition.

Permitted use. The 'permitted use' for land and buildings may well be the largest single factor governing value. Planning permission for development, which has been defined to include a change of use, is a vital weapon not only in planning control, but in its effect upon a building's value. Our present planning system leans heavily upon static 'use zoning' and does not always take account of the importance of its dynamic influence on property values. The economic consequences of each planning decision are in turn as important for the town as a whole as for the individual building, and a large development can have economic consequences even over an area far wider than its own town.

Planning brings powerful influences upon both supply and demand. The supply of land depends directly upon planning. Demand can also be affected, in that the planner can guide the available demand into those areas that offer the maximum benefit to the community.

An example of this at national level is the use of Development Areas, where new and expanding industries are firmly directed by Industrial Development Certificates and the payment of grants. Another is the control over office development through Office Development Permits (Fig. 65). Local planning authorities can influence the value and hence the future of property by channelling demand.

Location and environment. A building must be suitably located for its use, but the desirability of a particular location can be strongly influenced by wider planning schemes. For instance, better transport facilities elsewhere can diminish the value of a central location, and the reduced demand for housing in many town centres is due to easier daily travel from the suburbs. Conversely, better public transport and car parking in central areas can increase the demand for shopping space. The immediate environment is even more susceptible to control and improvement. Our recommendations for the Study Areas in Chester show some ways in which this can be brought about.

Design and suitability. The interior planning and layout of an historic building often make it unsuitable for modern needs. Its retention at the same time may preclude the fullest economic use of a site. All over Chester we find older buildings unsuited to current uses, where, for instance, the lower floors are occupied, but the upper ones are empty. On page 163, we suggest how some might be converted. Sometimes there is no economic solution for a single building, while a larger group may be susceptible to combined improvement. Fortunately those we have in mind in Chester are of high aesthetic quality; and this can also help their value.

Existing interests. These vary considerably and greatly affect value. Residential property is often beset by controlled tenancies which reduce the value far below that of similar buildings with vacant possession. The effects of the law of landlord and tenant make it uneconomic for private developers to build or convert residential accommodation to rent (except for expensive accommodation which is free from control). The private sector can therefore concern itself only with accommodation for sale to owner-occupiers and the purchase and improvement of property to rent is left to the public sector (including such non-profit-making organisations as Housing Associations).

Security. No purchaser will buy property whose future or whose neighbours' future is in doubt, and this situation is all too common in Chester. This insecurity is often the result of 'planning blight'. Many occupiers we have met complain of uncertainty, and are unprepared to invest any capital in their buildings. The result is decay.

Structural condition. This is a prime concern in the value of a building. It may be affected by past neglect, by the considerations outlined above, or by pure age. Historic buildings are often threatened by demolition even when they could be adapted for modern needs, because of the degree of deterioration and consequent high repair cost. (Fig. 66).

66 Good houses in Lower Bridge Street whose condition is fast deteriorating

67 A house in Upper Northgate Street, well converted into flats

2.6.3 Profit and incentive

If private owners and companies are to conserve historic buildings, the profit motive is essential. The city centre is the index of the quality of its civilisation and to put a cash value on the aesthetic, social and architectural merits of historic buildings is impossible. The difference between the cost of acquiring and converting property and its subsequent market value is simply the price society has to pay for these qualities.

Often, even when the economic incentive does exist, buildings are still not maintained but are allowed to deteriorate. An economic return is insufficient without security, that is, the confidence that the neighbourhood will not deteriorate, and that the value of the property will be maintained. For privately-owned houses, personal pride may be enough to secure their future. For others, adequate security must be added to economic repair cost.

In some instances, conservation may be hindered by slowly changing values. The property market is sometimes late in reacting to changed circumstances. Some owners' inflated ideas of the value of their property make them unwilling to sell unless they can obtain their price. In these circumstances the private developer, not being armed with compulsory purchase powers, cannot interest himself in purchase. Many owners, particularly owner-occupiers, are not motivated by financial profit: and if they can obtain a reasonable return, and the value of their property will keep pace with inflation, they need little encouragement to invest in repairs (Fig. 67). Where a local authority by its own activity and environmental planning shows reliability and inspires confidence, owners can invest in improvements (except to residential property subject to the Rent Acts) knowing that their investment is secure. This confidence brings an increase in demand which is in turn reflected in increased values and a further incentive for owners either to improve their property, or to sell out to those who are prepared to do the necessary work.

By public investment in environmental planning, such as removing detractions and providing open spaces, car parks and amenities, a local authority can encourage private owners to invest their own money on improvements and repairs.

There remains a class of property where an economic solution is incompatible with conversion at present, and seems unlikely to be so in the future. Here, either the property must go, or a subsidy in one form or another is required. This subsidy in effect is simply the cost to the community of retaining the aesthetic, social and architectural benefits given by the property. Improvement Grants are one good way in which the private sector has been encouraged to improve sub-standard houses. Current legislation will strengthen the hand of local authorities in conserving historic buildings. The Civic Amenities Act also gives authorities power to carry out work on listed buildings to save them from demolition.

We feel that local authorities must encourage rather than enforce co-operation from property owners. The partnership agreements which have been successfully adopted by private developers and local authorities for central area schemes are unlikely to be adopted for conservation schemes, unless these show a sufficient return.

Except for expensive accommodation free from rent control, private developers are only interested in residential development for immediate sale to owner-occupiers. We foresee little present opportunity in Chester for the developer in the commercial field. The market for good residential accommodation in the centre is untried; and it seems most unlikely that developers faced with comparatively high acquisition costs can afford to venture into this field at the moment. The City must lead the way, and encourage others to follow.

For large areas which cannot be redeveloped economically, a Government body is required, backed by considerable funds, and with initiative and enthusiasm. The formation, constitution and powers of such a body are suggested on page 246. Its job would be to purchase suitable properties and to sell or lease them at an appropriate figure, under suitable covenants, for development. Under its existing powers and given the finance, the Land Commission could in fact already act in the acquisition of areas requiring partial redevelopment, conversion and repair.

68 **New offices and shops in Watergate Street: many are still vacant several years after completion**

2.7 Land-use pressures in Chester

In this section, we study the principal land-use demands in Chester at the present time, and the trends that, based on our survey, we have assumed in the detailed treatment of study areas.

Land ownership. Land in central Chester still changes hands fairly frequently, but an increasing proportion is in public ownership of one kind or another. The County owns the Castle area and has purchased individual properties nearby. The City, which enjoys County Borough status, has acquired many older properties as a matter of policy, and now owns upwards of 26 acres of the area under study. This excludes the $15\frac{1}{2}$ acres of Grosvenor Park given to the City by the Marquis of Westminster in 1867. The Grosvenor Estates and the Dean and Chapter of the Cathedral each own considerable areas. Fig. 69 shows the principal land-ownership units at the time the survey was undertaken.

69 Land ownership in Chester

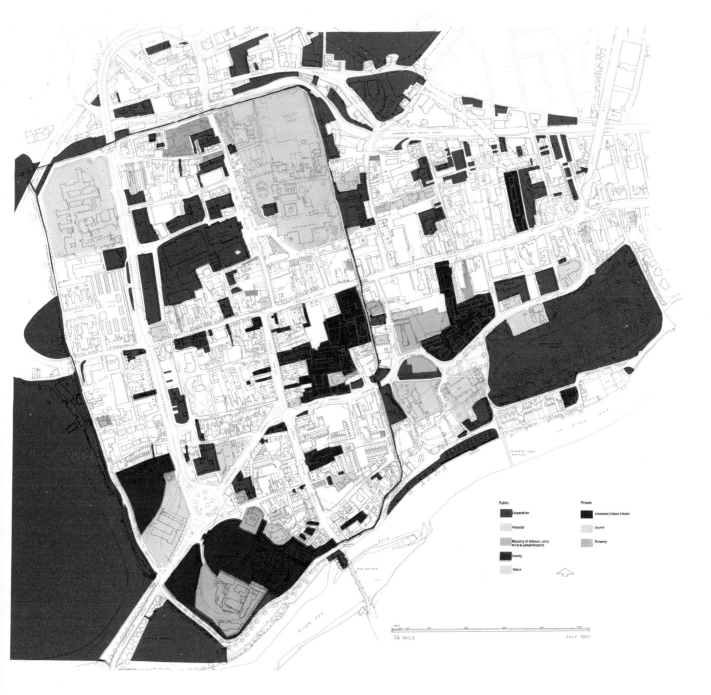

Railway
Canal
NORTHGATE
Canal
Inner Ring Road

EASTGATE

WATERGATE

SHOPPING
PRECINCT

Grosvenor Park

NEWGATE

The Roodee

River Dee

BRIDGEGATE

70 Land use in Chester

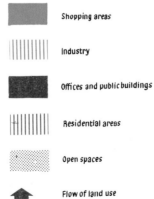

Shopping areas

Industry

Offices and public buildings

Residential areas

Open spaces

Flow of land use

2.7.1 Existing uses in the central area

The major present uses and trends are summarised in Figure 70 using a simple amoeba-like notation to stress the organic nature of urban geography. Existing uses are indicated on the Town Map as 'business, shopping, civic centre, parking, places of worship, schools and hospital'. As has already been mentioned, the Castle belongs to the County but it has been included in this study.

Industrial land. Land in industrial use includes the site of the present Chester Brewery in Northgate, and another within the south-east 'island' of the walled town. At present this contains a motor showroom, a garage and some Victorian terraced housing. These may not in our opinion be the best uses, and the point is discussed in more detail in the Bridgegate study area.

Residential. Most of the City within the Walls originally consisted of houses, but over the years these have gradually been converted to office and commercial uses, with fewer people living in the City centre. Few houses have been built here since the 19th century, but several domestic streets have been demolished for new roads or for slum clearance. In 1946 there were still about 3,000 residents, but now there are only about 1,000.

Open space. The overall ratio of public space is high (Grosvenor Park has $15\frac{1}{2}$ acres (Fig. 71) and the Roodee $65\frac{1}{2}$ acres), but this is patchily distributed over the town. The Town Map report of 1950 introduced a policy of increasing open space by clearing away development near the Walls—especially at the north and east, exposing a fine view of the Cathedral. The Chester Central Area Plan in 1964 again recommended opening up the Walls to view, but the estimated cost (at some £100,000 per acre) has frustrated this; and at least one cleared area has been re-used as a car park.

Civic Centre. For financial reasons, the planned construction of new municipal offices, central library, concert and conference halls, Museum and Art Gallery and Government Offices is likely to be 'a very long-term policy'.

Shops and offices. The Town Map report recommended that the existing central-area shopping was adequate, and zoned the remaining central-area sites as offices, with some retail warehousing.

New retail accommodation. Existing vacant premises and building already planned may at the time of survey be tabulated as follows:

a. Empty January 1967   30,800 sq. ft.

b. Due for completion 1967   89,000 sq. ft.

c. Likely to be completed by 1969/70   59,400 sq. ft.

d. Planning consents outstanding   12,320 sq. ft.

191,520 sq. ft.

Shopping in the centre. The old shopping streets are still the centre of commerce. In this Chester is fortunate. So often the high turnover shopping is in a new High Street, away from areas worthy of conservation.

Compactness. The central shopping area, including the new (Grosvenor Laing) Shopping Precinct (Fig. 72), is compact and well grouped mainly within the Walls (Fig 70). A visitor quickly grasps the plan, with its concentration of two-storeyed shopping, and its possibilities are often well exploited, for instance in one and two shops with offices over, or one store accessible from different levels.

Covered shopping. Chester has $7\frac{1}{2}$ acres of covered shopping. The Rows make it possible to walk easily through most of the central area fully protected from wind and rain. Compare this with Coventry's modern two-storeyed shopping which has higher stair access and less cover, and with Preston which has easier steps but again less protection from the wind. On The Rows, visibility is excellent both along and across the street and all the shops, their names and their goods can be clearly seen, and traffic and congestion avoided.

New offices. Accommodation being offered as a commercial speculation included at the time of survey:

a. Empty January 1967   32,200 sq. ft. approx.

b. Due for completion 1967   4,000 sq. ft.

c. Likely to be completed 1969/70   45,000 sq. ft.

81,200 sq. ft.

72 The covered and heated piazza is a focus of the new shopping precinct

2.7.2. Assessment of future residential demands

Using the basis of the Town Map report, we have attempted to assess likely future needs and demands in Chester. Residential demand in the City centre is not easy to assess. Estate agents report that while Chester is tending to become a dormitory for middle and higher income groups, they experience no demand for city housing. But equally, they rarely have any on their books. In the Market Area Development, 14 or 15 small flats will soon be on the market; and the response to these will be an indication of the demand. But the City Housing Manager finds a definite demand for flats from the professional classes at present accommodated at low rents in City-built tall flats at Newton. Many would pay higher rents if accommodation were available. Certainly Grosvenor Estates have found their well-designed flats at Handbridge to be popular. These let currently at annual rents of £185 to £300 for 1 to 3 bedrooms.

We have found that people do in fact enjoy living within the Walls, and while new houses with gardens could only be built at very high land cost, we should expect a demand for flats from upper-middle income groups—primarily those employed in the City, retired people who find Chester attractive and commuters to such places as Ellesmere Port and Runcorn.

Except for expensive accommodation free from rent control, private developers are only interested in residential development for immediate sale to owner-occupiers. We foresee little present opportunity in Chester for the developer in the commercial field. The market for good residential accommodation in the centre is untried, and it seems most unlikely that developers faced with comparatively high acquisition costs can afford to venture into this field at the moment. The City must, however, lead the way and encourage others to follow.

We cannot over-emphasise the importance which attaches to good planning. A basic function of planning is to guide natural economic trends by directing and controlling demand so as to ensure the fullest environmental benefit. The demand for residential accommodation is particularly sensitive to location and environment. Every effort should be made in Chester to encourage people wishing to live in the centre and this can be done both by improving the environment and facilities 'in town' and by giving every encouragement in planning consents to residential development in the heart of the City, rather than in the new outer areas.

2.7.3 A policy for Chester's shopping

The Chester Central Area Plan (1964) recommended that 'further commercial developments, involving large additional areas of retail shopping, should not be contemplated in the period to 1971' and were 'unlikely to be required' in the subsequent 10-year period. In March 1967 we carried out a street survey of shop premises which appeared to be empty – not including empty property obviously leased, but including newly-built but empty retail space. We found 33 street shops and 16 Row shops empty (Fig. 74). With the schemes under way or proposed, it seems Chester has for the moment reached saturation point for shopping premises. All the recent development schemes are tending to draw the central shopping area within the walls, at the expense of the Frodsham Street, Brook Street, and City Road areas; and these, with the northern part of Northgate Street, are in turn running down.

By far the majority of traders in the new Precinct are national 'multiples' (Fig. 75b). Two Chester firms moved in from primary and four from secondary positions elsewhere in the town, and two have started second branches. Empty shops elsewhere are not so much vacated by traders moving into the Precinct, as an indication of trade now lost in their part of the town.

New schemes tend to be located to the short-term advantages of the trade—but not necessarily to that of the town, and especially of an historical city centre. The vacated premises and the areas left to run down are often those of architectural or historical significance, which it is in the interests of the town's attraction to keep alive.

The figures for sales turnover per square foot support the assessment that Chester has reached saturation point in retail property. The C.C.A.P. showed that in 1961, before the Precinct was opened, the turnover in Chester shops was £10 per sq. ft. per annum, whereas 'an efficient average for new shops of all classes of retail trade' was at that time approximately £25 per sq. ft. Combining this with the projected new retail floor area, plus an increased population, it was surmised that a real increase in turnover of just under 90 per cent would be needed. In the Liverpool City Centre Plan, it has been assumed that sales turnover per square foot will increase, even within the same space.

With the shops at saturation point, no new big schemes for redevelopment should be given planning permission within the next five years or so. Chester must concentrate on providing departmental and specialist shopping.

75a The new covered shopping precinct within the Rows area

75b The new Market Hall

2.7.4 The future demand for offices

It seems very unlikely that Chester will ever become primarily an office centre. It is not one now, while Liverpool's offices are growing rapidly; and Runcorn and Warrington – Risley are likely to prove more attractive to big firms and decentralised concerns; both have better external communications than Chester. Apart from the block let to the Inland Revenue, all new premises have been let in small units. Grosvenor-Laing are fortunate to have let all their office space to the Council, and there appear to be many premises unlet (Fig. 75c).

Professional offices, as in so many towns, group together in the old streets like Whitefriars. Some of the Rows offices are used by building societies, estate agents and banks. Older buildings and prestige professional offices often go together; and this element of Chester's attractions may in the long run be more successful than the newer, glass-box speculations. If the County and City Councils expand into new premises, many present offices will be left vacant. Positive steps should be taken to keep the buildings they leave in good and attractive condition.

The Corporation plans to add 40,000 sq. ft. of offices by 1969/70; and the County office expansion policy is at present for 38,000 sq. ft. minimum, or 114,000 sq. ft. if several present premises are vacated. The Corporation similarly will vacate various premises when their new extension is completed. Much will depend on the findings of the Royal Commission on Local Government.

75c To let: office block in Hunter Street

75

2.7.5 Summary

Residential. The likely demand is difficult to assess. The supply of houses and flats has been very limited; and agents claim the future market is equally vague.

Shops. No further commercial developments involving large additional areas of retail shopping can be contemplated in the period to 1971, nor are they likely to be required during the subsequent decade.

Offices. The demand for new office buildings seems low and appears unlikely to grow. Many old buildings are capable of useful conversion for the purpose.

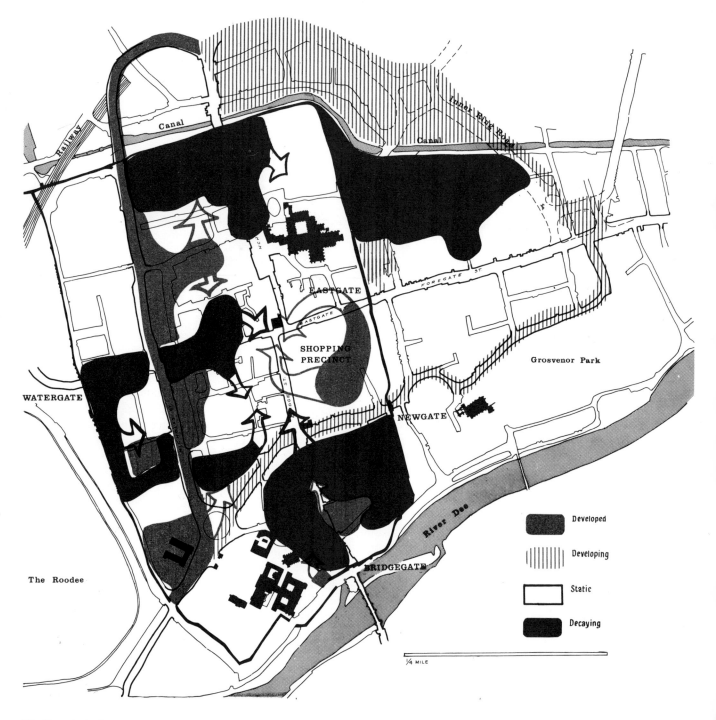

76   Trends in land use

2.7.6 Recreation and tourism in Chester

It is a combination of Chester's many and varied attractions that gives the City its magnetism within the region and to tourists. We asked Chester's hotels in a questionnaire what in their opinion were the main attractions. The Rows, the Walls and the River were quoted in every case. For most hotels, also, the Cathedral, the Races, the Regatta and the Zoo attracted their clientele.

The views of neighbouring planning officers. We also asked the County Planning Officers of adjacent counties and of Liverpool what they thought were Chester's chief attractions in their specific areas. All named the Zoo and the Races, although only Flintshire and Denbighshire mentioned the shops.

Liverpool and Lancashire had good shops of their own, and therefore quoted first the historic centre together with its restaurants and social facilities. As Liverpool said, 'Chester's advantages as a relatively prosperous and genteel town, together with its environmental assets, have enabled it since the war to grow in influence as a major shopping centre largely at the expense of Liverpool among the new Wirral population.'

77 Existing recreational facilities

- ■ Indoor sports, theatres, cinema, library
- ▨ Outdoor sports, parks, playgrounds, etc
- ■ Pubs, clubs, restaurants
- ▨ Betting shops

78a Promenade along the Dee

78b Grosvenor Park

The Cathedral. This attracts many visitors and is at present used for concerts when a large orchestra comes to Chester.

The River Dee (Fig. 78a). The river draws many visitors in summer when launches seating 70 to 100 passengers depart every 15 minutes, and rowing boats can be hired. Launches are often hired out to organised parties; and coaches, unwelcomed elsewhere in Chester, bring visitors to the river on day trips. The Regatta on Whit Sunday draws big crowds and there are many other river activities.

Grosvenor Park (Fig 78b). The park is a fine amenity visited by many who arrive at the riverside by coach.

The Roodee. The racecourse is owned by the Corporation. Race-meetings held three times annually bring an influx of visitors by car and by coach. For the rest of the year the Roodee is open to the public, and regular sports functions, tattoos and similar functions are held there, despite seasonal waterlogging (Fig. 79a).

79a The City Walls become a grandstand at Chester Races

Hotels and restaurants. The City Information Office lists 24 hotels in and near to Chester (1967) (Fig. 79b). These provide 698 bedrooms ranging from 20s. to 'from 75s.' per night. There are also 32 guest-houses, with 137 bedrooms, and four hostels with accommodation for at least 180. The Chester & District Junior Chamber of Commerce published in 1966 a study called *Chester: A Conference Centre*, which usefully compares Chester with other conference centres. Whilst it cannot compete with London or certain seaside resorts, the City does attract conferences, 50 to 200 being a normal attendance. Eight hotels, offering 445 beds between them, were at the time of the survey anxious to attract conference business.

The A.A. rating of Chester's hotels compared with some other cities is shown in Fig. 79b. As may be seen, the standard which Chester offers is high. Our questionnaire to the hotels showed that in summer, 80 per cent. of the clientele were tourists staying one to two nights. Out of season 80 per cent. of visitors are on business.

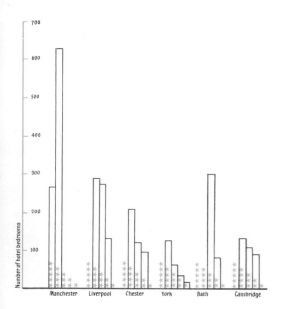

79b Hotel chart

80a Penny-in-the-slot machines (top left)

80b The Walls and Phoenix Tower from which Charles I watch'ed the battle of Rowton Moor (bottom left)

80c Roman columns re-set in the garden by the City Walls (top right)

80d Horse-drawn narrow boats are still to be found on the canal (centre right)

80e The old 'Bridge of Sighs' over the canal (bottom right)

Restaurant facilities.   Other than in hotels the restaurant facilities are limited. The demand is made up mostly of shoppers in the day, and clubs and business dinners in the evening. Local dining-out tends towards grill-houses in the country ; but a few good restaurants in the centre open at least until 11 p.m. and should find plenty of custom.

The old Gaumont Theatre, once occasionally used for concerts, is now a *Bowling Alley*. What was the Royalty Theatre is used as a *cabaret* and *a club.* There are three Cinemas, and a Bingo Hall. There is no sports hall or modern swimming pool, although the need for both is recognised.

Outdoor sports.   Chester 4th Division football team and the four 18-hole golf courses seem to be of mostly local attraction, except when there are big matches or competitions at home. Minor county cricket is played at the Boughton Hall Club ground.

2.7.7 A policy for tourism and recreation

Chester, with its many and diverse qualities, has every possible ingredient of a first-rate tourist centre ; but many of its attractions are undeveloped. Our recommendations for the improvement of existing tourist and recreational facilities in the City are explained in the various study areas in which they lie (see below page 105 *et sequitur*). We make, however, one general recommendation.

Tourist Office.   This is at present a summer-only office, sited in the Town Hall. We have used it as a base for the tourist map to be found on pages 84 and 85. It would be better still as a part of a new Transport Centre, where it could be open all the year round including weekends and evenings, and could give information on everything from coach tours to shopping.

2.7.8 Conclusion

Many people to whom we have spoken have no clear-cut reason for liking Chester. They think of it as a 'nice place'—not for any one particular feature, but for a combination of all the things that they find attractive. This is the secret of Chester's success. The place has something for everyone : the urban sophistication of the Rows with their busy shops, race days on the Roodee, a good museum, a Cathedral and churches, or ice-creams and boat trips on the Dee. Chester can cater for every interest, for every member of the family. Its potential for local people and for foreign tourists is enormous.

81 A Rows-eye view

82a The medieval mystery plays were part of Chester's first Arts Festival

2.7.9 Chester's cultural facilities

Chester is already a natural cultural focus for a large area. Visitors to the town for shopping and for recreation would welcome the additional attraction of a theatre and concert hall. Manchester and Liverpool both have repertory theatres and concert halls, for their own and visiting companies.

There is more than sufficient enthusiasm in Chester to support permanent entertainment. The local amateur symphony orchestra is well supported. Large orchestras, including the Hallé and the Liverpool Philharmonic, already visit Chester. The City's first Festival of the Arts in 1967 was highly successful and brought Chester to the notice of a large public (Fig. 82a). There were mystery plays on the Cathedral green, music, films, a Flower Festival, horse racing and a Festival Ball. As an annual event on its present scale, it could soon be of national significance and an enormous draw to the City, but at the present its future is undecided.

The Civic Theatre to seat 500, being built in the new Market Hall development, is planned as a repertory theatre. This is a good first stage in Chester's development as an arts centre. But it must be followed up with other facilities. There is a great need for a small concert hall for local societies and visiting companies. Attractively converted, the Town Hall Assembly Room would serve well. Restaurant and bar facilities could be combined with the new theatre and conference hall close by.   The latter could also be designed to give more suitable accommodation for larger concerts than is at present available in the Cathedral.

2.7.10 The City's future as a conference centre

Already a conference centre of local importance, Chester, with its multifarious activities, could support many more such gatherings. The main factor governing the choice of centre, other than tourist attractions, is the availability of suitable halls and hotel accommodation. Today, Chester is able to provide adequate meeting halls for up to 500 people in hotels where the delegates stay. But the only public hall available is the assembly room in the Town Hall, which seats about 450. This is often in use for exhibitions, and lacks good ancillary accommodation. Most comparable conference towns, like Buxton and Stratford-on-Avon, have halls big enough for 1,000 people. In Chester it is difficult to foresee a demand for more than two or three conferences a year of this size; but if the hall were used for other functions it could be made economically viable.

The best site for a Conference Hall is close to the City centre, although far enough away from the Cross to avoid traffic congestion. One good position would be immediately north of the Town Hall between Hunter and Princess Streets. This has easy and mostly covered approaches to the larger hotels, shops and restaurants, good access and parking facilities for cars and coaches, and public transport to and from the station (Fig. 82b). In promoting itself as a conference centre, Chester needs more publicity, both as a tourist resort and for its specific conference attractions.

82a The medieval mystery plays were part of Chester's first Arts Festival

82b A central site next to the Town Hall, ideal for a conference and arts centre

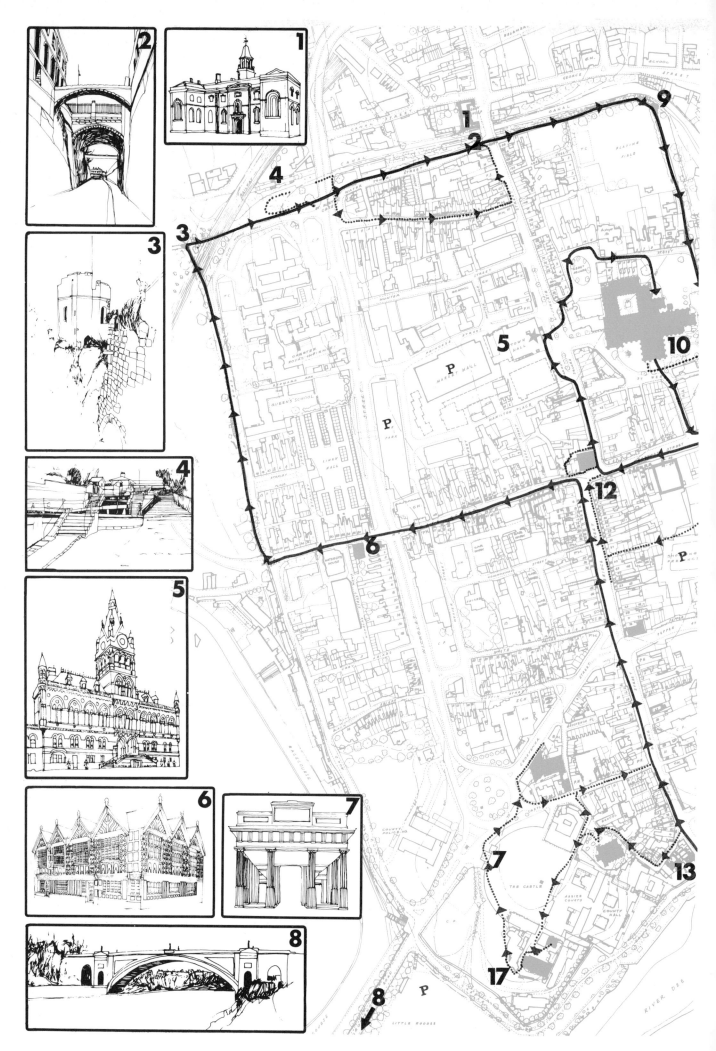

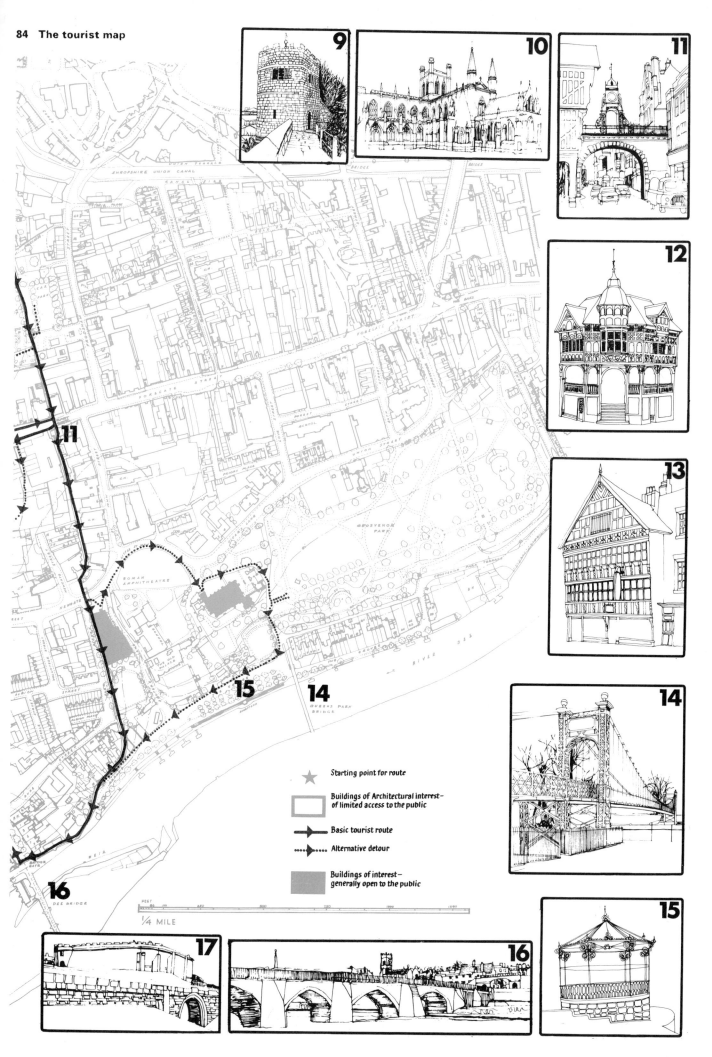

Starting point for route

Buildings of Architectural interest—
of limited access to the public

Basic tourist route

Alternative detour

Buildings of interest—
generally open to the public

¼ MILE

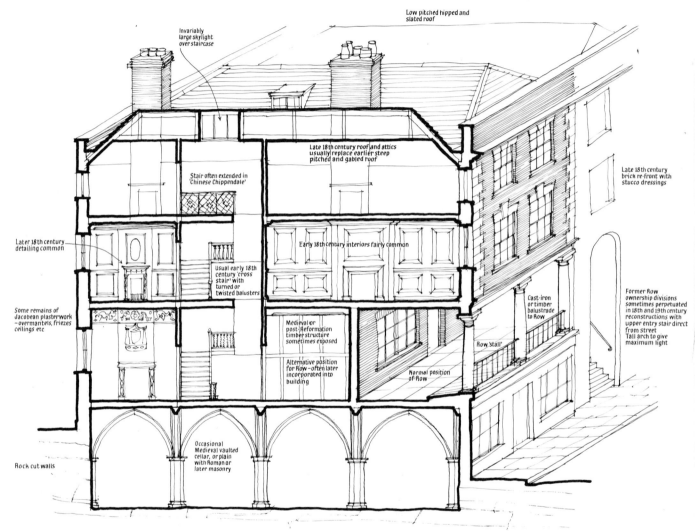

Low pitched hipped and
slated roof

Invariably
large skylight
over staircase

Late 18th century roof and attics
usually replace earlier steep
pitched and gabled roof

Late 18th century
brick re-front with
stucco dressings

Stair often extended in
'Chinese Chippendale'

Early 18th century interiors fairly common

Later 18th century
detailing common

Usual early 18th
century 'cross
stair' with
turned or
twisted balusters

Some remains of
Jacobean plasterwork
—overmantels, friezes
ceilings etc

Medieval or
post-Reformation
timber structure
sometimes exposed

Cast-iron
or timber
balustrade
to Row

Former Row
ownership divisions
sometimes perpetuated
in 18th and 19th century
reconstructions with
upper entry stair direct
from street
Tall arch to give
maximum light

Alternative position
for Row—often later
incorporated into
building

Normal position
of Row

'Row stall'

Rock cut walls

Occasional
Medieval vaulted
cellar, or plain
with Roman or
later masonry

Rock or Roman cobbled floor or later paving

86a Perspective drawing of a typical Rows building

86b A seventeenth-century plasterwork ceiling

86

2.8 Chester's old buildings

2.8.1 Architectural quality

Although Chester has much fine and complete single-period architecture, most of the buildings are in fact 'hybrids', which have developed gradually through the various phases of the City's history. Their form is remarkably consistent as a clearly recognisable Chester building type, and they occur, with minor variations, all over the City.

The characteristic elements are:

Cellars which vary from plain chambers hewn out of the rock to fully developed medieval rib-vaulted under-crofts. Sometimes these contain the remains of Roman structure. Often they are lined with fine, squared and tooled stone work.

Rows usually of the external type as in the main streets, but sometimes running within the building, one compartment behind the street front. Later, these internal Rows were often enclosed (by licence from the City Council) to provide extra rooms within the houses. Sometimes the separate ownership divisions of former Rows buildings have survived total later reconstruction.

Staircases running crosswise and occupying the whole of the building's centre. These are usually lit by a large roof skylight, and where space allows, the stairs have open wells to allow maximum light to lower levels. The earliest cross stairs are Jacobean, the latest Victorian. These stair wells are the most consistent feature of Chester's buildings.

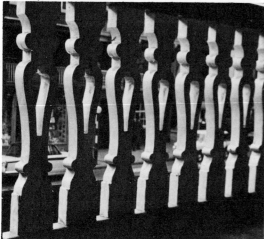

87a   Victorian cast-iron railing in the Rows (top)

87b   A wooden railing in the Rows dating from the Victorian period (bottom)

87c   Panelling in Bishop Lloyd's House

It has been said that 'Chester's face is its fortune', and old buildings are certainly the essence of this City. Their problems are a cancer that can destroy it: their health is vital to its future. A look behind the face of Chester's buildings reveals a widespread state of inner crisis, extending even to the heart of the City, the Rows. Defects in Chester's old buildings are fundamental, widespread and accelerating. In many cases they have reached a crucial state. The majority approach it, and some are sadly beyond it. If present conditions are allowed to continue, Chester's future status as one of Britain's foremost historic cities must soon be in jeopardy.

The basis of the problem is clear-cut: it is simply the disuse, under-use and misuse of valuable historic buildings throughout the City. Of the 442 buildings we have inspected during our survey, 44 were not only totally disused but also unusable in their present state, and have one or more storeys vacant or barely used. The result is neglect and deterioration of individual buildings. The 'blight' can spread rapidly from a single building to its neighbours, then to a whole street and finally to an entire area. This trend is most marked in Watergate Street and Lower Bridge Street. To halt and reverse it is, for Chester, a matter of the utmost urgency.

The only way in which this can be done is to reconcile the capabilities of fine historic buildings with the demands for use today. On the one hand are the problems posed by an old building's construction, condition and historic value; on the other are the demands and pressures of new standards and new uses. There are often acute difficulties of finance and of public control and policy. In considering a whole city, the problems of single buildings are further complicated. Groups of buildings must be considered in relation to each other and their environment. Their problems of use affect the whole population.

The situation is not one of allocating blame. The vital process of transforming problem buildings into real attributes must be a matter of compromise and 'give and take'. But to achieve this, it is first necessary to recognise and isolate the cause of decline.

The studies of individual areas that follow examine these problems in detail, but in general they stem from one or more of the following 'roots'.

88a A Jacobean staircase in 30 Watergate Street, the Old Assembly House (top)

88b 'Barley sugar' balusters: an early eighteenth-century staircase in the Grosvenor Museum (bottom)

88c Carved oak panels on the front of Bishop Lloyd's House

89a Design of a typical Rows building with inaccessible upper floors

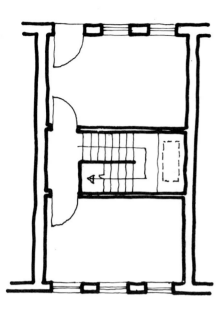

89b An internal 'cross staircase'

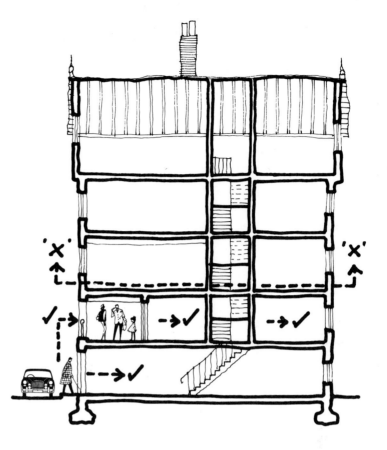

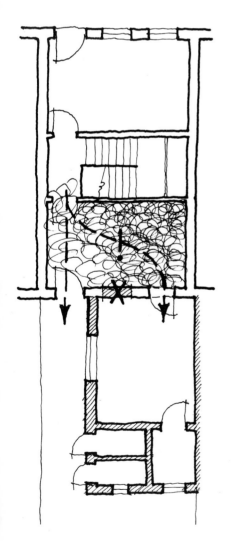

89c Rear additions destroy the form of buildings

2.8.2 The physical problems of buildings

Size. Chester buildings are usually large, with correspondingly generous rooms and high ceilings. The typical building has a large front and back room on each of three or four floors. It is usually terraced, with natural daylighting and ventilation from front and back. For historic and architectural reasons, the front is often unalterable; and so many buildings are unsuited, as they stand, for the smaller-scale needs of today, and have limited flexibility for conversion. Subdividing large original units into smaller ones brings practical problems of lighting and ventilation, and disturbs interiors and their architectural proportions.

Extensions. Later additions produced difficulties of use and maintenance. So often, attempts were made to deal with shortcomings by piecemeal additions. These are almost always at the rear and often of makeshift character. As a result, the original nucleus is often robbed of light and air, and burdened with maintenance troubles. Such additions bring anarchy and obsolescence, and complicate rather than help the possibility of future use (Fig. 89c).

Staircases. Vertical access within the buildings is usually by a single central staircase. The typical plan, with a central stair between front and back rooms, brings circulation and fire escape difficulties in any horizontal subdivision. Inhabitants at street or Row level naturally use upper floors from the bottom upwards, and often do not need them all. Top floors therefore tend to be disused or under-used (Figs. 89a/b).

External access. Entry is mainly restricted to the street side, and only at street or Row level. Access to upper floors can sometimes only be gained through the lower levels. Where these are shops (for example in the Rows), there are security and fire risk problems, since few users live above the shop.

H

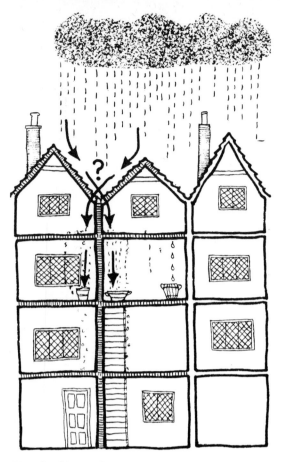

90a Leaking valley gutters cause rapid deterioration

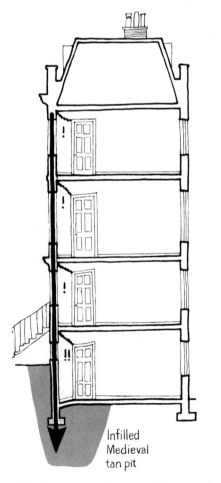

Infilled
Medieval
tan pit

90b Uneven settlement of foundations, for instance because of old Tan pits, also causes serious decay

Structural complexity. Old buildings have often been altered over the years, as in the Georgian brick refronting of an earlier timber structure. Chester's buildings have additional difficulties. Their basic form is of pitched roof units set at right angles to the street. This brings valley gutters over party walls, which are difficult to reach for cleaning and inspection and have problems of shared maintenance, in most cases unsolved. The result is leaking valley gutters, with wet penetration to lower levels (Fig. 90a).

Foundations. A particular problem in Chester is the effect of widely varying foundation conditions. Many buildings are founded on natural rock, but in some cases (especially on former Roman sites) the present buildings are partly on 'made' ground. Differential settlement has then occurred, and buildings have partially subsided (Fig. 90b). Proper maintenance is vital. For many, especially in tenanted buildings, the lack of it has brought decline and eventual disuse. Once a building is empty and neglected, its defects accelerate, and reconditioning costs rise.

2.8.3 The problems of the building's environment

Nuisances. Many of Chester's old buildings suffer from traffic noise, fumes and vibration. The best residential areas are all in the quieter streets—Abbey Street, the Groves, and so on—whilst noisy and narrow streets like Castle Street contain many houses that have been abandoned or are in decline.

Rear outlook and access. Outlook is sometimes constricted, with yards and gardens accessible only through buildings. This is largely caused by piecemeal rear additions. It is an important factor in the actual and potential use of buildings. For shops, rear servicing facilities are necessary, but the outlook is relatively unimportant. For offices, rear servicing, private car parks and a pleasant outlook are desirable, although not essential. For houses, an attractive outlook and space for a garden or drying yard are needed, while rear servicing is less important. Comparatively few old buildings have any of these simple basic functional needs.

Breweries produce smells as well as beer. New multi-storey buildings block the light from their neighbours, overlook their privacy, and dominate the view (Fig. 91a).

2.8.4 The ownership and use of buildings

When areas of structurally vulnerable buildings are all in single hands, a heavy maintenance bill can rapidly be built up. As a result available funds may either be spread thinly over the area as a whole, or spent only on selected buildings, with the rest left for 'another day'. The degree of maintenance naturally reflects the economic return, either in usefulness or in rent, and some estates in Chester now own more property than they need or can afford to maintain. The will is certainly there, but these estates have often to decide between financial stringency and the deliberate disuse of surplus property. Elsewhere, absentee landlords are unwilling to look after tenants or buildings, and financial considerations are paramount. These buildings rapidly pass to the debit side of the ledger, and are left to rot. Other valuable buildings are deteriorating because the war unhappily stopped reconditioning or even proper maintenance: financial restrictions since have made it impossible to close the gap. The situation has arisen purely because means have not been matched to intent.

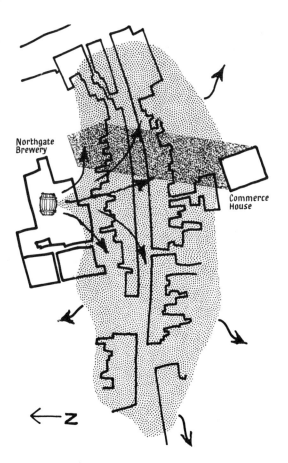

91a **Nuisance from neighbours: King Street is affected by brewery smells and is overshadowed by new office blocks**

91b **Neglect and under-use of a house in Watergate Street**

Uncertainty. One cause of area deterioration is uncertainty – the effects of doubt about future security. Often the cause is merely a premature announcement by owners of provisional redevelopment plans, as in the area of St. Mary's Hill. Here, proposals were frequently made but subsequently withdrawn or ultimately left in abeyance. The empty or deteriorating buildings remain, and so, even more damagingly, does the climate of growing anxiety and discouragement amongst adjacent owners or tenants. Many buildings are abandoned : others are neglected. The problem was clearly demonstrated for us by the situation of an elderly, poor but house-proud couple. Five years ago, they purchased wallpaper to redecorate. Ever since, under constant threats of dispossession, half-understood press announcements and rumours, the wallpaper has remained unhung. In this atmosphere of doubt, whole areas of valuable buildings go into a rapid decline.

Shared use. Dual ownership produces problems of shared use and repair. Many buildings in the Rows have separate freeholds at street and Row level. Complete agreement is obviously necessary on use and daily upkeep. While the building is fully occupied, all is well ; but as soon as any section falls vacant, the remaining freeholder loses all control. If the upper parts are empty, a leaking roof will soon persuade him to leave, and so the building falls.

Inappropriate use. Many good buildings in Chester have uses inappropriate to their architectural value. Although any sort of use, however inappropriate, is better than none, several fine interiors have been mutilated by misuse. This happens particularly where old houses are made to serve non-domestic purposes (Fig. 91b).

92a   Raw end of Kings Buildings exposed to the Inner Ring Road

92b   Hooligans speed the decay of an unused building, the Congregational Church in Queen Street

92c   Derelict property next to 'the gap' in Watergate Street

2.8.5 Compliance with modern regulations

We turn now to the statutory and other legal requirements as they affect old buildings. Two stages call for consideration: the first is when buildings are in 'passive' use or disuse and for some reason become a public liability, or simply 'in the way' of redevelopment schemes; the second or 'active' situation occurs when old buildings are to be reconditioned or altered, bringing them under the control of requirements earlier inapplicable. The following are some special problems that either do or could arise in Chester.

93 Egerton House, in Upper Northgate Street, was demolished to make way for the new roundabout

Demolitions

a. Comprehensive redevelopment – (*Town and Country Planning Act, 1962*). Chester has recently lost several valuable buildings through redevelopment in both the public and private sectors. Egerton House in Upper Northgate Street was an important Georgian building which had to make way for the new Northgate roundabout (Fig. 93). The Old Public Market has now been demolished in favour of the new Market Hall, and it is a pity that at least its facade could not have been preserved.

Permanent 'making good' for buildings adjacent to cleared sites is especially important in historic towns. For example, demolishing part of a terrace will create a new end elevation. Too often these remain raw, ragged and deteriorating just as they are left by the demolition gang (Fig. 92a). Nor is it sufficient merely to render over everything, chimney breasts and all, like an aftermath of war damage. Permanent and appropriate refacing is needed to heal these scars, although this clearly depends upon the co-operation of individual owners.

b. Private redevelopment – (*Town and Country Planning Act, 1962*). Thanks to the vigilance of the City Council, Chester has lost very few important buildings for private profit. But the increasing number of deteriorating buildings will make this a more pressing problem. Recent planning applications for example (1967) have involved the demolition of the Old Assay Office in Goss Street.

c. Disuse and neglect – (*Town and Country Planning Act, 1962 and Public Health Act, 1961*). Before the Civic Amenities Act became law in August, 1967, there was no redress if owners of historic property failed to maintain their buildings properly. If they became a public danger, the law required their demolition. Since the new Act, however, the responsible local authority has power to do the necessary work in certain limited circumstances. These powers may need to be strengthened further in subsequent legislation.

Chester has many buildings in neglect and decline (Figs. 92b/c). The early stages are graphically illustrated by the Chapel of St. John, in the south wing of the Bluecoat Hospital, Upper Northgate Street. The rest of the Hospital building is well used and maintained under lease by the City Corporation. But the Chapel, whose care remains with the owners, is disused and most clearly deteriorating.

94a Plumbing can be an eyesore if unplanned

94b Varied floor heights make conversion difficult

94c Large high-ceilinged rooms are not always sympathetically divided

Revitalising buildings

a. Planning and Development Control — (Town and Country Planning Act, 1962). So far as we are aware, little conflict arises from the City Development Plan on reconditioning old buildings. This is mainly because of the strikingly few applications that have in fact been made. It may also be partly due to the planning authority's understandable reluctance to refuse any application which would allow an old building's continued use. The future will bring more problems of this kind.

The facades of Chester's historic buildings can rarely be radically altered without violence to their character. But in fact external control often falls short in ignoring apparently minor alterations which can drastically affect the sensitive face of an historic building. External service pipes and the like can also cause great visual as well as physical damage (Fig. 94a). There is no planning control over architectural interiors, and many in Chester are ruined by insensitive sub-division (Fig. 94c).

b. Building regulations. The Regulations apply to old buildings when their reconditioning involves 'a material change of use, structural alterations or extension, or works consequent upon the installation of fittings'. Almost all the works needed in reconditioning Chester's historic buildings will fall into one or more of these categories. Conformity with the Regulations thus becomes a major problem.

Repair works will usually need consideration of Parts C (Resistance to Moisture) and D (Structural Stability). The commonest items are likely to be the lack of damp-proof courses and the limited weather resistance of external walls. Fortunately, modern techniques of damp proofing, for example by in-situ injection, can often help. Structural stability is less likely to cause problems due to Chester's rock foundations and to the generous and over-sized scantlings of much old timber construction.

In *Conversions*, the main difficulties may be from Part K of the Regulations, on Open Space, Ventilation and the Height of Rooms. To provide extra windows or enlarge existing ones may be impossible for architectural reasons. Ventilating internal stairways may be difficult in cases where conversions make them 'communal'. Statutory ceiling-heights could be a special trouble. At Row level for example, many of the storey heights are below 7 ft. 6 in., although elsewhere they are equally over-generous (Fig. 94b).

The Regulations provide for Dispensation or Relaxation on application to the local authority or against the decision of the local authority on appeal to the Minister. This must obviously be a matter for much intelligence and discretion.

95 The results of fire in an old building in Northgate Street

Fire resistance and means of escape

The Building Regulations 1965-66 include requirements for preventing the spread of fire and for means of escape, which pose problems for Chester's historic buildings. The City's Fire Prevention Officers make recommendations dealing with each case on its merits.

The *prevention of fire spread* is largely covered by the Building Regulations. The requirements were at first very stringent, particularly on fire-resistant 'compartments', and would have made impossible the economic sub-division of many buildings. The 1966 Amendments eased the situation considerably. It now appears that the regulations on the fire-resistance of 'compartment' floors and walls can normally be met by surface cladding rather than actual structural works.

But the enclosure of communal staircases will often be necessary in multiple conversions. This is a most important provision, as much to contain the spread of smoke as of fire. The generous staircases in Chester's larger buildings could mostly be adapted without difficulty in terms of space : but visually there are often difficulties in partitioning the grander architectural schemes. In Abbey Square, where this problem has already arisen when sub-dividing houses into flats, it has been solved with glazed partitions of good quality (Fig. 96a). The overall appearance can still be seen, even though it is now physically divided. This is certainly preferable to the major butchering of many good staircases which would otherwise be necessary.

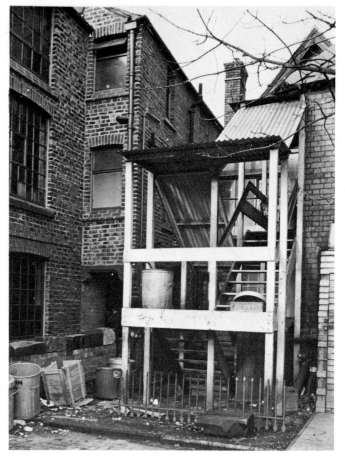

96a Glazed fire screens enclosing the stair-cases in Abbey Square

96b Unsightly rear fire escape in Watergate Street

96c A neat fire-escape door in a party wall in Whitefriars

Means of escape are usually a far more difficult matter: internally, a clear route must be provided within each sub-divided unit to its alternative means of escape. This is largely a matter of sensible planning, and can normally be fulfilled without too much difficulty.

Externally, the problem is to provide an alternative means of escape from each unit. Sometimes in Chester, this has been obtained over the roofs of adjacent buildings. It is simple where these are flat; but the pitch-and-valley roofs of most old buildings often rule this out. Several other means have been used, with varying degrees of success. External metal fire escapes direct to ground level are disliked. They are rarely properly maintained, and can be dangerous through inadequate lighting, and through icing-up in the winter. They are also almost always hideous (Fig. 96b).

A modified form of external escape is a metal 'balcony' which links adjacent windows across party walls. This has been tried in Abbey Square and elsewhere. It need not be unsightly but does raise problems of security and privacy. Where adjoining owners agree, it is a satisfactory method. Automatic lowering lines, chain ladders with rigid steps and the like are not approved since they are rarely well maintained and call for training in their use.

One of the best methods of escape between adjacent properties is simply an escape door through the party wall with emergency keys from both sides. This again requires agreement between adjoining owners (Fig. 96c), but it reduces security risks, involves no external alterations and is relatively cheap. It has been used most successfully for example in Whitefriars, and is particularly suitable for offices. A sand-built 'push-through' opening is another useful method suggested by the City Engineer.

2.8.6 A case study: the nine houses

circa 1650
A terrace of nine cottages was built (three-storeyed, timber-framed on a base of brick and stone). Five of these remain today in their original state.

mid 19th century
Two cottages at north end were rebuilt. These today are of less archaeological interest, but in sounder condition.

1957
An application received by the City Council to demolish the houses which were then all occupied, and to build a warehouse on the site.

The application was rejected on the grounds of unsuitable use in a residential area.

The plight of the houses was brought to the notice of local societies and the Society for the Protection of Ancient Buildings who recommended preservation.

1958
A proposal was put forward by the curator of Chester Museum to convert the terrace into a Folk Museum. This was well received by the City Corporation but negotiations with the owner were lengthy and difficult.

1959
The Local Public Health Inspector's report on the houses said that they could not be put in order at reasonable cost.

1962

An architect was appointed to convert the houses into a Folk Museum. By this time they had deteriorated, and all tenants had been moved to other accommodation.

The City Council asked for plans for alternative uses for the houses, including their conversion into .dwellings of a modern standard.

Negotiations were entered into with the owner, principally over the problem of building a rear-access road.

1964

As no agreement was reached, the Chester Civic Trust pressed for action on the situation.

The Historic Buildings Section of the Ministry of Public Building and Works was approached by the Council.

A report prepared by the SPAB underlined the historical and architectural significance of the houses and included plans for modernisation and repair.

1966

Negotiations with the owner continued, and another firm of architects was asked to consider the works involved. By this time the state of the houses was so poor that the consultants advised that restoration would not be economically viable in view of its high cost in relation to the likely return.

The City Council prepared plans for restoration and applied for an Historic Buildings Council grant towards the cost. This was successful, and a grant of £5,500 enabled the houses to be saved.

1967

The conveyance of the houses was completed and restoration and rebuilding work commenced. They will soon have been largely rebuilt.

98   The rear of the nine houses after a decade of neglect

2.8.7 Criteria for Study Areas

Chester's fine historic buildings give the City, firstly their intrinsic *architectural and historic* qualities, and secondly their *townscape* values, by their relation to one another and to the whole. To evaluate the comparative merits of Chester's historic buildings, we have categorised them as follows:

'Anchor' buildings. Those of such high intrinsic quality that no other tests need be applied. Many have special Cestrian characteristics and uniquely distinguish their City settings.

The Cathedral and the three important medieval churches are 'anchor' buildings (Fig. 100a); so are the Castle, and the Bluecoat Hospital in Upper Northgate Street. The City Walls, the Abbey Gateways and the Old Dee and Grosvenor Bridges also come into this category. Street buildings have been included only when their fronts are of exceptional quality and stand out even from distinguished surroundings, for example, the 'Bear and Billet' in Lower Bridge Street and Bishop Lloyd's House in Watergate Street. These are the cream of Chester's buildings and are indispensable.

Major townscape buildings. Those with major intrinsic qualities that contribute more to their settings than they derive from them.

The balance between buildings and setting is still weighted in favour of the building; they contribute more than they receive. This category includes most of Chester's best street buildings. Typical but differing examples are Leche House (Watergate Street), Oddfellows Hall (Lower Bridge Street), the Royal Insurance building (St. John Street) (Fig. 100b), and the houses in Abbey Square.

Minor townscape buildings. Those whose intrinsic and townscape values are balanced.

Here, their setting is as important as their intrinsic value. The Rows are mainly of such buildings. Their simple Georgian frontages are typical, as are those at the north end of Queen Street. These are Chester's 'bread and butter' historic buildings. They are a foil to those more individually important, and by their numbers and continuity make up the City's strong historical character.

Buildings of group value. Those of limited architectural value on their own, but which collectively combine into attractive townscape.

Examples include the major part of King Street (Fig. 101a) and the domestic part of the Groves. Environment here is often a major factor, for each building relies upon the others and the loss of one will devalue the rest.

Buildings of location value. Those that have no intrinsic merit but are important by virtue of their position.

The west side of St. Peter's Churchyard might be taken as an example, because it is a vital element in the enclosure of this miniature square (Fig. 101b). Gamul Terrace in Lower Bridge Street consists of small shops at street level, with a balcony to tenements above. Their two-level treatment is valuable to the character of the street. The function of these might equally be fulfilled by new buildings maintaining the same siting and form. But often they are in positions where rebuilding would be impossible, a situation that makes them literally irreplaceable.

100a 'Anchor' building: Holy Trinity Church, now the Guild Hall, is a landmark for much of Chester

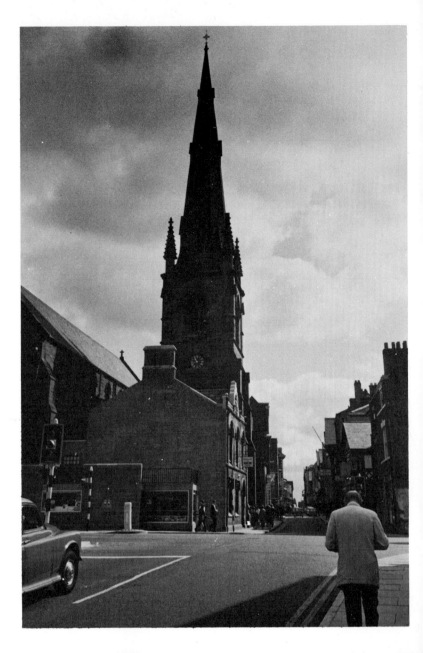

100b Major townscape building: 6 St John's Street gives character to an architecturally mixed street

101a   Building of group value: Georgian houses in King Street

101b   Building of location value: in St Peter's Churchyard, a quiet backwater close to the Cross

104

3 Chester: The Study Areas

We, now consider in detail the elements that make up the vital historical essence of Chester—the buildings and their environment—examine their present state, the problems that must be solved, and suggest policies that should be adopted for them.

Our criterion for detailed study areas has been a significant content of historic buildings, other than single monuments, or a special environmental character which contributes to Chester's status as an historic city. The definition of study areas has evolved from natural boundaries. Sometimes these are physical divisions, such as the City Walls or Nicholas Street: sometimes they are functional and sociological, for example, between the shops and commerce of Northgate Street and the Cathedral Close character of Abbey Square.

The characteristics and problems vary widely, and so consequently does the attention they require. The studies which follow are based upon a common analytical system, and then consider each individual area in detail.

DETAILED STUDY AREAS

1 City walls

2 Rows

3 Cathedral Precinct

4 Whitefriars

5 Bridgegate

6 Watergate

7 Northgate

8 Upper Northgate & canalside

9 Foregate

10 Riverside

OUTLINE STUDY AREAS

11 New market

12 Royal Infirmary

13 Castle

3.1 Study Area 1 : The City Walls

3.1.1. Townscape appraisal

The characteristics of the City Walls are principally visual, and are analysed in the following four pages.

106 Pictorial analysis of the City Walls

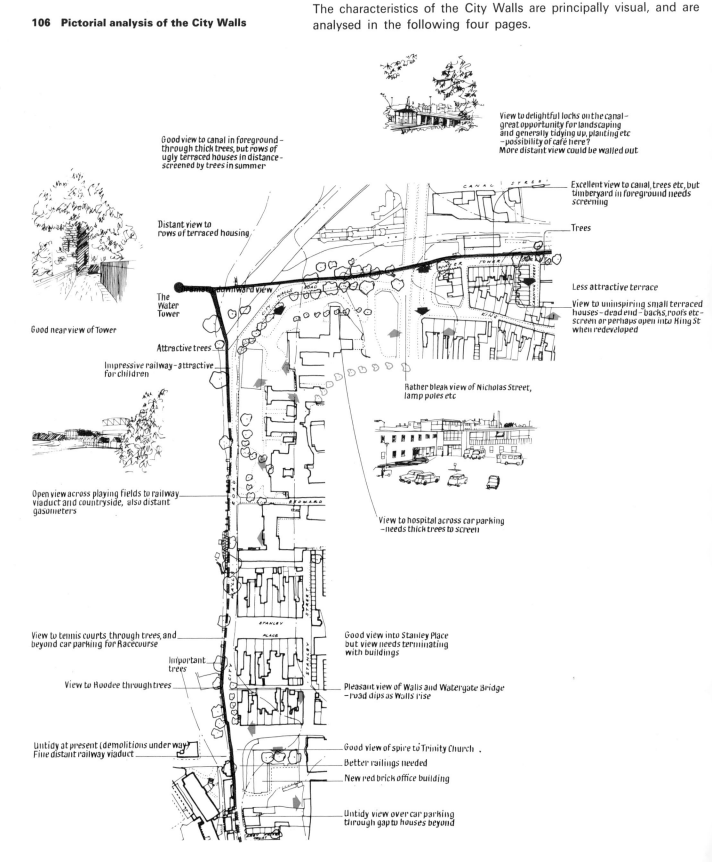

View to delightful locks on the canal –
great opportunity for landscaping
and generally tidying up, planting etc
– possibility of café here?
More distant view could be walled out

Good view to canal in foreground –
through thick trees, but rows of
ugly terraced houses in distance –
screened by trees in summer

Excellent view to canal, trees etc, but
timberyard in foreground needs
screening

Distant view to
rows of terraced housing

Trees

Less attractive terrace

View to uninspiring small terraced
houses – dead end – backs, roofs etc –
screen or perhaps open into King St
when redeveloped

The Water Tower

Dramatic downward view

Good near view of Tower

Attractive trees

Impressive railway – attractive
for children

Rather bleak view of Nicholas Street,
lamp poles etc

Open view across playing fields to railway
viaduct and countryside, also distant
gasometers

View to hospital across car parking
– needs thick trees to screen

View to tennis courts through trees, and
beyond car parking for Racecourse

Good view into Stanley Place
but view needs terminating
with buildings

Important trees

View to Roodee through trees

Pleasant view of Walls and Watergate Bridge
– road dips as Walls rise

Untidy at present (demolitions under way)
Fine distant railway viaduct

Good view of spire to Trinity Church

Better railings needed

New red brick office building

Untidy view over car parking
through gap to houses beyond

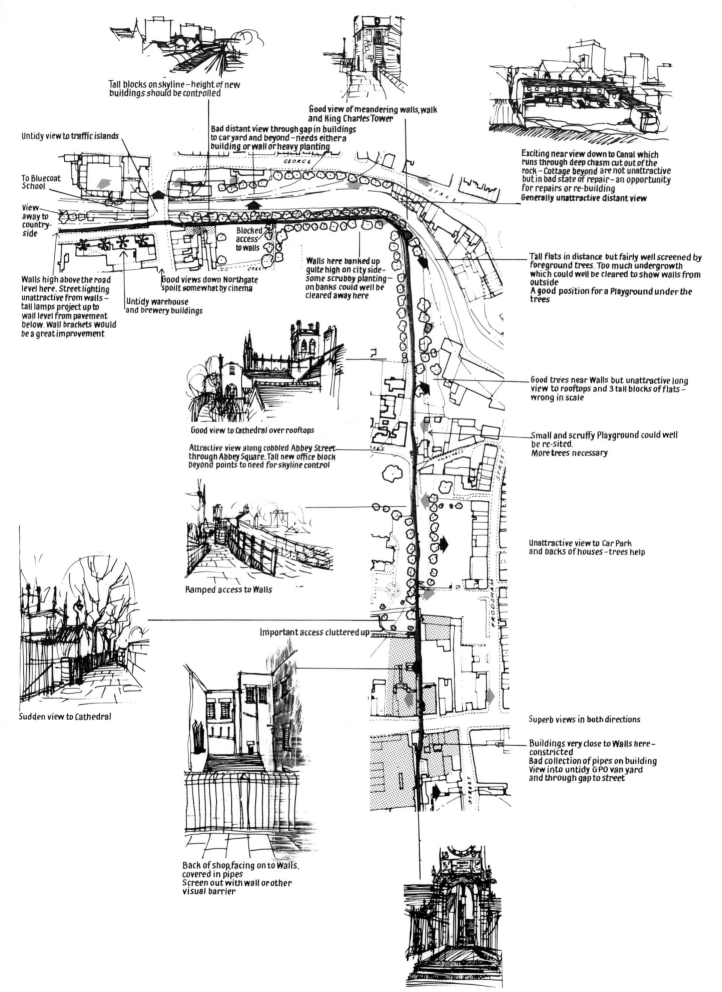

Tall blocks on skyline – height of new buildings should be controlled

Untidy view to traffic islands

To Bluecoat School

View away to country-side

Good view of meandering walls, walk and King Charles Tower

Bad distant view through gap in buildings to car yard and beyond – needs either a building or wall or heavy planting

GEORGE STREET

Exciting near view down to Canal which runs through deep chasm cut out of the rock – Cottage beyond are not unattractive but in bad state of repair – an opportunity for repairs or re-building
Generally unattractive distant view

Blocked access to walls

Walls high above the road level here. Street lighting unattractive from walls – tall lamps project up to wall level from pavement below. Wall brackets would be a great improvement

Good views down Northgate spoilt somewhat by cinema

Untidy warehouse and brewery buildings

Walls here banked up quite high on city side – some scrubby planting – on banks could well be cleared away here

Tall flats in distance but fairly well screened by foreground trees. Too much undergrowth which could well be cleared to show walls from outside
A good position for a Playground under the trees

Good view to Cathedral over rooftops

Good trees near Walls but unattractive long view to rooftops and 3 tall blocks of flats – wrong in scale

Attractive view along cobbled Abbey Street through Abbey Square. Tall new office block beyond points to need for skyline control

Small and scruffy Playground could well be re-sited.
More trees necessary

Ramped access to Walls

Unattractive view to Car Park and backs of houses – trees help

Sudden view to Cathedral

Important access cluttered up

Superb views in both directions

Buildings very close to Walls here – constricted
Bad collection of pipes on building
View into untidy GPO van yard and through gap to street

Back of shop, facing on to Walls, covered in pipes
Screen out with wall or other visual barrier

Looking North – view under attractive Clock Tower to trees and more open feeling beyond

FRODSHAM STREET

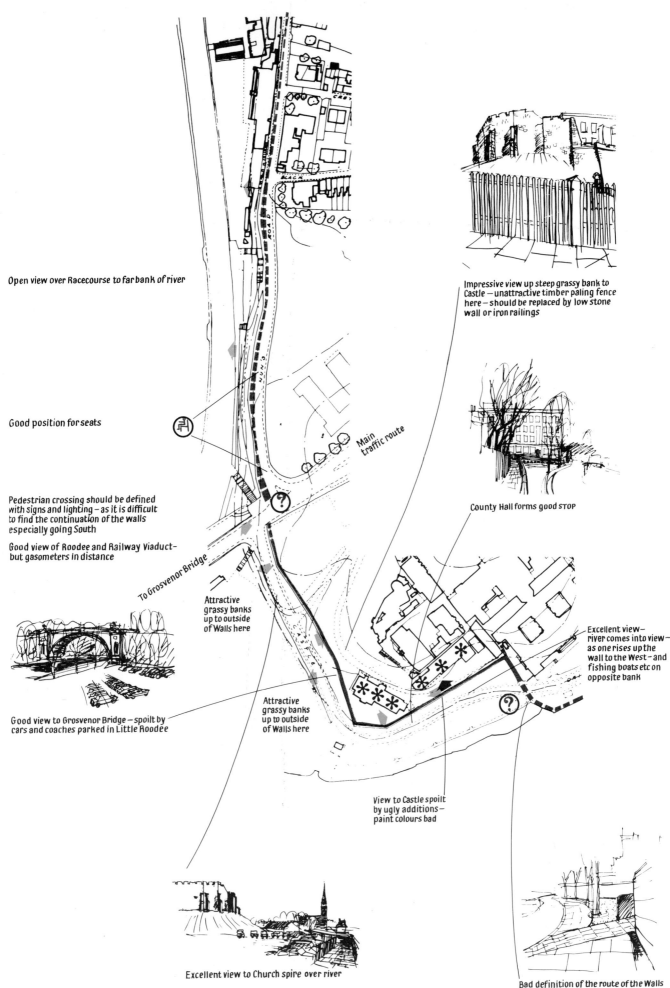

Open view over Racecourse to far bank of river

Impressive view up steep grassy bank to Castle – unattractive timber paling fence here – should be replaced by low stone wall or iron railings

Good position for seats

Main traffic route

County Hall forms good STOP

Pedestrian crossing should be defined with signs and lighting – as it is difficult to find the continuation of the walls especially going South

Good view of Roodee and Railway Viaduct – but gasometers in distance

To Grosvenor Bridge

Attractive grassy banks up to outside of Walls here

Excellent view – river comes into view – as one rises up the wall to the West – and fishing boats etc on opposite bank

Good view to Grosvenor Bridge – spoilt by cars and coaches parked in Little Roodee

Attractive grassy banks up to outside of Walls here

View to Castle spoilt by ugly additions – paint colours bad

Excellent view to Church spire over river

Bad definition of the route of the Walls at this point. Change in paving helps, this could be continued across road here and 'To the Walls' signpost desirable

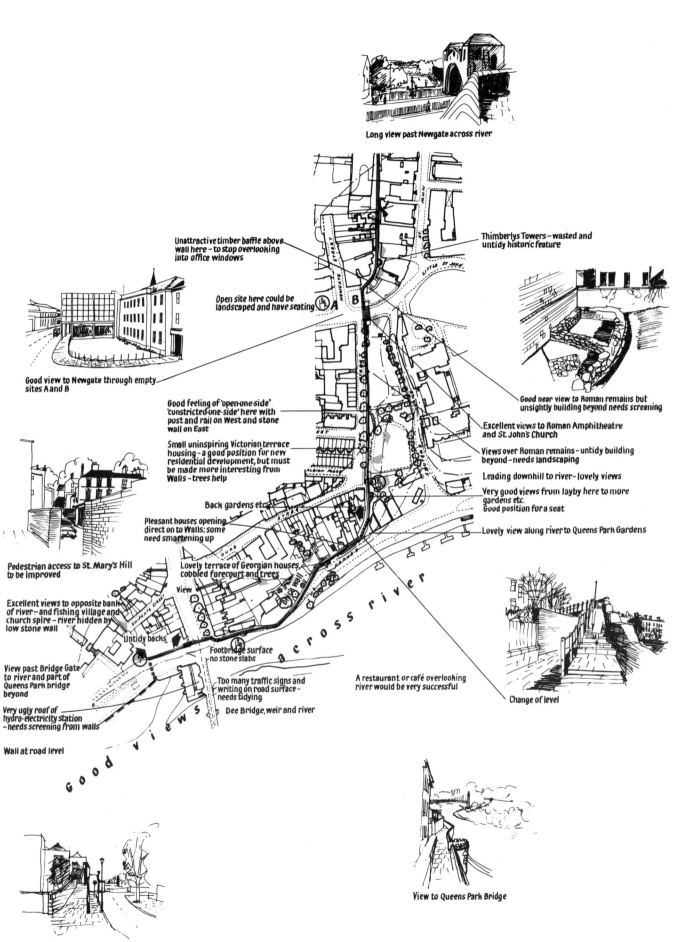

Long view past Newgate across river

Unattractive timber baffle above wall here – to stop overlooking into office windows

Thimberlys Towers – wasted and untidy historic feature

Open site here could be landscaped and have seating Ⓐ Ⓑ

Good view to Newgate through empty sites A and B

Good feeling of 'open-one-side' 'constricted-one-side' here with post and rail on West and stone wall on East

Small uninspiring Victorian terrace housing – a good position for new residential development, but must be made more interesting from Walls – trees help

Back gardens etc.

Pleasant houses opening direct on to Walls; some need smartening up

Pedestrian access to St. Mary's Hill to be improved

Lovely terrace of Georgian houses, cobbled forecourt and trees

View

Excellent views to opposite bank of river – and fishing village and church spire – river hidden by low stone wall

Untidy backs

View past Bridge Gate to river and part of Queens Park bridge beyond

Footbridge surface – no stone slabs

Very ugly roof of hydro-electricity station – needs screening from walls

Too many traffic signs and writing on road surface – needs tidying

Dee Bridge, weir and river

A restaurant or café overlooking river would be very successful

Wall at road level

Good near view to Roman remains but unsightly building beyond needs screening

Excellent views to Roman Amphitheatre and St. John's Church

Views over Roman remains – untidy building beyond – needs landscaping

Leading downhill to river – lovely views

Very good views from layby here to more gardens etc.
Good position for a seat

Lovely view along river to Queens Park Gardens

Good views across river

Change of level

View to Queens Park Bridge

Over Bridgegate

110a Eroded stone has been renewed at many stages

110b Some balusters need renewal

3.1.2 Condition and maintenance

The City Walls are the outstanding historical feature of Chester. Current repairs are done by the Corporation at a cost of £5,000 per year: but future conservation will call for increased expenditure.

Strengthening. The Walls have been rebuilt and repaired through the centuries and structurally speaking are no longer homogeneous. Several places show structural weakness and need priority repair before any actual collapse occurs. Between King Charles's Tower and Eastgate the Wall is spreading due to weakness of the core, and this needs strengthening within the original facing stonework. Another section to watch is immediately to the east of the new St. Martin's Gate, where a split through an old archway is again beginning to spread.

Stone renewal. The City Walls are built of local sandstone, and surface decay has been a constant problem due to its relatively soft nature. But this is very gradual, and only stones worn too thin for structural safety need renewal. At various times in the past, complete sections of the Walls have been refaced, often to a different profile from the original, and in stones of different sizes and textures (Fig. 110a). This can be seen on the south-east corner of the Walls by the Riverside, where a nineteenth-century refacing has been left 'keyed' for future extension. This wholesale refacing mars historical identity and could be avoided by the periodic renewal of individual badly eroded stones.

Gateways. The four historic entrance gateways (Northgate, Eastgate, Bridgegate and Watergate) are all solidly built but suffer from water penetration. Some of the cornices were formerly protected by flashings, but all leadwork has long since disappeared. If lead proves too much of an attraction for vandals, a less valuable material like asphalt can be used; but these cornices must be properly weatherproofed. Water penetration not only deteriorates the structure, but causes unsightly staining on the face of the stonework.

Regular washing would further help to remove City grime. Bridgegate and Northgate especially at present look more like the sooty portals of a railway tunnel, and would benefit enormously by careful cleaning of their stonework. Eastgate and Watergate would need to be cleaned much more carefully, owing to the soft nature of their red sandstone. Bridgegate when cleaned and waterproofed may need some strengthening of its south-east abutment, which is showing signs of movement.

Repointing. Old stonework needs careful pointing. Loose and open joints encourage water penetration, and the roots of shrubs displace and weaken the stonework. Large and fast-growing trees alongside the Wall can also disturb the footings, and should not be planted too close. Plants growing in and very near the Wall should be poisoned, and their roots removed. Then the areas affected should be deeply raked out and repointed with a suitably weak mortar.

Pavings. The natural stone pavings are essential to their character and should be retained. Wherever renewal is necessary, either stone slabs removed from other parts of the town, or else new York pavings are needed. Concrete slabs look incongruous and out of place on historic monuments like Bridgegate, and it would be desirable eventually to replace all of these with natural stone.

111a The undulating nature of the Walls adds to their interest

111b Stonework of high architectural quality

111c More and unobtrusive lighting is needed on the Walls

111d Clear signs are needed where the line is not obvious

3.1.3 Suggested improvements

1. *Access.* Blocked access points to the Walls (for example, from Abbey Green and east of the shopping precinct) should be reopened and made safe, by repairing steps, railings and so on and by better lighting.

2. *Continuity* (Fig. 111d). The identity of the Walls should be reinforced by good signposting and by retaining and completing their stone paving.

3. *Lighting* (Fig. 111c). A carefully designed system of lighting should be adopted for the Walls, from vandal-proof low-level sources, and especially at changes in level. The system should be continuous around the whole circuit of the Walls, again to give full value to their continuity.

4. *The outside of the Walls* should be cleared of redundant buildings and overgrown planting, especially on the north side, where much of the original Roman work can then be seen to better advantage.

5. *Tourist facilities.* A café, restaurant or even a good coffee stall could be a great asset at Walls level. An excellent position would be in one of the houses within the south-east corner of the Walls, overlooking the Dee.

6. *Seats.* More seats should be provided at the best viewpoints. For example, Thimbleby's Tower, at present neglected, could be floored over as an attractive viewing platform.

3.2 Study Area 2: The Rows

3.2.1 Townscape appraisal

The Rows are a thriving shopping centre in a magnificent architectural setting; the physical nucleus and social heart of Chester. They are the City's most individually characteristic element, and an outstanding reminder of the continued validity of good historic buildings for busy modern life.

The four main streets meet at the Cross and are continuously walled in all directions by tall buildings. Their strong definition and continuity are emphasised by the twin-level system of the Rows and by the dominant verticality of high, gabled facades.

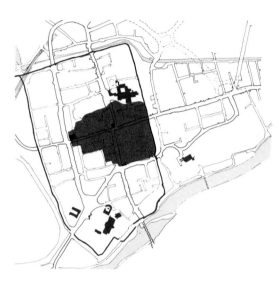

112a Study Area 2: The Rows

112b Aerial view of the Study Area

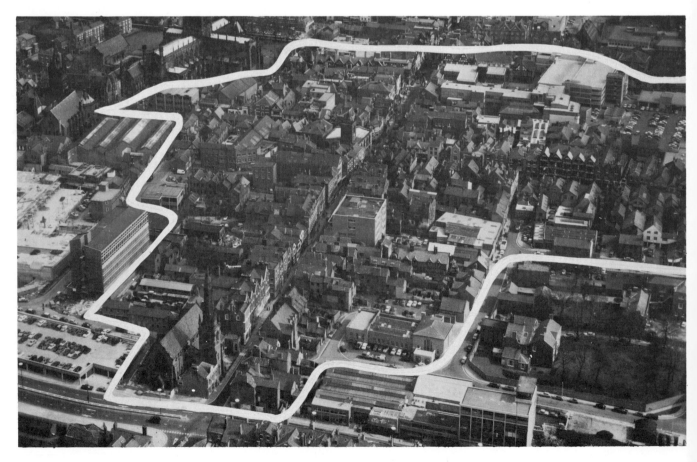

112

113a Townscape analysis

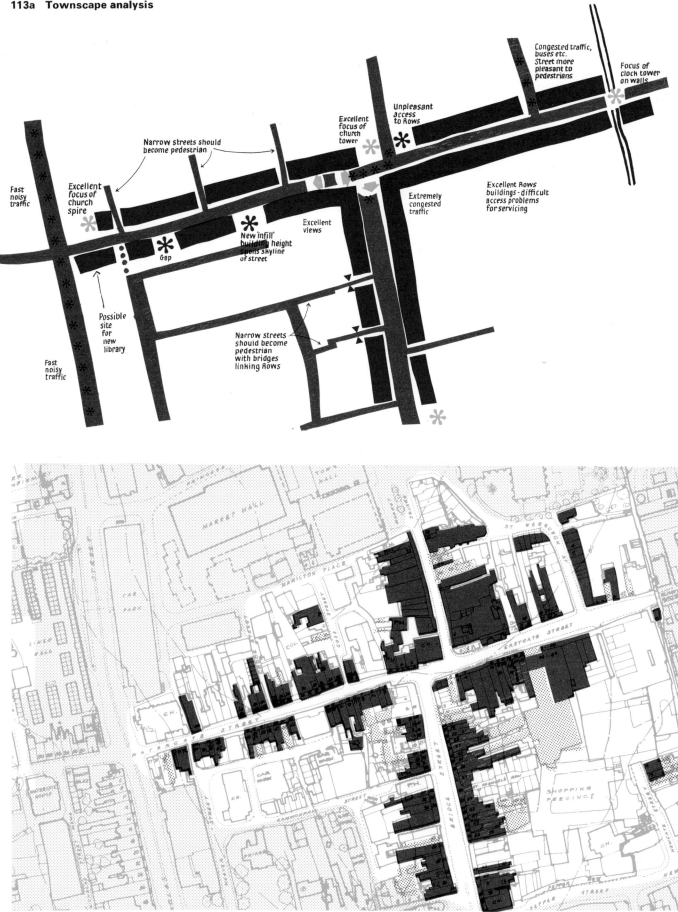

Congested traffic, buses etc. Street more pleasant to pedestrians

Focus of clock tower on walls

Unpleasant access to Rows

Excellent focus of church tower

Narrow streets should become pedestrian

Fast noisy traffic

Excellent focus of church spire

Extremely congested traffic

Excellent Rows buildings - difficult access problems for servicing

Excellent views

Gap

New 'infill' building height spoils skyline of street

Possible site for new library

Fast noisy traffic

Narrow streets should become pedestrian with bridges linking Rows

113b Buildings inspected

Buildings recommended for listing

Other buildings inspected

114a Victorian cast-iron railings

114b Row shop signs

This unity is achieved by the contrast of individual style and incident which gives interest, drama and excitement. The result is an intensely human character. There are three predominant building types: post-Restoration timber-framed fronts, mostly gabled; Georgian facades, plainer and with level parapets; and Victorian and Edwardian black-and-white reproductions, often of very high quality. To walk through the Rows is a unique visual experience; a changing sequence of levels, heights and widths, among a fascinating variety of railings (Fig. 114a), balustrades and pillars, shop signs, and fronts (Fig. 114b), and colourful window displays.

Each street of the Rows area has its own individuality:

Eastgate Street is Chester's most successful commercial street, except for one curious section of its north-side Row. The south side is one long line of prosperous shops westwards from the Grosvenor Hotel and includes Brown's Department Store and the entry to the new St. Michael's shopping precinct. The street vistas are extremely attractive and enhanced by a recent communal decoration scheme. A superb eastward stop is the fantastic ironwork of the Eastgate clock. To the west, the long view continues beyond the Cross and down Watergate Street to the Guildhall spire. There are few historic buildings earlier than the nineteenth-century replicas, but the combined effect of their grand scale and quality is supreme.

Watergate Street, on the other hand, is a street of fine individual historic buildings, but shows many signs of under-use and shabbiness. The splendid fronts of, for example, Leche House and Bishop Lloyd's House seem less attractive than they might, due to the gap further west. Here, neglect led to demolition. Refuge House is the only recent replacement, and its design illustrates the peculiar difficulties of infilling in the street. The street and its pavements are narrow and dangerous, and it runs downhill gently to the west. The Row system is continuous along the south side as far as Weaver Street. But on the north it is interrupted by Goss Street and stopped short by steep access stairs at Crook Street. Beyond, the splendid Guildhall spire sadly marks only the relentless barrier of Nicholas Street's cross traffic, and Watergate Street nowadays 'leads nowhere'.

114c A hanging shop sign in Eastgate

114d Feeling of enclosure in a low-ceilinged Row

115a Holy Trinity spire 'closes' Watergate Street

115b Cast- and wrought iron

115c An infinite variety of detail in Watergate Street

Northgate Street, within the Rows area, is a short link between the Cross and Town Hall Square. The constant battle between pedestrians and vehicles here is typical of Chester's traffic problem. The west side is arcaded over a single raised pavement. The east side has a fragmentary Row system, but this connects unsatisfactorily to the dark, uninviting entry into Eastgate Row; while to the north nondescript small shop buildings are mostly an unworthy prelude to the Cathedral.

Bridge Street, after Eastgate, is the most successful street of the Rows area. It combines good buildings with excellent and well-used shops. The street runs downhill from the Cross, but unlike Watergate Street it is sheltered and sunny, and its pavements are wider and less interrupted, especially on the east. The street view to the south is focused on St. Michael's Church, offsetting the inconclusive form of the road junction here. To the north, the view up the street is most splendidly stopped by St. Peter's Church. Bridge Street's buildings themselves are a fine amalgam of all Chester's architectural styles: from the exuberant facades of the Elizabethan 'Dutch Houses' through plain and decent brick Georgian to very fine Victorian timber framing. The variety and detailing of the Rows is at its most attractive.

The four quarters flanking the Cross vary greatly in character and use:

The north-east quarter is divided diagonally by *St. Werburgh Street*. This has splendid reproduction timber buildings and is partly arcaded, making a worthy setting for the Cathedral. But the triangle of buildings which it contains between Northgate and Eastgate Street has acute servicing problems.

The north-west quarter borders the site of the new market developments, south of which it meanwhile lacks form and cohesion. Careful integration will be needed. A delightful element is the quiet pedestrian way and miniature square behind St. Peter's Church, an attractive and practical alternative to the traffic of Northgate Street, which links directly to Watergate Street at Row level.

The south-east quarter is now filled to bursting by the highly successful new shopping precinct. Newgate Street retains a few good period building facades.

The south-west quarter is at present an unsatisfactory zone of under-used back land, but offers good potential rear service facilities to the Watergate and Bridge Street Rows.

115d Ironwork in Eastgate

116a Watergate Street, at present neglected

3.2.2 Architectural quality

The Rows present a complete cross-section of the architectural evolution of Chester. Each street has its own characteristics and qualities, reflecting varying degrees of prosperity. Perversely, success has often brought the renewal of buildings, while failure has generally allowed their survival.

Watergate Street recalls the importance of its origins, and of Chester's days as a river port. Thanks to declining commercial pressures, many buildings of outstanding high quality remain (Fig. 116a).

The oldest parts are the medieval cellars. Those below No. 11 are outstanding. Complete early buildings include sixteenth- and seventeenth-century Leche House, largely unaltered and with excellent original interiors, and early seventeenth-century Bishop Lloyd's House, with magnificent although restored carved timberwork (Fig. 116c). Many minor buildings also have good internal work of pre-Georgian date behind plain later fronts; for example the Deva Hotel and No. 36 Row.

The street's finest mainly Georgian building is No. 28-30 Row. This has a handsome facade, dignified and large in scale. The best work inside is early eighteenth century, and the building, although mutilated, is of the very highest quality. Good plain Georgian fronts and interiors elsewhere include Nos. 17, 46-48 and 68.

Due to its nineteenth-century decline, the street's only major example of a Victorian black-and-white replica is God's Providence House. The contribution of the present century has so far not been of any quality. The vacant sites westwards give scope for something better.

116b Leche House, Watergate Street, Chester's least-restored timber-framed building

116c Carved oak panels decorate Bishop Lloyd's House

116

117a The 'Dutch' houses are some of the earliest in Bridge Street

Bridge Street (Fig. 117c) has some fine early buildings, but its more sustained level of commercial success has brought with it a higher rate of replacement, especially to the east.

Roman Chester is represented here by a hypocaust under No. 35; and the cellars at No. 12 are medieval. The most important complete buildings of early date are Nos. 22 to 26 (the 'Dutch' Houses) (Fig. 117a) with their fine jettied and gabled facades and internal decoration. No. 49 is a good and mainly complete building of 1659; and No. 17 has good Jacobean features.

The eighteenth century produced many facades of mellow brickwork, with parapets and sash windows. But indoors, most of the Georgian quality has been lost in later alterations. Complete interiors like that of No 32 are now comparatively rare.

Bridge Street has at No. 36 one of Chester's best Victorian timbered reproduction facades with good and elaborate ornament. It has also one of the biggest, in the broad facade that spreads across the entrance to St. Michael's Row. Later work like the corner building at Watergate Street is of lesser quality. The contribution of the present century is almost entirely one of shopfitting, of varied standard.

Northgate Street (Fig. 117b) has as its most important building Harrison's City Club (1808), whose external stone Classicism and fine interiors are of great quality. The long, arcaded and 1900-ish reproduction terrace to the north is good of its kind. On the east side, No. 6 has historic interest in its sixteenth- and eighteenth-century remains and characterful early Victorian shopfittings. No. 8 is another notable Victorian black-and-white reproduction.

117b The southern end of Northgate Street, arcaded at ground level

117c Bridge Street, a variety of architecture terminated at the southern end by the tower of St Michael's

117

118a   Medieval cellars well used and displayed in a department store

118b   St Werburgh Street leads up to the Cathedral

Eastgate Street (Fig. 119a) has a good mixture of buildings, mostly Victorian. But the cellar of No. 60 is probably Roman, and so may be the one we inspected in No. 17. The thirteenth-century rib-vaulted and arched cellar of Brown's shop is outstandingly good (Fig. 118a).

The Boot Inn has a fine timbered front, most of which is original and very good seventeenth-century work inside. No. 32 Row retains Jacobean features of some quality and a typical Georgian staircase. Elsewhere the eighteenth century has left only minor plain facades.

This street is notable for its nineteenth-century work. It varies in quality from the early and pleasant Classical front of No. 23 Row and the much stronger 1828 section of Brown's shop through the adjacent High Victorian stone Gothic of 1859 front, to its ultimate in the magnificent timber-framed reproduction work of No. 2.

The twentieth century has contributed some good shopfronts, rare period replicas like the rumbustious baroque front of the House of Bewlay and the rebuilt Dutch gabled facade at the entrance to the precinct.

St. Werburgh Street (Fig. 118b) has only one early building, the thirteenth-century shell of what is now Lipton's supermarket. Its buttressed sandstone south wall is a sad reminder of the building's earlier importance and James Harrison's east front (1854) is somewhat meretricious Gothic Revival. Much of the rest of the street is splendid Victorian black-and-white reproduction work. The long east side terrace is particularly fine.

The lesser streets contain little of merit. In *St. Peter's Churchyard* the Commercial Hotel is a minor work of late Georgian date and acts as a foil to the more splendid rear facade of the City Club. *Goss Street* had the eighteenth-century Assay Office. *Newgate Street's* minor Georgian buildings are today dwarfed by the western flank of the shopping precinct.

The three churches of the Rows are distinguished in different ways. *St. Peter's*, at the Cross, has fourteenth- and fifteenth-century bulk and a good tower and small spire. *St. Michael's*, at the south end of Bridge Street, is attractive mid-Victorian Gothic, and its arcaded tower is visually strong. So is the spire of Watergate Street's *Holy Trinity*, now the Guildhall.

The area's largest and newest building is the shopping precinct, and with the exception of the Pepper Street frontage is little seen as 'street architecture'. Its visual attraction is mainly internal, deriving from the lively signs of success in its thriving shopping units. Its outward effacement to the established Rows buildings around it is the twentieth century's most sensitive contribution yet to the buildings of the Rows area, and sets an admirable standard for the future.

119a Eastgate Street, the busiest of the Rows   **119b Watergate Row**

119c Architectural value

Internal

 Major interiors

Good features

Unremarkable

External

Anchor or major streetscape

 Minor streetscape or group

 Location

120a   A fine seventeenth-century fireplace in a disused floor in Watergate Street

120b   Several Row houses are admirably used as antique shops

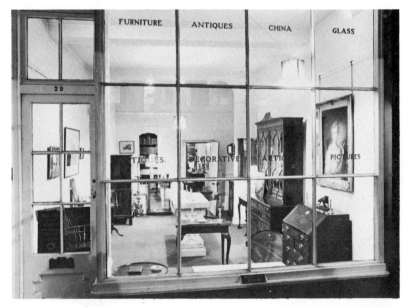

120c   The notorious 'gap' in Watergate Street contributes to the under-use of the street

3.2.3 Ownership, use and condition

The ownership pattern of the Rows area is as varied as the use of its many historic buildings. The two-level access has often resulted in a multiple ownership of individual structures. Some businesses have expanded horizontally through several properties, and many larger concerns own whole groups, or scattered premises throughout the area.

As a result of their policy of acquiring old property in the central area, the Corporation now owns several buildings on each side of Watergate Street, the most important of which is Bishop Lloyd's House. It is tragic that having bought these historic buildings with the best intentions of conserving them, lack of suitable tenants and insufficient funds should have resulted in the loss of Nos. 61-65 Watergate Row. Nos. 67 and 69, adjoining, are also in a ruinous state (Fig. 120c).

Use. The multitude of users includes not only shops, from the kiosk to department stores, but also printing works, clubs, laboratories, ballrooms and flats. Several properties have been converted as offices. Their upper floors, where they are used at all, are given over to a wide variety of commercial establishments, ranging from wigmakers to a secretarial college.

There tends to be a concentration of food shops at street level, especially in Bridge Street and Watergate Street, with speciality shops at Row level. Cafés are found at both levels. As well as the department stores, several types of shop such as stationers, toy, furniture and men's wear shops extend through several floors, and it is these buildings which are most fully used. At the other end of the scale, building society offices require only one floor, and unless the upper parts of such buildings can be let separately, they remain neglected and disused. The Row stalls were originally used for the display of wares, and nowadays some still contain additional display cases. Others became 'crystallised' as shops, one such remaining to this day in Watergate Row.

The new shopping precinct has achieved much success in attracting chain stores, but several premises in older buildings have been vacated and remain empty.

121a **Rainwater pipes and the removal of glazing bars destroy the facade of an otherwise attractive house** (below)

121b **Some Row houses are used as offices and the pavement is little used** (below right)

Suitability. Although the original use of the medieval undercrofts within the Rows is uncertain, by the eighteenth century most properties were still residential at Row level. Only a very few of these houses, for example 52 Bridge Street Row, remain unaltered.

Gradually more and more space at Row level was used for shops, while the shopkeepers continued to live above. A few still do, but in recent years many shops have been modernised and extended. Besides restricting access to the upper floors, this has removed many interesting features at Row level.

It is vital for the survival of these Row buildings that their use should be compatible with their architectural interiors. A department store surrounding Nos. 48 and 50 Bridge Street Row has preserved many of the original features of the buildings as a speciality shop and café, while Leche House in Watergate Street serves admirably as an antique shop. But the fine building on the north side of Watergate Street (Nos. 28-30 Row) contains laboratories and offices of institutional character, quite alien to its architecture. The medieval cellars are generally held in high regard, even if some are little used. But above, many splendid rooms with fine plasterwork and details are at present misused and mutilated.

Bridge St. West

Bridge St. East

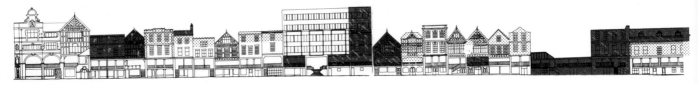

Watergate St. South

Watergate St. North

122a/b   Bridge Street, West and East; c/d Watergate Street, South and North. In these drawings, empty premises are shown by means of a solid red colour; those that are unsatisfactorily used by a red tint

The disuse of upper floors. The principal threat to many buildings in the Rows is the disuse of their upper floors. Often these have deteriorated with their decreasing use by retired shop-keepers. New occupants, with little incentive to put the whole building to full use, find it economical to modernise the property at street level but to abandon the remainder.

This disuse is not universal, but it is a tendency which if unchecked appears likely to spread. The natural cycle of misuse, under-use and disuse, with subsequent decay, dereliction, demolition and finally redevelopment, is demonstrated in Watergate Street, and is also a problem in much of Bridge Street. If this process continues, large parts of the Rows will be redeveloped, and the historic attraction of the central area will rapidly wane.

123 **'The house next door': Watergate Street**

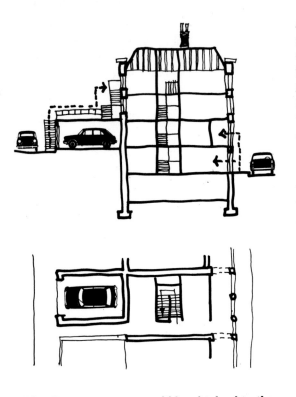

External access and servicing difficulties. Only a minority of properties have rear access and servicing facilities. Most rely entirely on front delivery at street or Row level. Access to the Rows is still further hampered by the limited and decreasing number of approaches, usually involving steep steps (Fig. 125b). Goods deliveries to Row level are difficult, and some tradesmen refuse to deliver at all to the 'second-rank' buildings set behind the main blocks. When repairs and alterations are in hand, builders must unload all materials from the narrow main streets below, causing congestion and delay.

Internal access difficulties. Frequently, modernised shops have sealed off the original staircases to the upper floors. These are now reached by devious routes through side entries and later buildings at the rear. Sometimes access to separate upper floors is still through the Row-level property, and their tenants must depend on the goodwill of the occupiers below. Otherwise, the top of the building becomes disused. Since nearly all the properties were originally single houses of modest size, they do not readily convert into multiple units with separate access. Even horizontal conversion, which is so successful in many parts of Chester, is difficult here owing to the diversity of floor levels. For all these reasons when only part of a Rows building is used, the rest often becomes inaccessible.

124a Separate access could be obtained to the upper part of Rows buildings from behind, where in many cases the ground is at Row level

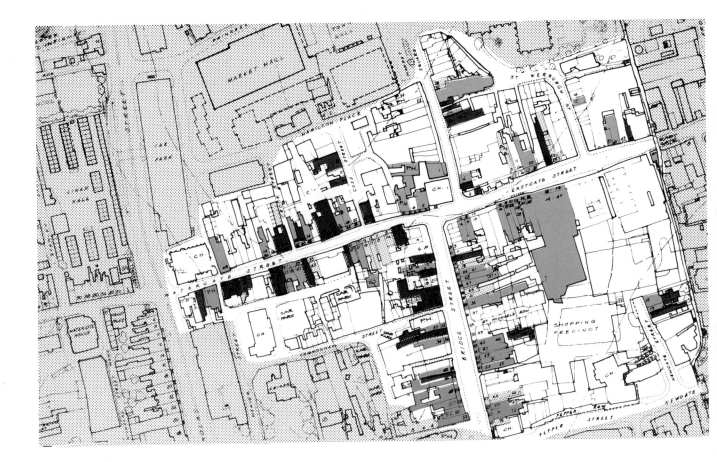

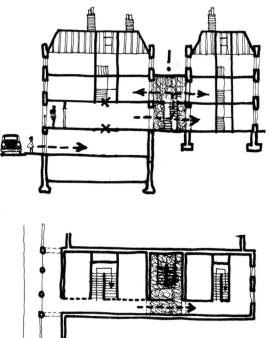

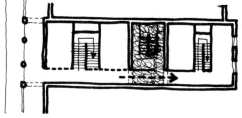

125a Typical Rows building showing difficulties of lighting and ventilation

124b Use and disuse

 Satisfactory

 Satisfactory if improved

 Unsatisfactory but suitable for change of use within present unit

 Unsatisfactory but suitable for use or change of use if combined

 Incapable of economic use or otherwise admitting of replacement

125b Break in Rows continuity handicaps easy use

Planning inadequacies.   Most of the planning deficiencies in the Rows buildings result from alterations and additions. Daylighting at the rear is often very restricted. Later sub-division of upper floors has created under-lit and odd-shaped inner rooms. The attics or old servants' quarters, although they may have fireplaces and dormer windows, are often underlit, and their sloping ceilings make these spaces really suitable only as stores. Some houses still have no bathrooms, but it would generally be simple to provide them. Fire prevention requirements and means of escape are here particularly difficult.

126a Leaking valley gutters cause typical damage in an upper floor

Condition. The architectural variety of the Rows produces especially numerous examples of Chester's party-wall maintenance problem. There is consequently much deterioration as a result of leaking valley gutters and general decay of roofs and chimneys (Fig. 126a).

These conditions can occur in fully occupied buildings. But, as always, the under-used and empty properties receive little or no maintenance. Fresh paint and attractive colour-schemes enhance the exteriors of Bridge Street, but some facades belie the true condition of the buildings behind, which are decaying as rapidly as those in Watergate Street.

Many of the most successful establishments, especially in Eastgate Street, are kept in immaculate condition, but there are other properties where the mantle of prosperity is only skin deep. The mask could melt away with surprising speed if the underlying symptoms of decay are not soon remedied.

The Rows area with its four quarters thus illustrates a whole range of problems in the use of old buildings. Watergate Street at present shows the dull side of the coin, and it is Chester's challenge to remedy this state of affairs so that all parts reflect the prosperity of Eastgate Street.

 Satisfactory overall

 Deteriorating in whole or part

 Individually serious defects

126b   Condition

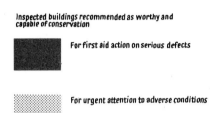

127a A more inviting treatment of the narrow passage behind Eastgate Street

Inspected buildings recommended as worthy and capable of conservation

  For first aid action on serious defects

For urgent attention to adverse conditions

For protection and care

Inspected buildings incapable of, or not in need of conservation

  For renewal, clearance or otherwise admitting of replacement

3.2.4 Conservation and action

The area needs much positive conservation, but the over-riding importance of the Rows makes their first-aid repairs of primary importance to Chester. Equally significant is the need for a solution to the disuse of upper floors. Once achieved this will create the right conditions for proper building care. Many unused upper floors, well converted, could make good flats. Full and appropriate use should be encouraged by all possible means, like the pruning of unwanted additions. A good and thorough standard of repair is needed.

To allow the separate conversion of upper floors, new access and servicing facilities will be needed in Watergate Street and Bridge Street (west).

Maintenance.   90 buildings (Fig. 127b) call for better maintenance, especially at valley-gutters between roofs of the Rows terraces. This could be done by a regular maintenance programme, organised for an Owners' Association.

Site for a public building.   It is vital for Chester that this divided street should now be brought back to life. This will quickly develop if a new and strong attraction is provided, to bring people regularly to it.

127b   Recommendations

128a Watergate Street gap-site redevelopment: plan at second- and third-floor levels

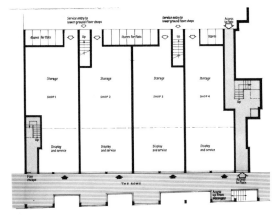

128b Plan at Row level

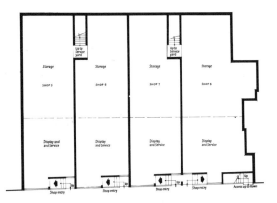

128c Plan at Watergate Street level

Action sites: Watergate Street

The corner site opposite the Guildhall would be a distinguished site for a good building at the gate, as it were, to the street, and well-served by pedestrian and road access and car parking. The Corporation here has a splendid opportunity to revitalise this valuable part of the City by allocating to this site the new library which Chester so much needs.

Gap site redevelopment (Figs. 128a/b/c)

The present *Public House* at the west end could then be re-sited with great success, at street and Row levels in a new building in the 'gap' site to the east. Alternatively, eight *shops* could be provided at the lower level. In either case five 2-person and three 1-person *flats* could be provided on two upper floors.

The public house or shops, and the flats would have access both from Watergate Street and the rear service road. Car parking is nearby, integral garages actually on this site being an uneconomic use of land.

The Cross. Two present corner buildings (north-east and south-west) at the cross are less than worthy of their important positions and complicate pedestrian movement and use. The earliest opportunity should be taken to redevelop these sites with good modern buildings.

128d Elevation to Watergate Street

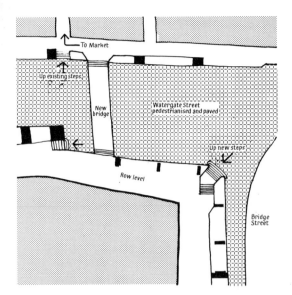

129a **A new footbridge between the Rows and a more inviting entry south-west of the Cross**

129b **Watergate Street closed to traffic** (right)

Environmental improvements

Watergate Street for pedestrians (Figs. 129a/b). This proposal should be completed as soon as possible. Re-surfacing could be combined with bridging of the Rows where these are interrupted by side entries, and between the Rows at north and south. The pedestrian underpass below Nicholas Street would give safe access from lower Watergate Street.

Bridging of Bridge Street Rows. Side-entry interruptions to Bridge Street Row (west) should be bridged, and a new access formed at the present cul-de-sac south end.

Street improvement schemes. The programme recently completed in Eastgate and Bridge Streets should be extended to the rest of the Rows, and arrangements made for regular re-painting. The enclosed Rows passage along the north side of Eastgate Street calls for urgent improvement.

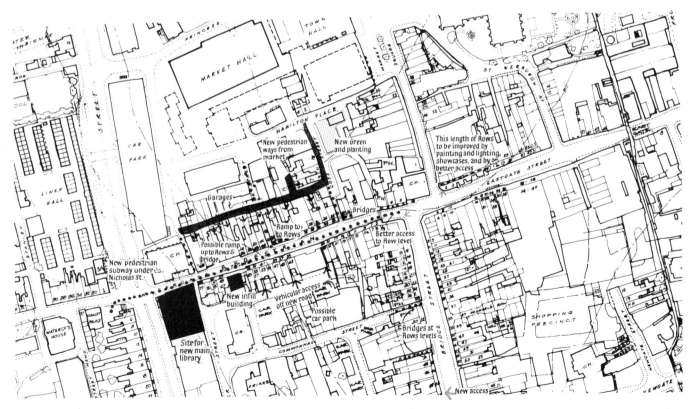

129c **Analysis of recommendations**

3.3 Study Area 3: Cathedral Precinct

130a Study Area 3: Cathedral Precinct

130b Aerial view of the Study Area

3.3.1 Townscape appraisal

This area is in effect Chester's Cathedral close—a quiet enclave to the north of the Cathedral, defined to the east and north by the City Wall and screened behind Northgate Street from the noise and bustle of the City.

The main traffic access is restricted to a rigidly controlled entry through the Abbey Gateway. This provides access for residents and limited parking in Abbey Square. Little Abbey Gateway gives separate entry to minor garaging and service ways in Abbey Mews. A similar separate approach from Northgate Street serves Abbey Green. Otherwise, the area is exclusively pedestrian, entered through the Cathedral or down steps from the City Wall.

The atmosphere of the area is thus totally withdrawn from the City's noisy daily life. To enter Abbey Square from Northgate Street, through the momentary darkness of the Abbey Gateway, is a dramatic transformation to quiet, with cobbles underfoot, grass and trees, in an architectural enclosure of Georgian nobility and Cathedral grandeur.

131a Townscape analysis

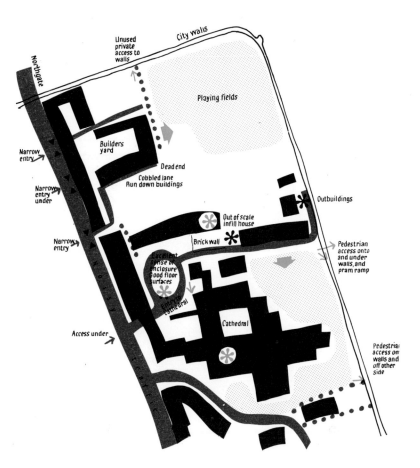

Unused private access to walls

City Walls

Playing fields

Northgate

Narrow entry

Builders yard

Dead end

Narrow entry under

Cobbled lane
Run down buildings

Outbuildings

Out of scale infill house

Narrow entry

Brick wall

Pedestrian access onto and under walls, and pram ramp

Excellent sense of enclosure
Good floor surfaces

Enter cathedral

Cathedral

Access under

Pedestrian access on walls and off other side

131b Buildings inspected

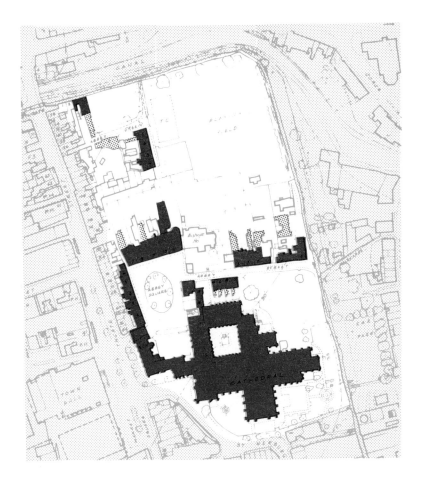

Buildings recommended for listing

Other buildings inspected

132a   Cobbles in Abbey Square

Abbey Square is the area's principal and finest element and is Chester's nearest approach to a formal Georgian Square. Its central space has a simple but effective treatment of raised grass, surrounded by cobbles, in which the carriageways are attractively defined with smooth pavings (Fig. 132a).

Abbey Street to the east continues the square's theme with cobbles underfoot and mainly Georgian architecture, although of a more informal character. The street vista is effectively enclosed by the City Wall, and the whole makes a most attractive setting and foil to the Cathedral.

Abbey Green   (Fig. 132b), to the north of the square, has as its heart a terrace of four charming houses overlooking the playing field and City Wall beyond. But around them at present is an oddly random and formless back area, a visual muddle of run-down workshops, ancillaries and waste land.

132b   Abbey Green

132c   The Cathedral from the playing fields

132d   Abbey Gateway

132e   The Choir School, by Sir Arthur Blomfield

3.3.2 Architectural quality

Chester Cathedral is one of the nation's historical treasures; and its twelfth- to fifteenth-century work is the City's greatest architecture. Its history has earlier been described. The surrounding precinct is also architecturally most distinguished.

Abbey Square (Fig. 133a) has a superb fourteenth-century gateway (Fig. 133b) with the sympathetic nineteenth-century 'Gothic' Choir School adjoining. Except for one pair of early, small seventeenth-century houses, the buildings are Georgian. The northern terrace is the finest and of grand scale. Splendid and varying doorcases and enriched window surrounds distinguish the exteriors. Within are spacious, beautifully ornamented rooms, arranged around the elaborate central staircases. The western terrace is similar but of lesser quality in planning and detail.

On the east side is Abbey Chambers – a good, detached building of the eighteenth century (Fig. 133c). The present Bishop's Palace is withdrawn in its courtyard and has a pleasant Regency flavour.

133a Abbey Square (right)

133b Abbey Gateway (below)

133c Abbey Chambers (bottom right)

134a Abbey Street

Abbey Street's eighteenth-century facades (Fig. 134a) often mask seventeenth-century houses. They are varied and most attractively informal. Many houses have fine rooms and splendid features, especially in some excursions into the 'Gothick'. The small modern house at the entry to Abbey Square, set back almost as if to foreshadow some street widening scheme, is a very great pity. The south side has a short terrace of early nineteenth-century houses of no great quality, but pleasant and harmonious with their setting.

Abbey Green is late eighteenth century, a fine terrace of spacious houses with an attractively proportioned facade and pleasant interiors.

134b Architectural value

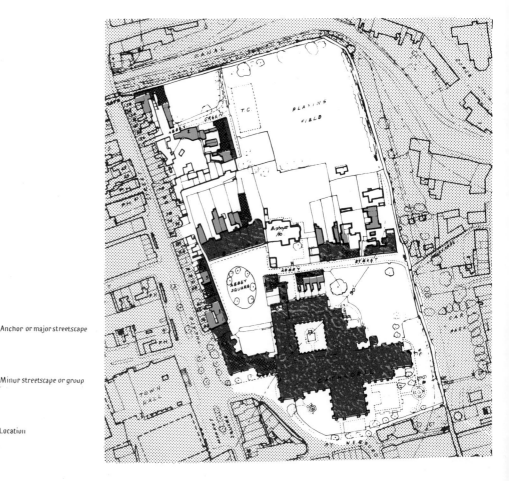

Internal		External	
	Major interiors		Anchor or major streetscape
	Good features		Minor streetscape or group
	Unremarkable		Location

134

135a Abbey Mews, built on the site of an old quarry, is little used

3.3.3 Ownership, use and condition

Ownership. This area is largely owned by the Cathedral, with whom many residents have strong connections. It is quiet and predominantly residential, but a few houses have been converted into offices. Most of the central buildings are reasonably well used, but the standard falls significantly towards the edges. Considering its position, the land is remarkably under-used, and includes many derelict sites, especially around the Abbey Mews (Fig. 135a).

Suitability. Those houses still used as single dwellings (and they make delightful family houses) present no real problems. But some of the larger ones have been subdivided into flats, and here difficulties arise when delicate eighteenth-century interiors are altered. Sometimes, successive alterations over the years have brought anomalies, which now prevent any proper utilisation of the available space. For instance, part of No. 2 Abbey Square has been combined with No. 3 and some of the remainder divided into flats leaving the residual space almost unusable. In several cases subdivision has provided flats of unequal standard in the same house. Buildings of this quality deserve the most careful conversion, enabling their architectural merits to be enjoyed to the best advantage.

135b Use and disuse

Satisfactory

Satisfactory if improved

Unsatisfactory but suitable for change of use within present unit

Unsatisfactory but suitable for change of use if combined

Incapable of economic use or otherwise admitting of replacement

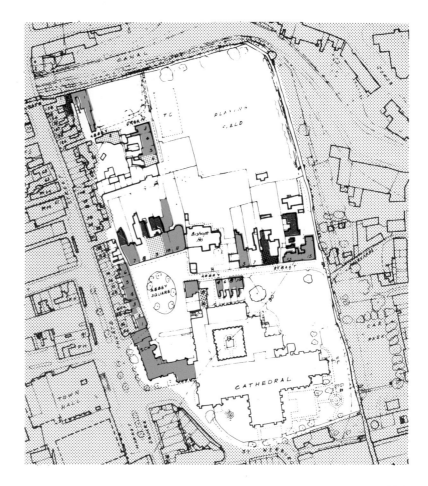

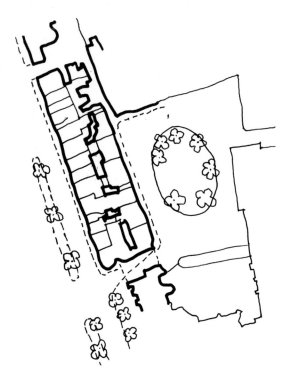

Servicing and access. Bounded by the Walls of the City and of the former Abbey precinct, this becomes an entirely self-contained area. Yet the three points of entry do not interconnect with one another. Rear servicing of the west side of the square is made impossible by the proximity of the Northgate terraces (Fig. 136a), and this tightly-packed area has become almost a single, complex building. But elsewhere good service roads must be provided as a part of any scheme to realise the full potential of the area.

Planning inadequacies. The successful subdivision of buildings is difficult where, as on the north side of the Abbey Square, separate access to each floor is required without marring the fine staircases that occupy much of the centre of each house. In smaller units, like those of the Abbey Green and the west side of Abbey Square, the provision of first-floor access sometimes restricts accommodation on the ground floor. These smaller buildings are best used as single units. Again, extensive rear wings of later date now darken some of the original houses on the north side of Abbey Square·and prevent their suitable use (Fig. 136b).

136a Back-to-back houses make rear access impossible

136b Unused rear additions to good houses in Abbey Square`

136c Abbey Square today, marred by car parking

137a   Ceiling under leaking roofs

Condition.   Some buildings, and the clergy houses in particular, are maintained in immaculate condition. But by and large, standards tend to fray at the edges. The cost of maintaining a large group of historic buildings is heavy, and insufficient funds are available to keep each and all in good repair. The repair of the Cathedral is, of course, rightly the first responsibility and concern of the authorities. But the survival of buildings in Abbey Square, together with both sides of Abbey Street and Abbey Green, is equally of great importance to the City.

A good redecoration programme in this area is helpful in maintaining the facades, but leaking roofs and gutters (Fig. 137a) with rising damp, are often unseen and lead to more serious threats. Any old building needs to be kept dry, and every leak calls for prompt attention. Chimneys in particular are often neglected. Pointing decays more rapidly here than on less exposed places, and several stacks are leaning quite badly. Several walls have settled or bulged. Where all movement has not ceased, as apparently in the end walls of No. 3 and No. 6 Abbey Green and No. 6 Abbey Square, careful watch must be kept to determine the cause of movement and the most appropriate repair. Rebuilding need only be undertaken as a last resort, since this

137b   Condition

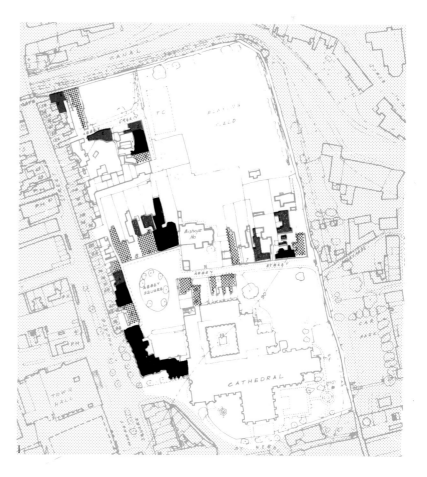

   Satisfactory overall

Deteriorating in whole or part

Individually serious defects

not only destroys the building's authenticity, but may not in itself answer the problem. The new end wall of No. 3 Abbey Green for example, although rebuilt, bears every sign of a renewed movement.

Fine features deserve careful maintenance just as much as the structure, for when a building deteriorates these are the first to suffer. The many splendid doorcases need regular attention, especially to their protective lead flashings; and in sash windows the original panes of crown glass should be retained wherever possible with their delicate glazing bars (Fig. 138b).

138a Twisted and damaged downpipe harming the stonework of the Cathedral

138b A fine terrace, although damaged in scale by the loss of glazing bars

3.3.4 Conservation and action

Many buildings are well suited to their present residential and office uses but most would benefit by removal of later additions, and by careful conversion within the original building units.

Maintenance. Some 27 buildings (Fig. 139) call for better maintenance, for example by a routine system of inspection, as already carried out for most ecclesiastical property.

139 Recommendations

Inspected buildings recommended as worthy and capable of conservation

 For first aid action on serious defects

 For urgent attention to adverse conditions

 For protection and care

Inspected buildings incapable of, or not in need of conservation

 For renewal, clearance or otherwise admitting of replacement

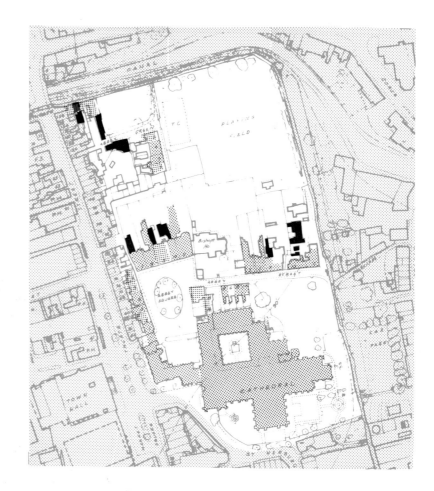

140a   Suggested new houses for Abbey Mews

Action site

The area suggested is of surplus, sub-standard and low-density buildings between Abbey Green and Northgate Street.

Selective redevelopment could include 14 shops and 16 upper *maisonettes* (for 5 persons) to Northgate Street, with rear service and covered car standing facilities, and 30 three-storey *houses* (for 5 persons), with integral garages and private or combined gardens.

Access would be from Northgate Street, and by existing and extended pedestrian ways from Abbey Square and Abbey Street, and a reopened gate from the City Wall. Within the layout, all houses would be served by access roads, vehicle standing and turning spaces.

Environmental improvement

Road and paving surfaces.   The cobbled ways in Abbey Square and Abbey Street need maintenance. Items like this should surely qualify for grant aid from the Historic Buildings Council.

Trees and planting.   Existing valuable trees require special protection. More planting would screen the outbuildings behind Abbey Street (north) and the small house on its western flank. The untidy lesser bushes and shrubs beyond the playing field would be better thinned and cleared.

140b   Townscape recommendations

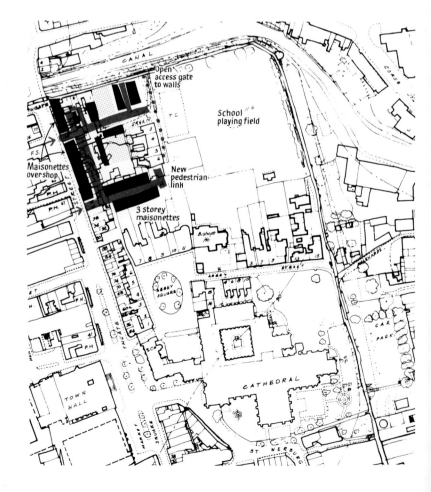

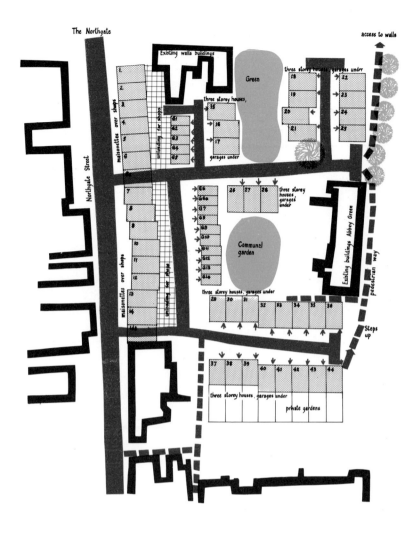

The Northgate

access to walls

Existing walls buildings

Green

three storey houses, garages under

three storey houses,

maisonettes over shops

unloading for shops

garages under

Northgate Street

three storey houses garages under

Communal garden

Existing buildings Abbey Green

pedestrian way

maisonettes over shops

three storey houses, garages under

Steps up

three storey houses, garages under

private gardens

141 Proposed new housing in the Abbey Green area

3.4 Study Area 4: Whitefriars

142a Study Area 4: Whitefriars

142b Aerial view of the Study Area

3.4.1 Townscape appraisal

This inner sector of the City contains contrasting elements:

Whitefriars itself shows all the signs of the proper treatment of distinguished historic buildings. The street is a straight run eastwards to Bridge Street, its vista well closed by the Rows. But westwards the view to the developing area across the inner ring road is for the present open and indeterminate. The street's merits derive entirely from its buildings. On the south these are continuous, with only very slight variations in the frontage line. They are mostly Georgian, with strong historical unity. On the north, the continuity of the eastern section has few interruptions. Then comes a valuable contrast in two large, detached and distinguished houses. Walled gardens maintain the street line; and there are fine trees, especially around The Friars.

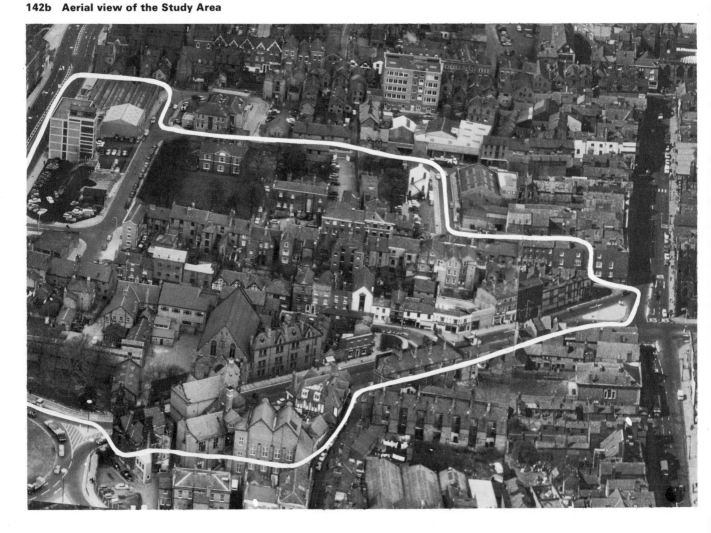

143a Townscape analysis

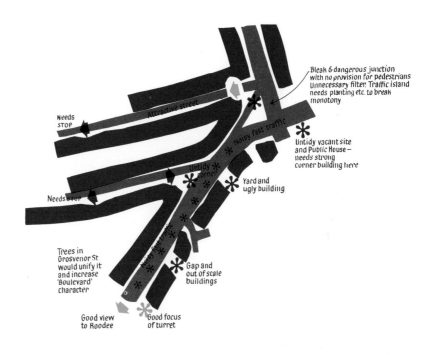

Bleak & dangerous junction
with no provision for pedestrians
Unnecessary filter. Traffic island
needs planting etc. to break
monotony

Needs
STOP

Attractive street

Noisy fast traffic

Untidy vacant site
and Public House –
needs strong
corner building here

Untidy
corner

Yard and
ugly building

Needs STOP

Trees in
Grosvenor St
would unify it
and increase
'Boulevard'
character

Noisy fast traffic

Gap and
out of scale
buildings

Good view
to Roodee

Good focus
of turret

143b Buildings inspected

Buildings recommended for listing

Other buildings inspected

143

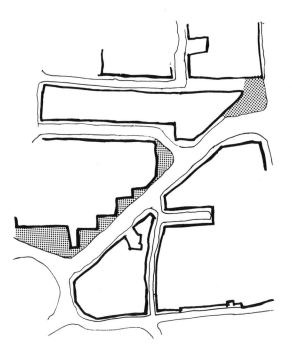

Cuppin Street, by contrast, has mainly poor buildings in obsolescent condition. The very position and alignment of the street prevents any usefulness of its own or to adjacent buildings. Its north side is only about 100 ft. from the backs of Whitefriars, giving insufficient space for itself and cramping the latter, which it also debars from rear access. Architecturally, Cuppin Street is almost totally undistinguished.

Grosvenor Street's straight and uncompromising diagonal has never become integrated with the surrounding areas. The conception was presumably one of a wide boulevard, designed to lead straight from the glorious entry of Grosvenor Bridge to the heart of the City. But as a result of subsequent failure to endow it with correspondingly worthy buildings, it remains bleak and unattractive. At its north-east end especially, it drains space from Bridge Street in an awkward and shapeless junction (Fig. 144a). The south-west end is better defined and more distinguished, thanks mainly to the well-conceived modern Grosvenor roundabout.

144a   Grosvenor Street's diagonal line creates 'feather-edged' junctions and awkward plot shapes (top left)

144b   Older houses in Whitefriars (bottom left)

144c   Junction of Grosvenor Street with Bridge Street (top right)

144d   Savings Bank in Grosvenor Street, by James Harrison (bottom right)

145a Architectural value (below)

145b The Friars: a house containing the remains of a medieval friary (below right)

145c Heraldic overmantel in 8 Whitefriars (bottom right)

3.4.2 Architectural quality

Whitefriars (Fig. 144b) is the area's only street of consistent quality. The building of earliest origin is The Friars, fine and detached with vestiges of the medieval Carmelite Friary, but now mainly of the eighteenth century (Fig. 145b). Bank House, next to it, is another large and pleasant Georgian building.

Nos. 1 and 8 have very good Jacobean features (Fig. 145c), but Whitefriars is typified by minor Georgian buildings, designed for comfortable domestic use. Nos. 9 and 11 are good early examples; Nos. 5, 13, 16, 23 and 25 are later types; and No. 14 is a rather grander element. The remaining houses are in fact of the early nineteenth century, but they echo the Georgian manner and make the whole an attractively homogeneous street.

Grosvenor Street's only notable building is the Trustee Savings Bank, a splendid essay in Victorian Gothic both inside and out (Fig. 144d).

Cuppin Street has little of value, apart from some very minor eighteenth-century fragments.

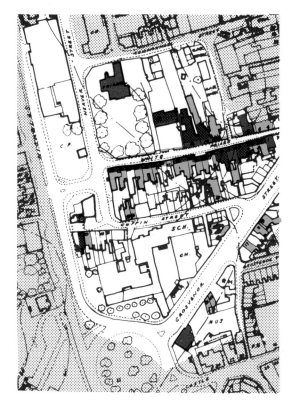

Internal		External	
	Major interiors		Anchor or major streetscape
	Good features		Minor streetscape or group
	Unremarkable		Location

146a Grass growing in hopper heads

3.4.3 Ownership, use and condition

Most of the buildings in this area are owner-occupied, sometimes with upper floors let as separate offices. In consequence, most are fully used. The exceptions are some of the smaller units in Whitefriars and the deteriorating property at the west end of Cuppin Street.

The two principal streets, Whitefriars and Cuppin Street, have sharply contrasting uses. Whitefriars is one of the best established business streets in the City, but Cuppin Street contains mostly substandard housing. Most large houses in Whitefriars have been well converted into offices, some of which have extensions sensitively added. The difficulties in this street lie in the smaller buildings. Some of the smallest, for example Nos. 5, 7 and 9, are still in residential use but lack bathrooms, and might well one day be combined to form more viable units. Nos. 4, 6 and 8, formerly cottages, are now used merely as stores. This is incompatible with the rest of the street; and No. 8 especially deserves a better use, commensurate with its architectural quality. Other small houses, for example Nos. 19 and 21, although sufficient for residential use, really have too few rooms on each floor to make them economical for their present use as offices and might benefit by horizontal combination with each other. Houses in Union Court and at the west end of Cuppin Street are very small, of no particular interest, and would be better redeveloped.

The north side of Whitefriars has good service access from Commonhall Street, but the south side has only a few pedestrian alleys leading through from Cuppin Street. Similarly, the south side lacks parking facilities for occupants or visiting clients.

Being well used, most buildings in Whitefriars are reasonably well maintained. But one notable defect affects most buildings on its south side. They stand on the line of the former Roman City Wall, and settlement in many of their rear walls is probably due to their foundation on the infilled Roman ditch (Fig. 147a).

146b Use and disuse

 Satisfactory

Satisfactory if improved

Unsatisfactory but suitable for change of use within present unit

Unsatisfactory but suitable for use or change of use if combined

Incapable of economic use or otherwise admitting of replacement

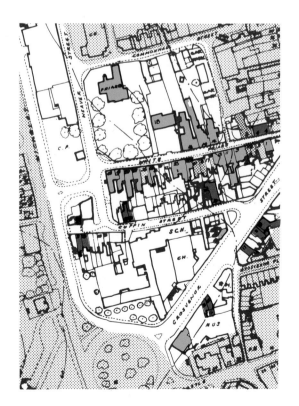

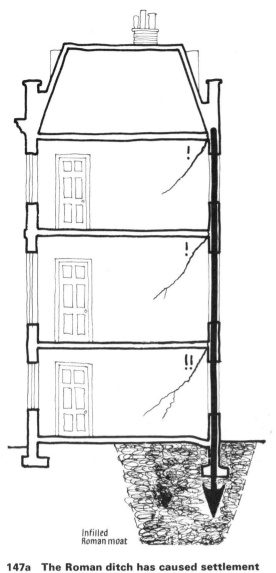

147a The Roman ditch has caused settlement in many houses in Whitefriars

147b Outbuildings behind the south side of Whitefriars show dipping brickwork courses

147c Condition

  Satisfactory overall

Deteriorating in whole or part

Individually serious defects

147

3.4.4 Conservation and action

Comparatively little attention is needed to buildings in Whitefriars. The current predominance of office use is satisfactory and should be encouraged. The smaller houses need some improvement; and repairs are needed to cope with the settlement of rear walls on the south side.

Cuppin Street as a whole appears to have no viable future, and its few and minor historic buildings do not, on analysis, warrant preservation.

Grosvenor Street has no buildings with a strong case for conservation apart from the Savings Bank. The remainder will require individual attention if retained. But none is irreplaceable.

Opportunity area: Cuppin Street and Grosvenor Street

The complete clearance of Cuppin Street and its realignment to the north of its present line would bring several benefits to the area. It would remove the problem of obsolescence in Cuppin Street's north side buildings. The restrictions to the rear of Whitefriars buildings would be removed and opportunity given for proper rear servicing. Good car parking facilities would be provided, given careful and adequate screening. On a larger scale, the currently somewhat wasted site between Grosvenor Street and Cuppin Street would be enlarged and might be comprehensively redeveloped. The present piecemeal and 'feather-edged' buildings on Grosvenor Street should be redeveloped with buildings better fitted to the Chester grid. With this type of careful treatment, carried eventually to the south side also, Grosvenor Street could, at last, achieve a distinction and sympathy with the rest of the City.

148 Recommendations

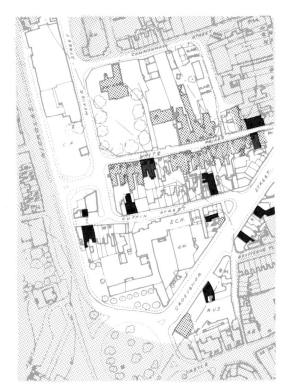

Inspected buildings recommended as worthy and capable of conservation

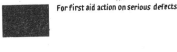
For first aid action on serious defects

For urgent attention to adverse conditions

For protection and care

Inspected buildings incapable of, or not in need of, conservation

For renewal, clearance or otherwise admitting of replacement

Environmental improvements

At the Grosvenor Street-Bridge Street junction, and as part of the traffic management proposals recommended, the left-hand filter from Grosvenor Street into Bridge Street would be closed. This could also enable the pedestrian island to be enlarged and given better floor textures and planting. Good trees would vastly improve Grosvenor Street, and we suggest planting groups of trees so as to reinforce its Boulevard character (Fig. 149a). This could readily be done in conjunction with the comprehensive redevelopment of the north side. Trees in the angled forecourts between rectilinear buildings and the diagonal line of the street would give a very much more unified and interesting appearance.

149a Suggestions for improving the junction of Bridge Street and Grosvenor Street

149b Townscape recommendations

3.5 Study Area 5: Bridgegate

3.5.1 Townscape appraisal

This is a southern sector of domestic streets within the City Walls. The terrain falls steeply southwards to the river, and there are long views from the upper part of the neighbourhood.

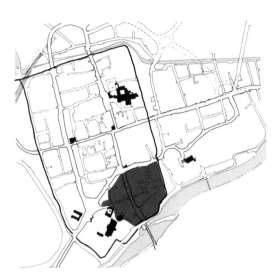

150a   Study Area 5: Bridgegate

150b   Aerial view of the Study Area

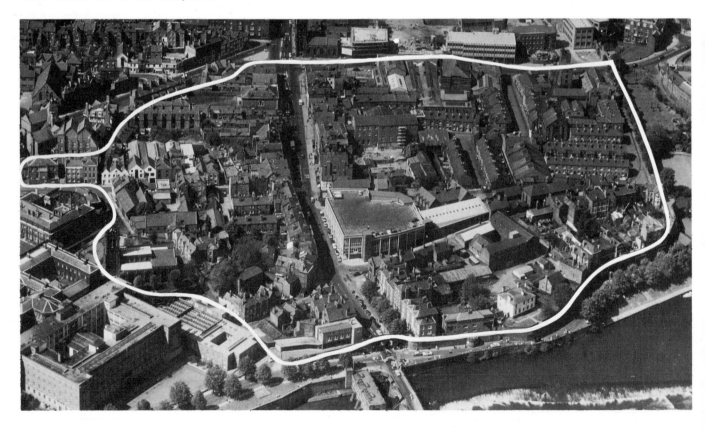

151a Townscape analysis

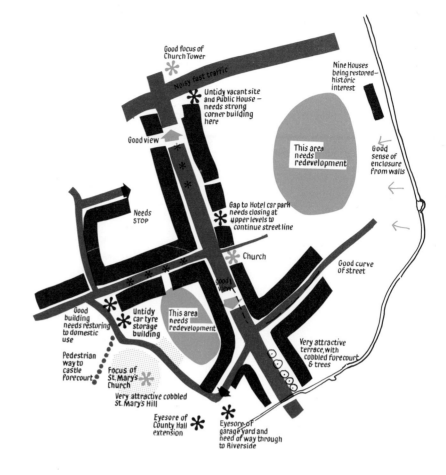

Good focus of Church Tower

Noisy fast traffic

Untidy vacant site and Public House – needs strong corner building here

Nine Houses being restored – historic interest

Good view

This area needs redevelopment

Good sense of enclosure from walls

Needs STOP

Gap to Hotel car park needs closing at upper levels to continue street line

Church

Good curve of street

good view

Good building needs restoring to domestic use

Untidy car tyre storage building

This area needs redevelopment

Very attractive terrace, with cobbled forecourt & trees

Pedestrian way to castle forecourt

Focus of St. Mary's Church

Very attractive cobbled St. Mary's Hill

Eyesore of County Hall extension

Eyesore of garage yard and need of way through to Riverside

151b Buildings inspected

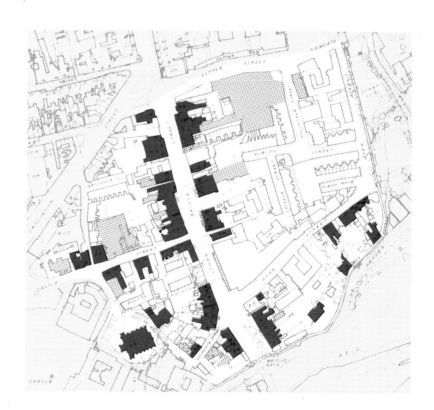

 Buildings recommended for listing

Other buildings inspected

152a Lower Bridge Street

152b The car park breaks the continuity of the street

Lower Bridge Street is the spine of the area, running southwards downhill from Bridge Street to Bridgegate. On the eastern side, this strong visual stop is softened by fine trees fronting an attractive Georgian terrace. To the west, it is distinguished by the well-timbered facade of the Bear and Billet. Immediately beyond is the medieval Old Dee Bridge, hard against the City Walls, a strong echo of the old days of the fortified City. Within the Walls, the view up Lower Bridge Street has another decisive focus—this time in the tower of St. Michael's Church. The promise of enclosure here proves illusory on closer approach, when all sense of space leaks uncontrollably away at the junction with Grosvenor Street.

Lower Bridge Street (Fig. 152a) was earlier lined almost continuously with good, tall seventeenth- and eighteenth-century fronts, including several important buildings. Only its west side still remains complete, and this is of considerable architectural importance. But on the east side, recent demolition has brought a disastrous gap in the former continuity of the street (Fig. 152b). Nearby to the south, an adjoining redevelopment has been set back with little respect for the street.

But the street's main characteristic is unfortunately the visual poverty resulting from its fundamental problem: the disuse and decay of many of its fine buildings. This is one of Chester's worst examples of area decline, and a solution is urgent.

Shipgate Street curves away at the lower west side. It retains period continuity, but with a sudden and engaging miniaturisation of scale. On the north are pretty, three-storeyed Georgian cottages, but from uncertainty about their future, these are now deteriorating sadly. On the south are what were once customs buildings and the like, but are now decayed or derelict, and retain only vestiges of their former interest. The street's western terminal is unfortunately the very unattractive exposed rear end of County Hall, but the view up St. Mary's Hill is magnificent.

St. Mary's Hill (Fig. 153) climbs steeply north-west from Shipgate Street. The stepped pavement, cobbled textures and dramatic slopes and levels, together with adjoining St. Mary's Church and its fine churchyard trees, combine to give to Chester an extremely attractive and characterful element of townscape. The west side is marred by the back clutter of County Hall; but the east side, from its small Georgian tenements at the bottom to the engaging Victorian school at the top, is all attractive. Halfway up, the old Rectory of St. Mary's has a large garden with some fine trees, but this at present gives graphic views over the clutter and decay behind Lower Bridge Street.

Castle Street, to the north, runs west from Lower Bridge Street. From an acutely constricted junction, quite unsuited for the buses that now thread through it, the street widens imperceptibly westwards to finish grandly at the Castle outfliers and forecourt. Its buildings are a contrast in date, form and use, but enough continuity remains to make this a predominantly historical street. Some of its best buildings show the effects of their serious misuse and the blight spreading from the precarious planning situation around Shipgate Street.

The area north of Castle Street, into which *Grosvenor Place* pushes an indecisive cul-de-sac, has no buildings of historic quality. East of Lower Bridge Street, the section around *Albion Street* has only substandard Victorian terraces and the derelict Lion Brewery, and is ready for redevelopment. *Park Street*, however, runs attractively alongside the City Wall and is distinguished by the gabled frontage of the Nine Houses, and its line of good trees.

Duke Street, to the south, rises uphill eastwards from Lower Bridge Street, and contains some good period buildings. It is a pity that those at its eastern end, where the street runs strongly and attractively to the City Wall, have deteriorated so much. The houses along the south side are unusual for Chester in having attractive and spacious back gardens, some with access to the City Walls and with good views to the river beyond. This is a most pleasant and well-used corner, eloquent of the advantages that could result from future domestic use in favoured sites within the walled City.

153 St Mary's Hill, a steep and attractive pedestrian way

3.5.2 Architectural quality

Like Watergate Street, the Bridgegate area has many fine historic buildings, untouched by commercial pressures but decimated by serious neglect.

Lower Bridge Street (Fig. 152a) has good examples of all periods, from interesting medieval remains at Nos. 30 and 53 to the attractive late-Georgian urbanity of Bridge Place. The best individual buildings are of the sixteenth and seventeenth centuries. Tudor House (Fig. 155a) and the Bear and Billet have magnificent timbered facades; and the Old King's Head is another fine timber-framed building, although somewhat over-restored externally. Gamul House has splendid Jacobean features (Fig. 155b). The Oddfellows Club, The Talbot and No. 51 all remain in essence late eighteenth-century major town houses, the first especially having interiors of great quality.

The background historic buildings of the street have a predominantly Georgian character, although they are often basically earlier. These are the typical Cestrian minor town houses, terraced and parapeted with central cross stairs and other good details. They contain many vestiges of forgotten Rows, often now internal or enclosed.

Castle Street (Fig. 154a) has further good buildings, mainly of the seventeenth and eighteenth centuries. These are small in scale, and many have been mutilated by the change from their original domestic use. Good features remain, especially in No. 23 (seventeenth- and eighteenth-century plaster-work and fireplaces), No. 25 (fine early eighteenth-century panelling and staircase), and the Golden Eagle (robust seventeenth- and eighteenth-century timbering and panelling).

154a   Small Georgian houses in Castle Street

154b   Terrace of eighteenth-century houses in Bridge Place

155a   Tudor House, a well-used building sensitively restored

155b   The derelict Jacobean interior of Gamul House

155c   Varied architecture in Lower Bridge Street

156a   St Mary's Hill: The Old Rectory

156b   Harmonious materials in Lower Bridge Street

156c   Shipgate House, at the foot of Lower Bridge Street

Shipgate Street and St. Mary's Hill are notable more for their form than for their architectural detail, except for the fifteenth- and sixteenth-century splendour of St. Mary's Church. *Shipgate House* (Fig. 156c) is a good early eighteenth-century building with an excellent staircase and good plasterwork. No. 4 next door is a delightful small Georgian-fronted villa.

The Old Rectory (Fig. 156a) in St. Mary's Hill has good eighteenth-century features in an attractively rambling building. Otherwise the Hill has minor houses in the Georgian vernacular.

Duke Street possesses good Georgian terraced buildings. No. 4 is in almost original condition, with good interiors; and Nos. 22 and 30 are similar but on a larger scale. The other buildings are mainly of a later period.

In *Park Street* the structural form of the famous seventeenth-century Nine Houses is unique in Chester.

The large garage and the tyre store in *Pepper Street* contain intact remains of the former Methodist and Baptist Chapels on these sites.

157 Architectural value

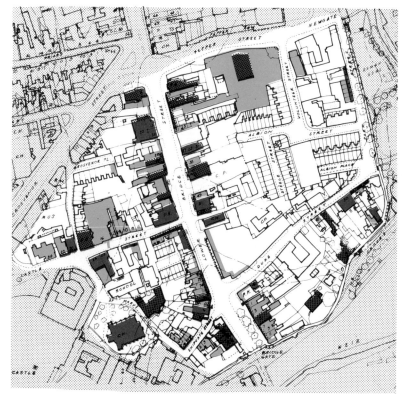

Internal

 Major interiors

 Good features

 Unremarkable

External

Anchor or major streetscape

Minor streetscape or group

Location

158a **A garage in Pepper Street incarcerates a Classical church**

158b **Gamul House, now used as a warehouse**

3.5.3 Ownership, use and condition

Most of the property in this area is in private hands, and some landlords own several groups of buildings. The Grosvenor Estates hold a number of sites on the east side of Lower Bridge Street, and the County Council have a considerable interest in property on the west side.

Use and suitability. Many of the buildings are empty or seriously under-used, but those still occupied mostly remain in residential use. Castle Street, Lower Bridge Street and Pepper Street have shops and commercial premises as well. But shops, especially in Lower Bridge Street, are declining and in Pepper Street the Brewery stands empty and awaiting demolition. Inns like the Old King's Head and the Bear and Billet attract attention, and several small cafés flourish. The Talbot, used as overflow accommodation during recent alterations at the Grosvenor Hotel, is now an hotel in its own right. Several other historic buildings have recently been converted to modern use. Tudor House, earlier divided into three tenements, has been restored as one; and No. 23 Castle Street is being converted into two good flats. But these are exceptions.

A most significant pointer to the social decline of this part of Chester is the plight of many noteworthy buildings at the present time. It would be difficult to think of a less appropriate use for the fine terminal building at the west end of Castle Street than its present function as a tyre store (Fig. 160). The Great Hall of Gamul House survives partly empty (Fig. 158b), and partly as an upholsterer's store. Several other fine early houses are at best used now merely as stores, or as poorly converted one-roomed dwellings.

Lower Bridge St. East

Lower Bridge St. West

Lower Bridge St. West

159a/b/c Lower Bridge Street: (from top) East; West (south end); and West (north end). In these drawings, empty premises are shown by means of a solid red colour; those that are unsatisfactorily used by a red tint

159d Use and disuse

 Satisfactory

 Satisfactory if improved

 Unsatisfactory but suitable for change of use within present unit

 Unsatisfactory but suitable for use or change of use if combined

Incapable of economic use or otherwise admitting of replacement

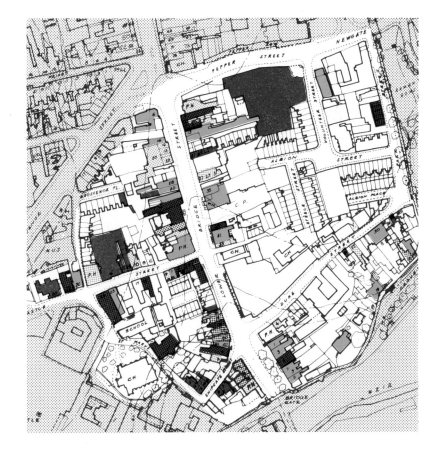

159

This problem, which is prevalent throughout Chester, is here a major blight. Many good houses, particularly in Lower Bridge Street, stand empty or seriously under-used. Derelict cottages and overgrown gardens occupy much land between the main streets.

A long history of neglect has produced this situation. More recently, the County Council earlier pursued a policy of acquiring properties around Shipgate Street and have announced successive schemes for extending the County Offices as far as the west side of Lower Bridge Street. Outline application has also been made for private redevelopment on adjacent land north of Castle Street. In both these cases, property has fallen empty as tenancies have lapsed and is frequented by tramps and meths drinkers who disturb neighbouring residents. The fear of compulsory purchase also hangs over those owners who remain. Uncertainty about the future has naturally discouraged owners from maintaining their property. Nor can prospective tenants or purchasers find the individual buildings physically or economically attractive. Additionally, the new shopping precinct, with others that are planned, is attracting shopping away to the central area. Lower Bridge Street has been even more detached from the central area by the busy inner ring road, and many shops have closed.

These are extra difficulties to those encountered in the central area. Problems like access to upper floors, properties too large for convenient subdivision, or others too small for economic use, the lack of bathrooms and other facilities, are found here as elsewhere. Few properties have any rear servicing facilities.

160 This building, in Castle Street, is used as a tyre store

161a Broken windows in the nine houses

161b Almost collapsed: the roof of Gamul House

161c Condition

Condition. The deteriorating state of many buildings is a direct result of their misuse or disuse and of the ever-present threat of demolition. The complex form of many buildings makes their maintenance more difficult. A few buildings inspected were well maintained, but these stand in marked contrast to the remainder. Leaking roofs and gutters have led to excessive water damage in many empty buildings (Fig. 161b), and there are extensive outbreaks of wet rot. The risk of dry rot is fortunately at least reduced by ventilation through the many broken windows (Fig.161a). The rooms are often wantonly damaged and filled with rubbish by intruders. In partially occupied buildings, attempts have been made to hold back the tide by an assortment of bowls and cans at strategic positions on the staircase and abandoned upper floors, but the water still pours in through the roof and ceilings. Where ventilation is lacking, for example in rooms used as stores, dry rot has developed and is rife in several valuable buildings.

Good buildings do stand up to an amazing amount of punishment, and surprisingly few are beyond repair. Shipgate House, for example, has safely withstood the weight of many thousands of books on its deteriorating structure, and some reports on this and other properties in County Council ownership are in our opinion exaggeratedly pessimistic.

It is important that repairs are put in hand by order of priority. This has not always been done, and examples could be cited where an annual maintenance budget has been expended on the unnecessary decoration of divided attics, while serious basic faults in the structure remain unattended.

 Satisfactory overall

Deteriorating in whole or part

Individually serious defects

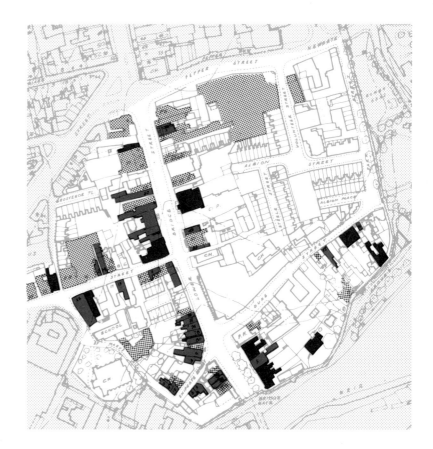

162a Terraced house in Lower Bridge Street, with a typical Georgian facade, suitable for conversion to residential use

3.5.4 Conservation and action

Throughout this area, residential conversion is desirable, with selective redevelopment. A wide variety of flats and houses would result. A typical conversion scheme is illustrated on these two pages. This shows a terraced house in Lower Bridge Street with a typical Georgian brick facade and good seventeenth-century plasterwork and panelling. It has been poorly converted into two shops and dwellings and is now empty and semi-derelict.

A new service 'core' would enable it to be converted into four flats and two shops, with rooms of good size, retaining and re-expressing all its good period features. This is typical of the form, state and possibilities of many such buildings in Chester. But little can be achieved without major financial support for buildings of this kind (see page 246).

Maintenance. Some 66 buildings call for improved maintenance (Fig. 162b). In Lower Bridge Street this could best be carried out as a combined scheme.

162b Recommendations

Inspected buildings recommended as worthy and capable of conservation

 For first aid action on serious defects

For urgent attention to adverse conditions

For protection and care

Inspected buildings incapable of, or not in need of, conservation

 For renewal, clearance or otherwise admitting of replacement

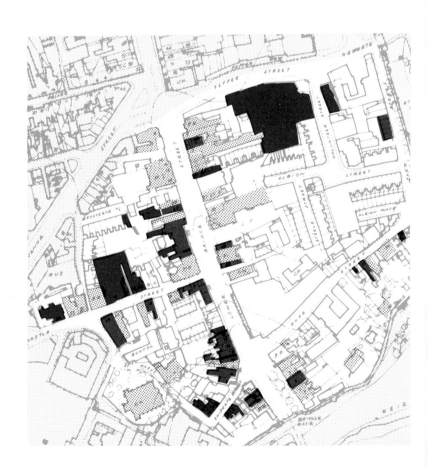

162

163 Suggested conversion of the building shown opposite

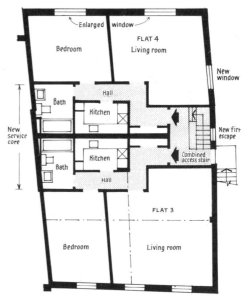

Brickwork open jointed

←Inadequate daylighting→

Severe wet penetration through roof

Defective valley gutter

No bathroom or services

Good stair

Partition detracts from interiors

✳ Blocked window
Brickwork open jointed

2nd floor

←Enlarged window→

FLAT 4

Bedroom

Living room

New window

Bath

Hall

Kitchen

New fire escape

Kitchen

Combined access stair

Bath

Hall

New service core

FLAT 3

Bedroom

Living room

2nd floor

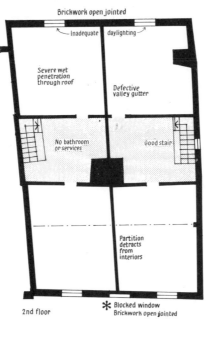

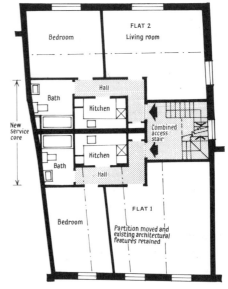

Brickwork open jointed

Inadequate existing stair

Good stair

Disused fireplaces

Partition detracts from interiors

✳ Blocked window

1st floor

FLAT 2

Bedroom

Living room

Bath

Hall

Kitchen

Combined access stair

New service core

Kitchen

Bath

Hall

FLAT 1

Bedroom

Partition moved and existing architectural features retained

1st floor

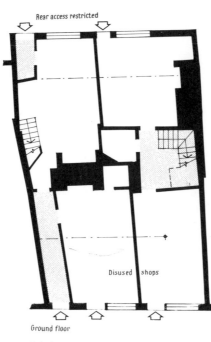

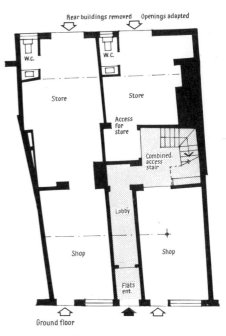

Rear access restricted

Disused shops

Ground floor

Existing

Rear buildings removed   Openings adapted

W.C.

W.C.

Store

Store

Access for store

Combined access stair

Lobby

Shop

Shop

Flats ent.

Ground floor

Proposed improvements

163

Environmental improvements

The line of the street should be completed by infilling existing gaps. The most important is the Talbot Hotel car park, which could be developed over a street-level access to the car park behind.

The south-east corner of the Lower Bridge Street and Grosvenor Street crossroads is at present an empty lot. A building of some size is needed here to form a strong corner. This should be at least as high as the adjacent buildings in Lower Bridge Street.

These improvements and general attention to surfaces, planting and painting could transform Lower Bridge Street into one of Chester's most attractive entries.

Action site: Shipgate Street and Castle Street

The area suggested is the back land between Shipgate Street and Castle Street. Perimeter buildings would be rehabilitated or replaced, according to their architectural or historic value.

Selective redevelopment would include:

New buildings: 8 flats (2-person)
                      5 maisonettes (4-person)
                      51 flats (3-person)
                      4 small shops
Converted buildings: Approximately 40 flats.

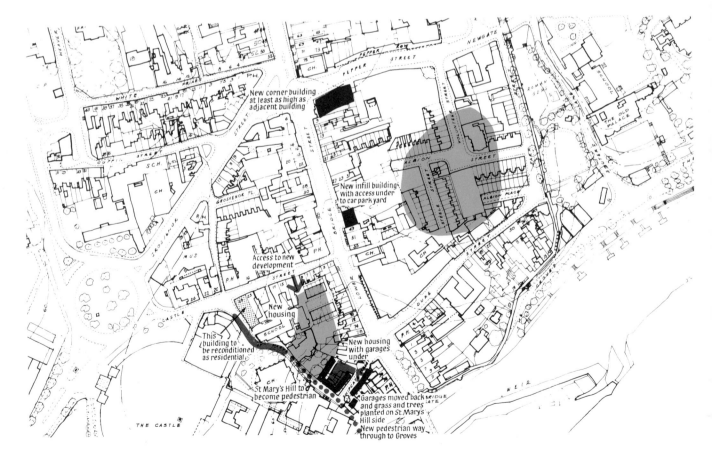

164 Townscape recommendations

Covered car spaces could be provided for all dwellings. Vehicle access would be from Castle Street, upper St. Mary's Hill and Shipgate Street, with internal distributor and service areas. Pedestrian access would be from Lower Bridge Street and lower St. Mary's Hill.

Residential blocks would be arranged to take full advantage of site levels and views, grouped around and within planted gardens, and linked by footpaths with surrounding streets.

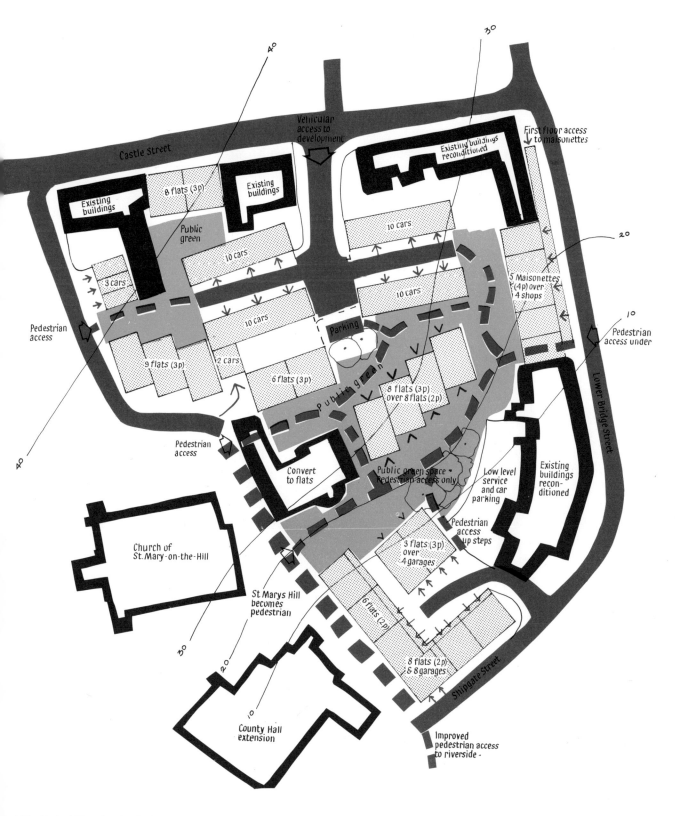

Opportunity area: Albion Street site

This area is at present mainly nineteenth-century terraced cottages, now at the end of their useful life. We show below some outline suggestions for redeveloping this site for flats and maisonettes.

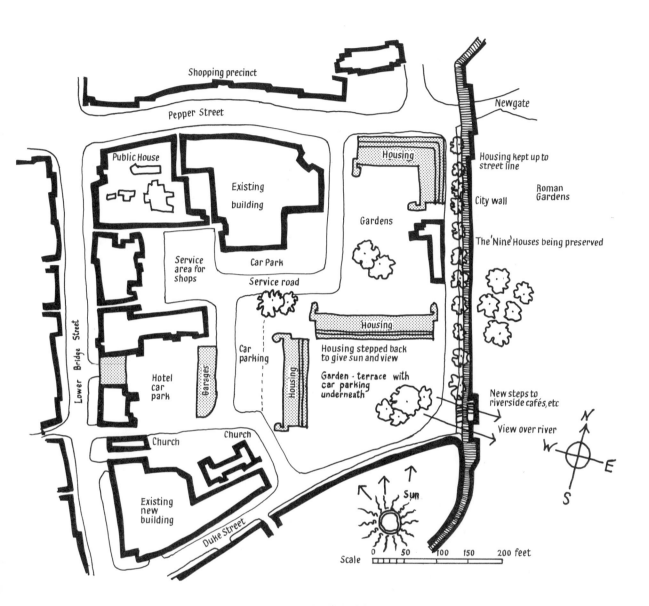

Shopping precinct

Pepper Street

Newgate

Public House

Existing building

Housing

Housing kept up to street line

Roman Gardens

City wall

Gardens

The 'Nine' Houses being preserved

Service area for shops

Car Park

Service road

Housing

Housing stepped back to give sun and view

Car parking

Lower Bridge Street

Garages

Housing

Hotel car park

Garden - terrace with car parking underneath

New steps to riverside cafés, etc

Church

Church

View over river

Existing new building

Duke Street

Sun

Scale 0 50 100 150 200 feet

N W E S

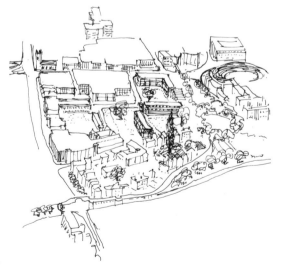

167c Albion Street site as existing

3.6 Study Area 6: Watergate

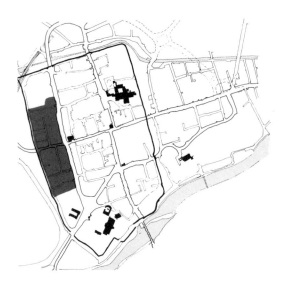

168a Study Area 6: Watergate

3.6.1 Townscape appraisal

The Watergate area echoes the Cathedral precinct as a self-contained entity within the City Walls. To the west and north are the long-established barriers of the City Walls and the Hospital. The south and east boundaries are recent. The former is the new County Police Headquarters: the latter, the new inner ring road along Nicholas Street. This especially forms a real barrier to the remainder of the City.

Within its boundaries the area is remarkably successful, despite its exposure on the one flank to Chester's prevailing westerly winds and on the other to the traffic noise. There are deep-seated and favourable antidotes: long use, the attractive views to the distant Welsh Hills, and peace and quiet within.

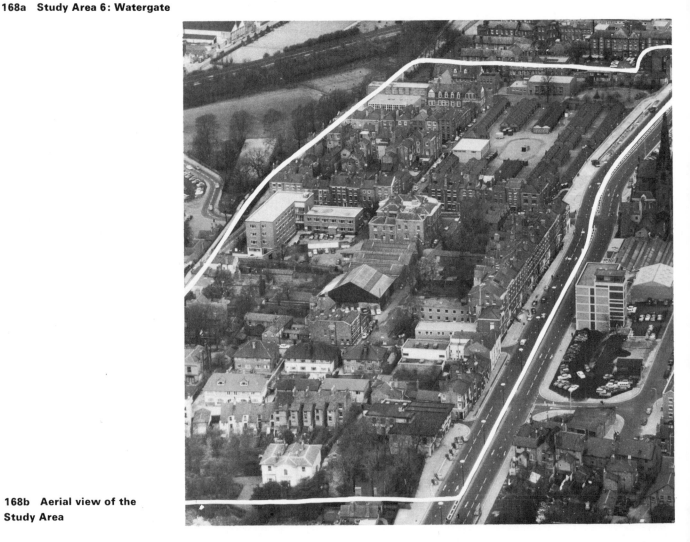

168b Aerial view of the Study Area

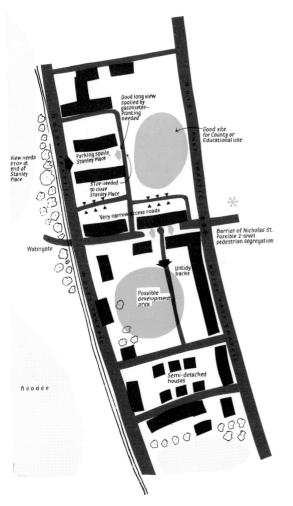

169a   Townscape analysis

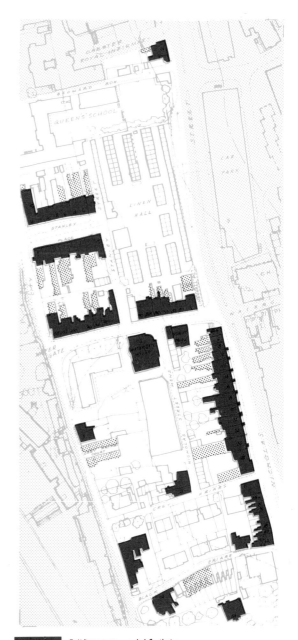

 Buildings recommended for listing

 Other buildings inspected

169b   Buildings inspected

M

Stanley Place (Figs. 174b/c), like Whitefriars, is a successful example of the intelligent and beneficial use of old buildings. It consists of two short and straight Georgian terraces facing each other across a grass strip; wider than a street, narrower than a square, and very attractive. To the west is a superb long view towards the Welsh Hills, but unhappily the foreground is decisively wrecked by a large gasholder. To the east, Stanley Place has a weak and indecisive stop in the single-storey stables on the site of the Linen Hall, increasingly an opportunity for redevelopment. To the north is the Queen's School which has grown naturally into a neighbouring part of Stanley Place.

Lower Watergate Street (Figs. 170a/b) has been divorced by Nicholas Street from the main section leading to the Cross—even though from the west the two halves are still visually continuous. Westwards it tends unfortunately to look out beyond the Watergate itself at the muddled prospect of the Sealand Industrial Estate. Its northern side is a good eighteenth-century terrace. This is interrupted only, and not unpleasantly, by the arrival of Stanley Street, but many of its buildings show signs of misuse and neglect. The south side is an odd amalgam of buildings, weakened at the west by the setting-back of modern Norroy House.

Nuns Road, Blackfriars, Greyfriars and Nicholas Street Mews form a mixed backland area with a miscellany of buildings, many of them strange bedfellows. All are interspersed with good trees, and these, with the quiet backlane character of the roadways, give a curiously rural atmosphere. Despite its architectural anarchy much could be made of the area by careful and selective redevelopment. To the south is Thomas Harrison's own house, set in a garden of mature trees.

Nicholas Street is a busy, noisy traffic route. All the demolition needed to make way for it was on the east, and, at the time of the survey, this was in a visually raw state of truncated ends and spasmodic rebuilding. But its west side buildings are undisturbed. It is a tribute to their qualities and established use that so far they have not apparently been impaired by exposure to the passing traffic. The long Georgian terrace retains its grandeur and provides strong central cohesion to what is otherwise now either fragmented by the Old Linen Hall site, with Queens School ground and Royal Infirmary to the north, or frail in the minor terrace to the south.

170a   Watergate Street, looking west

170b   Watergate Street, looking east

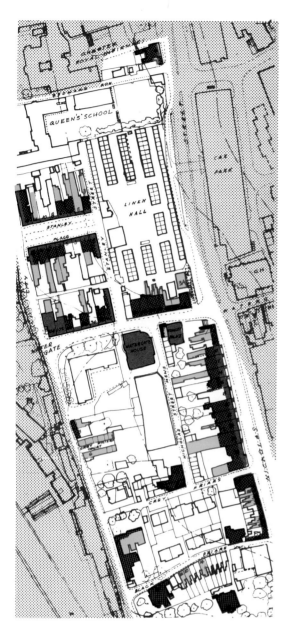

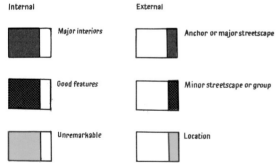

Internal		External	
■	Major interiors	□	Anchor or major streetscape
■	Good features	□	Minor streetscape or group
■	Unremarkable	□	Location

171a Architectural value

171b Georgian terrace in Nicholas Street
(top right)

171c Stanley Place, Watergate Street
(bottom right)

3.6.2 Architectural quality

Watergate Street (*West*) is the oldest in origin. But apart from Roman and medieval cellars, it retains only one early building, which is Stanley Place (Fig. 171c). Although heavily restored, this has much good work of the early seventeenth and eighteenth centuries. The street's other notable building is Watergate House (c. 1810)—a good example of the work of Thomas Harrison. Otherwise it has largely eighteenth-century terraced houses of the 'central cross-stair' type, which become grander as they reach the Watergate.

Stanley Place is another set piece of late eighteenth-century architecture. Its terraced houses are big in scale and have good and well-proportioned fronts. But inside they have disappointingly little real quality, even though they are pleasant and usable buildings.

Nicholas Street has a long and large-scale terrace of Georgian buildings on its western side (Fig. 171b). These are mostly of high quality inside, and many have particularly fine staircases and decorated ceilings. Further north, a small group of eighteenth-century houses once formed part of St. Martin's Fields. The lesser terrace to the south has pleasant minor buildings of the same century. Beyond them Harrison's house has great distinction for its simple but assured interiors.

Nuns Road, Greyfriars and Blackfriars have some good houses of the eighteenth and early nineteenth centuries, but these are set amongst later buildings of less interest. The period buildings are set cheek by jowl with the central City's only post-war semi-detached speculative housing, and a large asbestos motor coach shed.

3.6.3 Ownership, use and condition

Many buildings are privately owned and cater for a diversity of uses. Several on each side of Stanley Place are combined to contain part of Queen's School; and parts of the long Nicholas Street terrace are similarly combined as offices. Indeed as in Whitefriars, most premises are used now as offices with a scattering of clubs, surgeries, and a substantial minority of residential units. Most of the smaller houses in the area, for instance in Blackfriars and Nuns Road, are still used as single units; but many of the larger houses still residentially occupied in Nicholas Street, Watergate Street and Stanley Place have now been subdivided into flats.

Use and suitability. Many buildings illustrate that, whilst the use of an historic building may change many times during its lifetime, it is important that new uses are appropriate and sympathetic to the original design. Unhappily several buildings in Watergate Street have suffered unsympathetic alteration, and their present use augurs ill for the future. The fine rooms of the largest houses, for example, have been awkwardly subdivided, one as offices, and another as a hostel (Fig. 173b). Both are now largely empty, so the position could soon be remedied. Several others, now serving as flats, deserve a better standard of use, more compatible with their architectural quality. Watergate House itself is splendidly appointed, but several fine upper rooms find only desultory use as overflow stores.

By contrast, some other buildings in this area are splendidly used for a variety of purposes. For example, several houses in Stanley Place have been most suitably converted as prestige offices; and one of the terrace houses in Nicholas Street has become a doctor's surgery, with three excellent flats.

Many eighteenth-century properties here have later wings which have since become redundant. Unlike most Chester houses, those in the Nicholas Street terrace often have long staircase halls at the side. These make it difficult to subdivide the houses into separate floors. The alley between Watergate Street and Stanley Place is just too narrow to admit a lorry, and this prevents effective rear servicing of these premises.

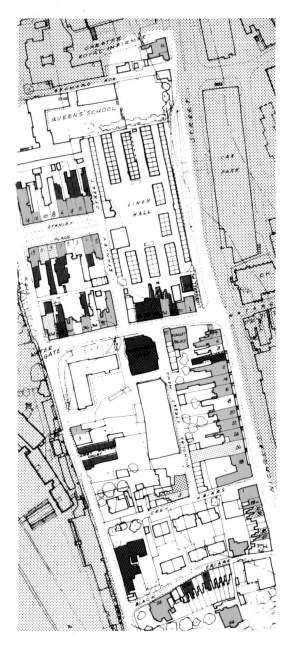

 Satisfactory

 Satisfactory if improved

 Unsatisfactory but suitable for change of use within present unit

Unsatisfactory but suitable for use or change of use if combined

 Incapable of economic use or otherwise admitting of replacement

172 Use and disuse

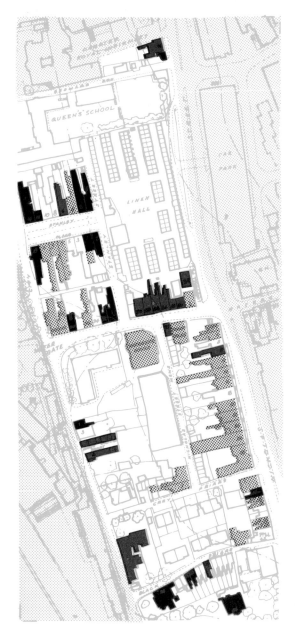

Condition. As one might expect, the structural condition of these buildings varies sharply. Few are empty; but under-used property, for example in Nicholas Street and Watergate Street, is suffering severely from water penetration, so that any dry rot which arises could easily spread into the better-kept neighbouring houses. Difficult roof access often prevents proper maintenance: many slopes are slated and pointed with cement, and have neglected roof lights, lead valleys and gutters, all admitting water. Many of the rear wings are in a poor condition, and it seems incredible that some in Nicholas Street can still be used for office purposes. Happily, several houses in Watergate Street have recently been renovated, but much remains to be done. Fortunately, the whole of the north side is so far intact, but urgent work is needed to save these terraces.

 Satisfactory overall

Deteriorating in whole or part

 Individually serious defects

173a   Condition

173b   Fine rooms now sub-divided in Watergate Street

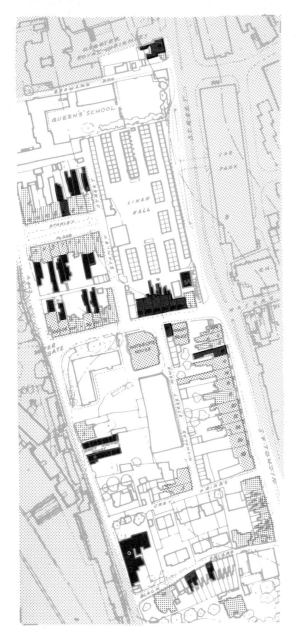

3.6.4 Conservation and action

The best-used buildings of *Stanley Place* need no more than attention to individual structural defects. The south side would benefit from the removal of their long and mainly unwanted rear additions. This would enable the very restricted rear lane to be widened as a proper service road. The road would also serve at the rear the north side of *Watergate Street.* Many buildings here need urgent repair and conversion, especially those partly empty or unsuitably used. Separate access to upper storeys could be arranged over new rear service additions, as previously suggested for the Rows. Nicholas Street buildings mainly need no more than individual repairs, as do the comparatively few remaining historic buildings elsewhere.

Maintenance. Some 44 buildings demand better maintenance (Fig. 174a). The terraces would be well served by regular joint maintenance schemes.

174b Stanley Place, looking west

Inspected buildings recommended as worthy and capable of conservation

For first aid action on serious defects

For urgent attention to adverse conditions

For protection and care

Inspected buildings incapable of, or not in need of, conservation

For renewal, clearance or otherwise admitting of replacement

174c Planting would help, and would screen the gasometer

174a Recommendations

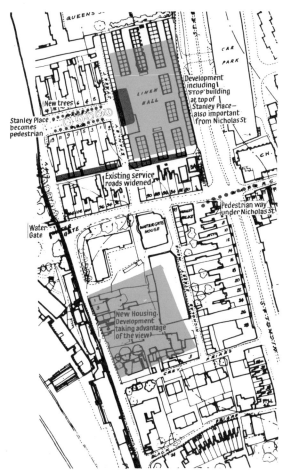

175a   Townscape proposals

Opportunity areas: Old Linen Hall site
This valuable site is under-used by its present occasional function as racecourse stables, especially in relation to its now important position on Nicholas Street. If this accommodation could be provided elsewhere, the land could serve a much more effective purpose in the City (possibly for local government offices for the County). A new building would need careful design, especially in relation to Stanley Place, to which it would form an eastern termination.

Greyfriars Court site
The site between Greyfriars Court and the western end of Greyfriars is at present under-used, its few buildings being substandard and uneconomic. This would be an excellent housing site, with its good outward views and trees, around which the layout could be planned. The site could include that of the present inappropriate coach shed in adjoining Nicholas Street Mews.

175b   A pedestrian underpass linking Watergate Street beneath the new Ring Road

175c   Stables now occupy the Old Linen Hall site

3.7 Study Area 7: Northgate

176a   Study Area 7: Northgate

176b   Aerial view of the Study Area

3.7.1   Townscape appraisal

Northgate Street is the least attractive and successful of all the approaches to the City centre. The contrary northward view is more successful only by virtue of the splendid strong stop of the Northgate (Fig.177b). Some good seventeenth- and eighteenth-century buildings on the west side are attractively arcaded over the pavement. But except for the Abbey Gateways, the east side is undistinguished, and its few decent Georgian upper facades struggle in vain to overcome the monotonous confusion of the small, terraced, and sometimes run-down shops below.

177a   Townscape analysis

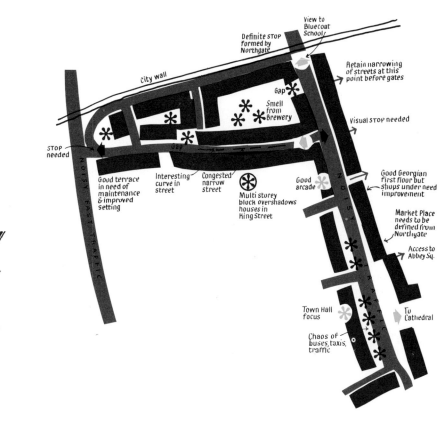

View to Bluecoat School

Definite stop formed by Northgate

Retain narrowing of streets at this point before gates

City wall

Gap

Smell from Brewery

Visual stop needed

Stop needed

Gap

Good Georgian first floor but shops under need improvement

Good terrace in need of maintenance & improved setting

Interesting curve in street

Congested narrow street

Multi storey block overshadows houses in King Street

Good arcade

Market Place needs to be defined from Northgate

Access to Abbey Sq.

Town Hall focus

To Cathedral

Chaos of buses, taxis, traffic

NOISY EAST TRAFFIC

NOISY TRAFFIC

177b   Northgate, by Thomas Harrison, 1808

177c   Buildings inspected

Buildings recommended for listing

Other buildings inspected

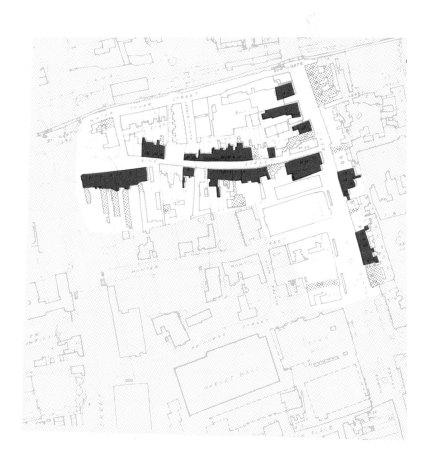

178a   The gentle curve of King Street

King Street (Fig. 178a), predominantly of small houses with some offices, is by contrast an attractive period street. Its hill form is narrow and interestingly sinuous, giving changing vistas although badly closed at both ends (Figs. 178b/c). Its attractive seventeenth- and eighteenth-century houses front continuously on to the narrow pavements. From the rear, the street is subject to strong external pressures on each side. On the north, the Northgate Brewery inevitably causes some disturbance; and the Victorian tenements of Water Tower and Canning Streets are a physical restriction. To the south, the Hunter Street office block dominates and overshadows the houses—an unfortunate object lesson in relations between new and old.

Kings Buildings at present links King Street with Nicholas Street, but its terraced splendour is at odds with the busy traffic route to which it is now exposed (Fig. 178b).

178b   West end of King Street 'opened' by the new Ring Road

178c   Weak stop at the inner end of King Street

178d   Northgate Street

179a The Pied Bull Inn has some of the remaining arcading in Northgate Street

3.7.2 Architectural quality

The Northgate area has individually good and representative work of most periods. The majority of its historic buildings are, however, of minor quality. The most noteworthy are concentrated in King Street.

Northgate Street retains disappointingly little of its original quality. Exceptions are No. 65 (formerly the Bluebell Inn), which has excellent fifteenth- and seventeenth-century work, and the Pied Bull with its very fine Jacobean detail and strong external form (Fig. 179a).

No. 53 (ffolliot House) is a good eighteenth-century building with fine and typical interiors including a good cross-stair. Other buildings, mainly on the east, retain minor Georgian elements. But most have lost their architectural value through drastic alteration.

179b Architectural value

Internal		External	
	Major interiors		Anchor or major streetscape
	Good features		Minor streetscape or group
	Unremarkable		Location

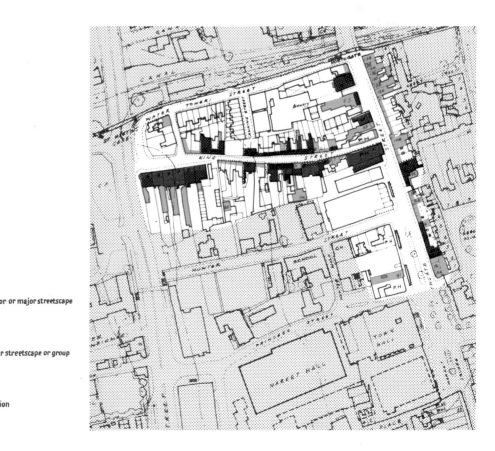

King Street has much more architectural distinction. Nos. 28 and 30 are interesting small seventeenth-century cottages; and No. 9 is a fine example of the eighteenth-century expansion of a small earlier building, with domestic interiors of very good quality (Fig. 180a). Most of the street's historic buildings are in fact Georgian terraced houses of one bay, three storeys high, with central cross-stairs and other characteristic features. Nos. 14, 15 and 18 are typical and No. 21 is a larger version.

Kings Buildings is a fine Georgian terrace of six houses, still only of three main storeys, but bold in scale and with correspondingly grand staircases and fine interiors. They give real distinction to the area whose merits are otherwise in a lower key (Fig. 180b).

180a   Georgian houses in King Street

180b   King's Buildings

3.7.3 Ownership, use and condition

Most properties here are individually owned, but few are owner-occupied. Some landlords live in distant parts of the country, and much daily maintenance is left to the goodwill of tenants. The Northgate Brewery has extensive premises and owns a number of adjoining properties. Several vacant properties at the east end of King Street have been acquired by the Corporation; and one, the former Bluebell Inn in Northgate Street, has been restored for occupation.

Servicing and access. Both *King Street and Northgate Street* are narrow two-way streets, yet nearly all the buildings depend on front access for servicing. North of King Street, rear access is restricted by the Brewery: east of the Market Square, the shallow buildings have become knitted together with those over the Abbey wall and fronting Abbey Square, making rear access impossible. Pedestrian alleys serve many yards, but very few have vehicular access.

Use and suitability. Nearly all the terraced houses on the east of Northgate Street once had living accommodation above ground-level shops. But planning inadequacies have resulted in disuse of many upper floors, unless required for storage by the shops. A few have been converted as offices, but their small size mostly makes this uneconomic. The street caters for local rather than regional shoppers, and few units need more than one floor. Thus the smaller buildings at the north end of Northgate Street tend to be more fully occupied than the higher terraces towards the Market Square.

The ideal size of a living-unit varies from time to time, and according to the changing status of the area. In the Northgate area many houses remain eminently suited to the size of today's families, but some have grown too large, and others that are now too small have consequently become vacant and neglected (Fig. 181c). Neighbouring buildings of merit can sometimes be combined into larger units. Several buildings in King Street might qualify for this treatment, but others of no particular value could be more economically renewed, maintaining the continuity of the street. In Northgate Street, many properties with only one or two poorly used rooms on each floor and steep staircases lend themselves to horizontal conversion as attractive flats.

181a   Little Abbey Gateway, its stonework much neglected

181b   Small cottages in King Street (below)

181c   One of the many disused rooms in King's Buildings (below right)

Redevelopment pressures on this area have so far been kept at bay, and many buildings are still used for their original purpose. It is important to find appropriate uses for houses which are too large for a single family unit. No. 9 King Street (Fig. 182a), for example, is well and fully used as a doctor's house and surgery; and the former Bluebell Inn has been pleasantly converted as a small shop.

Some buildings suffer from inappropriate use. The upper rooms of No. 53 Northgate Street are for the most part neglected, and there are only a few offices on the ground floor. The stately rooms of Kings Buildings deserve a more worthy use than the flatlets or institutional quarters into which some are divided.

182a A well-kept house in King Street

182b King's Buildings: some are now empty or badly sub-divided

182c Use and disuse

 Satisfactory

Satisfactory if improved

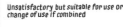 Unsatisfactory but suitable for change of use within present unit

Unsatisfactory but suitable for use or change of use if combined

 Incapable of economic use or otherwise admitting of replacement

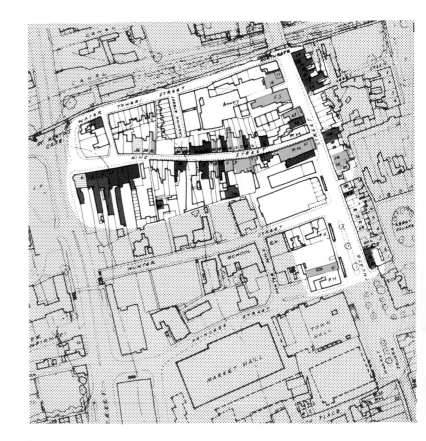

183a   Cracks in King's Buildings: the front wall is falling out due to settlement

Condition. Most buildings in the Northgate area are in reasonably sound structural condition. But individual properties show the typical problems of historic buildings whose maintenance is hampered both by absentee landlords and the problems arising from rent control. Where buildings are only partially occupied, their condition is as always closely related to the amount of use made of them. As this diminishes, deterioration tends to set in at the roof and upper floors and spread downwards.

Thus, owner-occupied houses tend to be the best looked after. Next come buildings, such as those on the north side of King Street, whose maintenance is falling short due to lack of funds or interest of their non-resident owners. A further stage comes when part of the building is disused, as at No. 53 Northgate Street, where the disused upper floors are fast approaching dereliction. This happens also to houses which have become vacant, like parts of Kings Buildings. Unless repairs are put in hand promptly, these would quickly decay beyond the point where restoration is worthwhile, and the Corporation is already taking action.

Particular problems of repair arise in individual cases. Settlement in the front wall of Kings Buildings for example needs specialist treatment (Fig. 182b). Another problem here is that of party-walls exposed by the demolition of adjoining property. These are not only unsightly but are structurally weak and admit the weather. A bad example of this kind of exposure is the west wall of No. 6 Kings Buildings, where not only is there a large crack in the upper part of the wall, but the cold water main to the demolished property has been left exposed and a waste-pipe severed, so that both have been saturating the end wall.

Nevertheless, more often it is the unseen defects like leaking gutters and roofs which lead to the most rapid and serious decay.

183b   Condition

 Satisfactory overall

 Deteriorating in whole or part

Individually serious defects

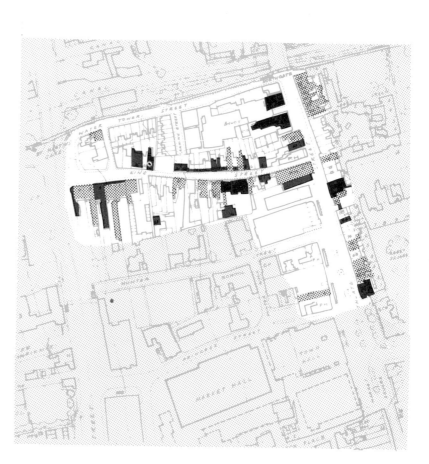

3.7.4 Conservation and action

In *Northgate Street,* the few buildings which warrant conservation are mostly suited to their present uses. The residential character of *King Street* should be strengthened by all possible means. This will mean combining uneconomically small units and reconditioning others. For houses backing on to the Northgate Brewery, especially where rent-controlled, this may not for some time be possible. It is meanwhile important that they should not be allowed to deteriorate any further. *Kings Buildings* need urgent repair and conversion. With selective pruning of their long rear additions, they could become excellent flats.

Maintenance. Here, 32 buildings demand better maintenance (Fig. 184). Where this is beyond the means of individual owner-occupiers, grant-aid will be needed.

184 Recommendations

Inspected buildings recommended as worthy and capable of conservation

 For first aid action on serious defects

For urgent attention to adverse conditions

For protection and care

Inspected buildings incapable of, or not in need of, conservation

 For renewal, clearance or otherwise admitting of replacement

185a   The front wall of King's Buildings has been extensively shored

185b   Townscape recommendations

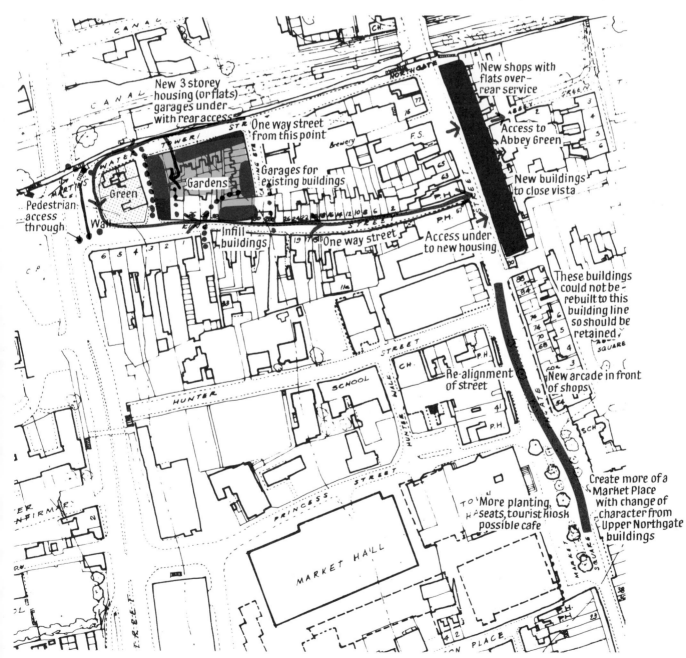

New 3 storey housing (or flats) garages under with rear access

New shops with flats over – rear service

One way street from this point

Access to Abbey Green

Garages for existing buildings

New buildings to close vista

Pedestrian access through

Infill buildings

One way street

Access under to new housing

These buildings could not be rebuilt to this building line so should be retained

Re-alignment of street

New arcade in front of shops

More planting, seats, tourist kiosk possible cafe

Create more of a Market Place with change of character from Upper Northgate buildings

MARKET HALL

Action site: King Street and Water Tower Street

Some housing is nearing obsolescence between the western ends of King Street and Water Tower Street. A residential redevelopment scheme is suggested.

The scheme would provide 13 houses (5 to 6 persons) and three flats with garages and small private gardens. The western terrace of new houses would face on to a new walled garden square with Kings Buildings to the south. Other new houses would have access from Water Tower or King Streets with rear service circulation (Figs. 186 and 187).

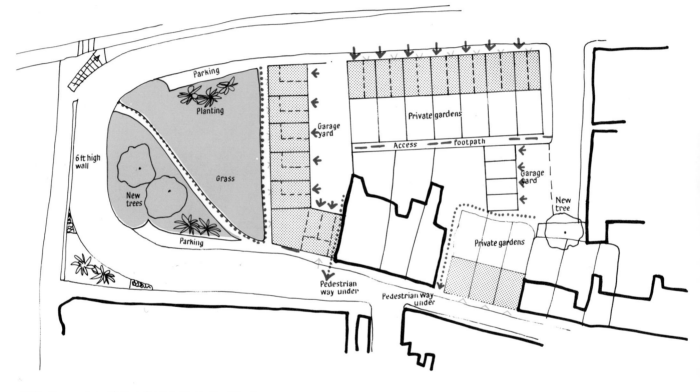

186 A new housing scheme opposite King's Buildings, and in Water Tower Street

Opportunity areas: Northgate Brewery site

If and when the present brewery removes to a more convenient and appropriate site, the kind of housing layout previously suggested to the west could be extended. Proper reconditioning of the retained building in King Street (north) would also then be possible.

City centre site

The land between the Town Hall and Hunter Street is at present wasted. This would be an excellent and central position for an important civic building such as the suggested Conference Hall.

187 Perspective drawing of the proposed housing scheme opposite King's Buildings

3.8   Study Area 8:
Upper Northgate and Canalside

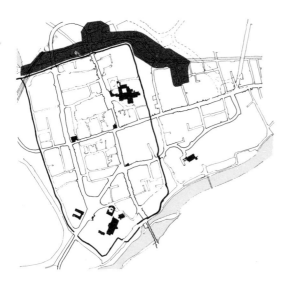

188a   Study Area 8: Upper Northgate and Canalside

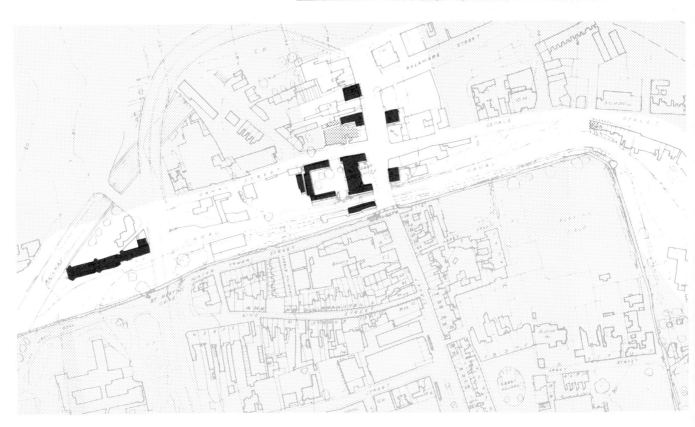

189a Aerial views of the Study Area

189b Buildings inspected

  Buildings recommended for listing

Other buildings inspected

190a Outwards from the Walls: Upper Northgate Street

3.8.1 Townscape appraisal

Upper Northgate Street continues the axis of Northgate Street through the gate and City Walls to the new inner ring road and its roundabout. It passes over the Shropshire Union Canal, but the relationship here is remote with no physical connection.

Southwards, the street has a splendid vista of the strong entry through Northgate itself, flanked by the distinguished Georgian architecture of the Bluecoat Hospital. From the Northgate Bridge there are dramatic views down into the canal gorge below.

Northwards, as yet, the view towards the new roundabout and its fountains is less good, although new proposals are being considered. Minor Georgian terrace buildings on each side are interspersed with mediocre public and commercial buildings. At the roundabout, the building pattern is for the moment understandably loose and fragmentary, with an overwhelming predominance of roadway and traffic paraphernalia.

190b Townscape analysis

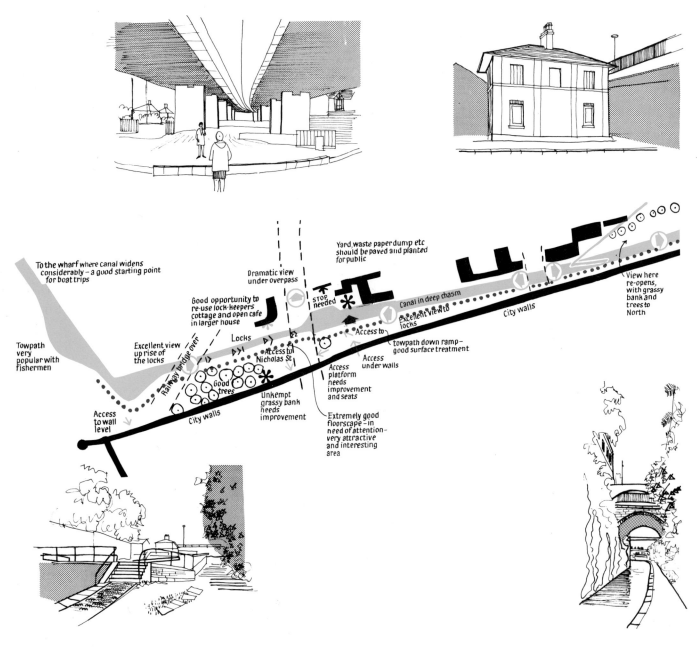

The Shropshire Union Canal runs from east to west, just north of the City Walls. The canal basin is to the north-west, under the railway bridge and Nicholas Street flyover. A bold rise of three locks has lost none of its character with the new traffic overhead: the nineteenth-century detailing and engineering work is splendid. Here is the history of whole centuries of traffic engineering. The canal then enters a deeply-cut gorge, under the lee of Northgate and Bluecoat Hospital. This is narrow, deep and intensely dramatic, with sheer rock walls rising vertically on either side. Overhead is the graceful arch of the so-called Bridge of Sighs and a more substantial bridge carrying Upper Northgate Street.

Continuing eastwards, the canal's north bank sets back as it drops, and is further softened by the green grass and planting fronting George Street. But the south side rises sheer to the City Walls as far as their north-east angle and King Charles' Tower.

The terrain on both banks then drops to canal level, and Frodsham Street passes over it on a flattish bridge. The surroundings are mainly industrial, except at the end of Queen Street where the scene becomes fleetingly domestic.

Queen Street runs directly northwards to a right-angled junction with the canalside. The canal setting is attractive, despite the blank brick hind-parts of the modern cinema opposite. Union Walk has minor period character, and runs westwards to Frodsham Street. This is a small and relatively unimportant group, but it has a historical cohesion in an otherwise barren and nondescript area. To the east, recent clearances have produced an area of desolation, temporarily used for car parking.

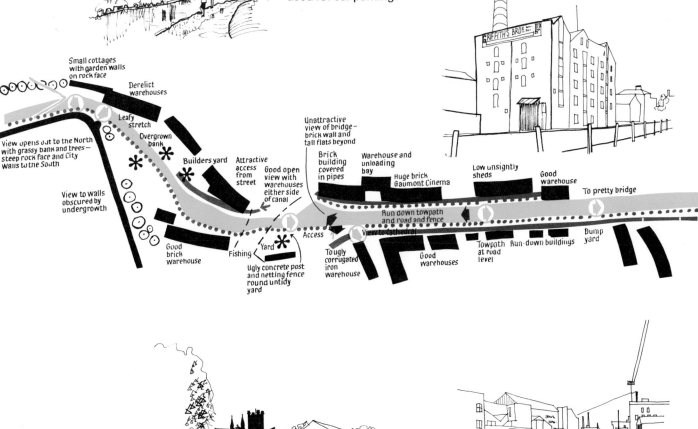

3.8.2 Architectural quality

The best architecture here is concentrated in *Upper Northgate Street* (Fig. 193b). This contains good eighteenth-century buildings, especially the Bluecoat Hospital (1717). Externally this has a strong form and excellent detailing, but the interiors are plain. The south wing, formerly used as Little St. John's Church, has been stripped internally. Behind the main building is a simple quadrangle of small nineteenth-century almshouses, set in an attractively quiet backwater. Further north in the street are some good eighteenth- and early nineteenth-century town houses at one point arcaded over the pavement. *Canal Street* has a pleasant late eighteenth- or early nineteenth-century house, set in a good garden, and the lock-keeper's cottage of about 1772.

The Oddfellows Arms in *Frodsham Street* is a cheerful eighteenth-century pub with engaging details. *Union Walk* has minor late-Georgian houses; and early warehouses along the canal have an industrial grandeur.

The north end of *Queen Street* has some minor late-Georgian terraces with pretty doorcases and typical interiors. The old Congregational Church has considerable quality, and the strong stone classicism of its exterior and assured delicacy inside strongly suggest an attribution to Thomas Harrison (Fig. 193c).

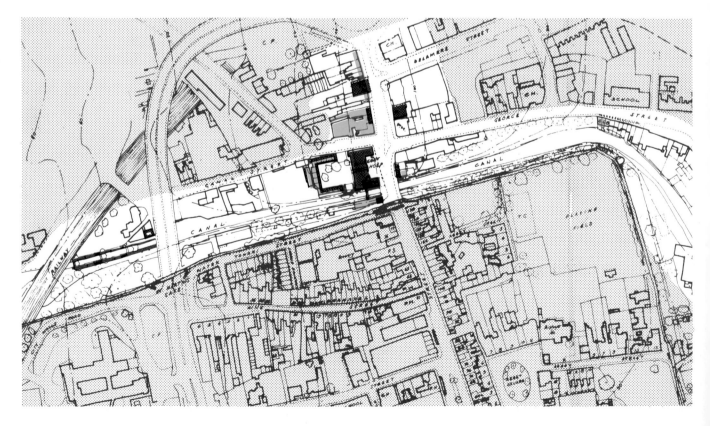

193a Canal cottages in George Street

193b Upper Northgate Street (top right)

193c The old Congregational Church and school (right)

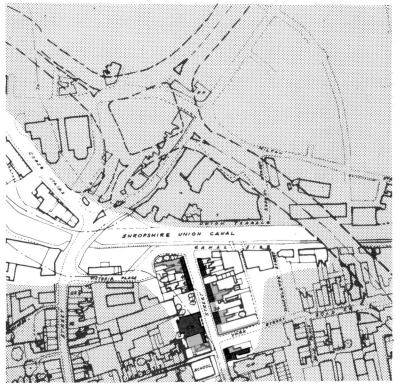

193d Architectural value

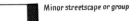

Internal		External	
	Major interiors		Anchor or major streetscape
	Good features		Minor streetscape or group
	Unremarkable		Location

194a 10 Upper Northgate Street, shortly to be demolished

3.8.3 Ownership, use and condition

The property in *Upper Northgate Street* shows how the survival of historic buildings depends on sympathetic ownership. For example, two private houses face one another across the street. No. 13 on the west has been well converted into flats, but No. 10 on the east is neglected and likely to be replaced by a garage (Fig. 194a).

Most houses at the north end of *Queen Street* are individually owned, and nearly all are still residential. The majority are fully occupied, but southwards several on the west have been altered and are now disused.

Use and suitability. Upper Northgate Street is the link between the town centre and northern Chester, but the street has itself only a few smaller service shops, with insurance offices and the like, several clubs and some residential accommodation.

Most of the buildings have been suitably converted to their present use. The best example is No. 13, well arranged as three flats with a shop below. But No. 10, once a good house, is now poorly used as a store for garage miscellanea.

Few buildings in Upper Northgate Street present any special difficulties in planning. The relatively narrow, terraced eighteenth- and early nineteenth-century houses have mostly become offices. A more efficient and convenient use of the available space would be obtained by horizontal conversion.

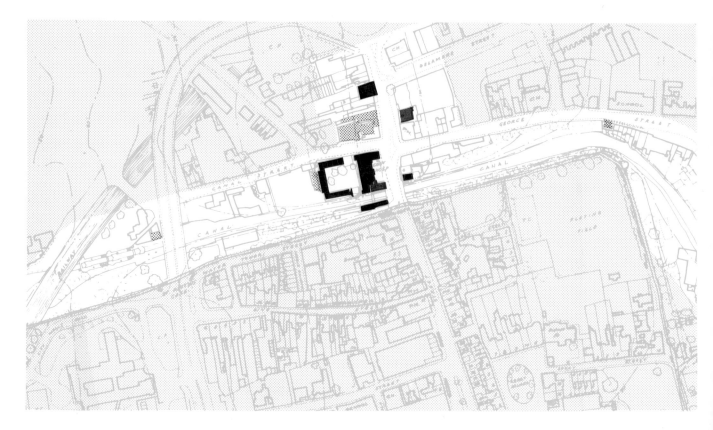

The cottages in *George Street* are an attractive group facing the north-east corner of the City Wall and overlooking the canal. But the present units are too small and lack modern amenities.

Many houses in Queen Street remain eminently suitable as dwellings. But the former Congregational Church, later used as a theatre, was for a long time empty and partly derelict.

Several of the better houses at the north end of Queen Street have been equipped with modern services, and have good well-lit rooms of adequate height. But the standard deteriorates sharply southwards on the west side of the street. Cramped terraced units lead from communal alleys, and poor and crowded, ill-lit rooms have an almost Dickensian flavour. It is very doubtful whether the cost of modernising could possibly be justified.

Condition.   The state of most buildings is closely related to their use. Many are in reasonable structural order, and the poorest are the Bluecoat Chapel and No. 10, the latter now saturated by rain pouring through the roof.

The cloud of indecision and threat of pending demolition hangs low over Queen Street. The terraces have been 'eaten away' by demolitions, and roofs have been left with ragged edges, hastening the deterioration of neighbouring buildings. The chapel and some of the empty houses are in serious disrepair; but many better houses at the north and on the west are well maintained.

195a   Derelict end house of a good terrace in Queen Street

195b   Condition

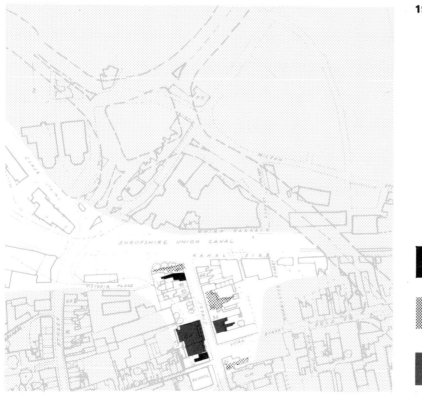

  Satisfactory overall

Deteriorating in whole or part

  Individually serious defects

195

3.8.4 Conservation and action

The rescue and reconditioning of the Bluecoat Chapel is of prime urgency. The whole of the building will come under the care of the City Corporation as soon as the legal difficulties can be cleared.

The cottages in George Street on the Canal bend have little intrinsic historical value, but they have a picturesque quality almost impossible to replace. Each pair could be combined into an attractive small house, and their especially good setting should make these readily saleable.

The old Congregational Church could be converted and incorporated in a group development, such as might be sought by the YMCA when they vacate the Old Bishops Palace.

Maintenance. Nineteen buildings call for improved maintenance (Figs. 196 and 197c).

Environmental improvement
Canalside. The canal with its towpath deserves much more use than it yet receives. A thriving canal traffic could be encouraged in pleasure craft, canal buses and private boats. An ideal starting-point for passenger trips (for example to the Zoo) would be from Canal Street, where an empty site is available. The old lock-keeper's cottage could be converted into a restaurant, and the locks become one of Chester's most interesting 'places to go'.

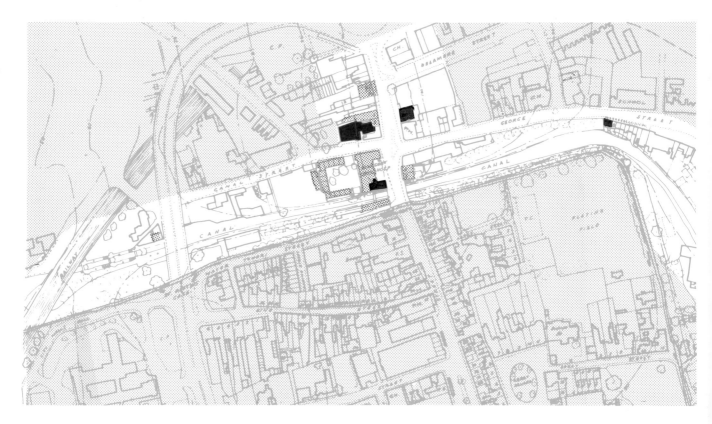

Opportunity area: Upper Northgate roundabout

The roundabout is for the moment over-large in scale for its surroundings, and the general atmosphere is incomplete and untidy. This is a good position for new buildings, and we suggest the policy should be to complete it by a stepped layout underlining the basic east-west grid of the City. This would give back a sense of enclosure, contrasting on the west with the views of the Welsh Mountains.

197a   Disjointed area around the new roundabout in Upper Northgate Street

197b   The proposals for unifying the area

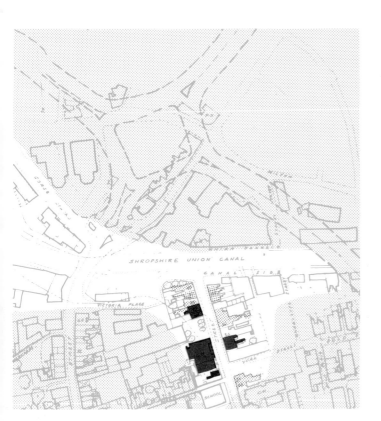

197c   Recommendations

Inspected buildings recommended as worthy and capable of conservation

 For first aid action on serious defects

 For urgent attention to adverse conditions

 For protection and care

Inspected buildings incapable of, or not in need of, conservation

 For renewal, clearance or otherwise admitting of replacement

3.9 Study Area 9: Foregate

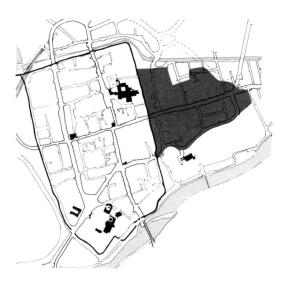

198a Study Area 9: Foregate

3.9.1 Townscape appraisal

The Foregate area is large, loose-knit and barely held together by Foregate Street, which drives straight and uncompromisingly inwards to Eastgate. To the north is the commercial character of Canalside; to the south, the softer recreational spirit of Grosvenor Park and the Riverside. But the area between lacks established character. Its buildings are mostly mediocre, relieved only here and there by small enclaves of quality.

198b Aerial view of the Study Area

199   Buildings inspected

 Buildings recommended for listing

Other buildings inspected

200 An open view of the Cathedral from the car park in Frodsham Street

Foregate Street itself should be a splendid approach to the walled City through Eastgate. It has all the basic attributes and is long, straight and wide. The vista towards Eastgate calls up visions of the splendour beyond. But Foregate Street's own lack of distinction is a sad contrast. Looking back eastwards, the scene is a disappointment, emphasised by a counterpart of Grosvenor Street in the 'feather-edged' junction with diagonal City Road, but this will shortly be removed for the new roundabout.

Good individual buildings still remain to echo the former quality of the street as do a few trees, but they are neither numerous nor cohesive enough to establish satisfactory character. Overall, the street is rather restless and disjointed, and lacks the architectural unity and distinction it deserves.

Frodsham Street runs parallel with the City Wall, northwards from Foregate Street, and has similar characteristics but on a smaller scale. It too has a largely undistinguished and disjointed street scene, consisting mainly of small shops. Northwards, it narrows and curves slightly to a more characterful end at the canal. Otherwise it has few cohesive features, except for good momentary views over the City Wall to the Cathedral (Fig. 200), of which new buildings should take every advantage.

St. John Street leads south from Foregate Street and is altogether more purposeful. It has a fine southward view to the amphitheatre and Roman gardens. Its large-scale public buildings are of various styles, dates and merits, but invest the street with a certain quality. Good opportunities offer at the south for new buildings overlooking the amphitheatre site.

Queen Street (*south*) arrives abruptly at the north of Foregate Street in a narrow right-angled junction. The street widens progressively to the north until it reaches the more distinguished area around the canalside. The southern section is now mainly derelict and consists only of terraced tenements, albeit with a Georgian flavour, and small industrial premises.

Bold Square and its environs (Bold Place and York Street) will virtually disappear when the inner ring road is completed. The square itself has some small and once pretty early-Victorian villas, marooned in a sea of cleared sites, car-parks, and makeshift premises.

Grosvenor Park Road, Union Street, Vicar's Lane and Little St. John Street, along the southern flank of the Foregate area, combine into a busy traffic route as the southern link of the inner ring road, entering the walled City at Newgate. The recreational and tourist attractions of Grosvenor Park, St. John's Church and the Roman amphitheatre lead on to the riverside. On the north side of the route a preponderance of red brick Victoriana has its own distinction, but gives little cohesion as a street.

Love Street, Bath Street, Priory Place and Forest Street are back streets between the southern link and Foregate Street. This is an almost entirely nineteenth- and twentieth-century area of small tenements, commercial and public buildings, with minor and mutilated remnants buried in it. It has very few merits and no sense of place.

The Headlands, at the east, is a tiny backwater with pretty cottages and a delightful cobbled and treed approach from Dee Lane. Its merits are perhaps mostly as a reminder of what must once have been the character of the area, and its future is perilous.

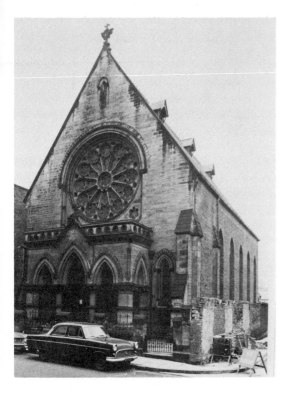

201a High Victorian Welsh Chapel, in St John's Street

201b Good timber-framing in the District Bank, in Foregate Street

3.9.2 Architectural quality

This area is extremely varied in the age, character and quality of its buildings.

Foregate Street has the remnants of good buildings although often heavily restored. For example the Old Nag's Head (1597) was rebuilt in 1914, and the Old Royal Oak Hotel (1601) was completely reconstructed in 1920. The buildings which have in fact retained their historical integrity are, therefore, the more valuable. The earliest is No. 70. This is a small timber-framed house of the late sixteenth century with original and seventeenth-century work inside. Another is No. 77, half of a timber building in relatively unaltered condition, but later and plainer in character. There are also some seventeenth-century internal elements at No. 63.

The eighteenth century is represented by a few buildings in an almost complete state like No. 105 and by several partial interiors, as at No. 71 and Nos. 126 to 130. Plain Georgian buildings like No. 65 achieve added importance from their poor surroundings.

Foregate Street has a few notable nineteenth-century buildings. These include a good Classical Revival example in Lloyds Bank and the black-and-white replica fronts of Nos. 2, 4 and 6. But its later buildings are undistinguished except for the District Bank (Fig. 201b) and the new building at the corner of Bath Street which sets a good standard for the future.

St. John Street has one very notable building exterior—No. 6. This has a splendid brick-and-stone front of mid-Georgian date, but is disappointing inside. Conversely the Methodist Church has a bad 1906 exterior masking a pleasant Regency interior with galleries. The Welsh Church is wholeheartedly 1870 inside and out (Fig. 201a). Some buildings near Newgate are unworthy of their position.

Vicar's Lane has one key building in the detached eighteenth-century rectory, now the Grosvenor Club (Fig. 202b), with an especially good exterior. Its red brick Victorian neighbours are good of their kind.

Love Street has only one good historical building, the large eighteenth- and early nineteenth-century Forest House. Although superficially mutilated, this large two-part building has excellent features both inside and out.

Frodsham Street contains only minor historical remnants of little value. *Queen Street* (*south*) has also lost almost all its historical value. Its plain late eighteenth- and early nineteenth-century tenements were never more than of minor interest and have been further devalued by dereliction.

202a   Forest House, in Love Street: a good under-used building defaced by plumbing

202b   Grosvenor Club, in Vicar's Lane (right)

202c   Cottages in Bold Square, spoilt by the insertion of new windows

203 Architectural value

Internal

■ Major interiors

■ Good features

▨ Unremarkable

External

□▨ Anchor or major streetscape

□■ Minor streetscape or group

□▨ Location

3.9.3 Ownership, use and condition

The main property owners in Chester, the Corporation, Grosvenor Estates and several of the larger multiple stores (for example, Chester Co-operative Society) all own parcels of land in this area. But most buildings of historical and architectural value are still owned by individual occupiers.

Many in *Foregate Street* are well used as shops or offices, but problems arise when the upper floors are excessive to requirements or are too small or inconvenient (for example, No. 65) to convert economically as separate offices. The upper parts then tend to become neglected, and the consequent disrepair becomes a threat to the future. Empty floors have on several occasions assisted burglars in breaking through into occupied adjoining property.

Similar conditions are found in most of the area north of Foregate Street. The houses particularly on the west side of Queen Street and in Union Walk are very small, and several are empty and derelict. But there are established communities here and in Seller Street, Bold Place and Bold Square, to be carefully rehoused in any redevelopment.

Building uses to the south of Foregate Street are much more varied. In *St. John's Street* they are mostly public or professional and include the Public Library, the Post Office and two churches. Although on the east some gaps have been cut for rear access to the south of Foregate Street, the rest are well used, as are the neighbouring good buildings in Vicar's Lane.

Forest House in *Love Street* has had a chequered history and still enshrines in its upper floors an abandoned NAAFI Canteen (Fig. 202a). Although it provides accommodation for a restaurant, much of this potentially fine property is still under-used or empty. Elsewhere south of this side of Foregate Street many buildings are substandard, and their sites small, making their improvement uneconomic.

3.9.4 Conservation and action

No comprehensive scheme of conservation can be carried out here, but special attention is needed for the better buildings, where rarity gives them added value.

Maintenance. Sixteen buildings call for better care, and for more awareness on the part of individual owners (Fig. 205).

Environmental improvement
An overall scheme of tree-planting and maintenance would further help to reunify Foregate Street, making it visually more attractive and providing a softened approach to the strongly urban City entry at Eastgate.

Opportunity area: Foregate Street
On the redevelopment of this area we concur with the proposals of the 1964 Central Area Plan, but with the inclusion of the proposed Central Bus Station (52 and 53). A carefully controlled combination of comprehensive and piecemeal redevelopment can regain the character of Foregate Street, encouraging an arcaded treatment of new buildings. Special care will be needed to integrate new building with the few historically valuable ones, so that the latter do not become anachronistic.

204a Neglect in Queen Street

204b Disused rear additions in Foregate Street area

205 Recommendations

Inspected buildings recommended as worthy and
capable of conservation

For first aid action on serious defects

For urgent attention to adverse conditions

For protection and care

Inspected buildings incapable of, or
not in need of, conservation

For renewal, clearance or otherwise
admitting of replacement

3.10 Study Area 10: Riverside

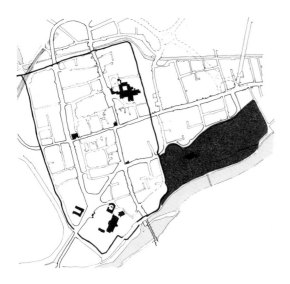

3.10.1 Townscape appraisal

This area, from the Old Dee Bridge to the rowing club, is served by three access roads: from the Bridge; down Souters Lane; and from the east around Grosvenor Park. Three attractive pedestrian footways descend to the river by steps from the north. There are very attractive views in all directions, across and along the river, and between Dee Bridge and the Queen's Park footbridge.

206a   Study Area 10: Riverside

206b   Aerial view of the Study Area

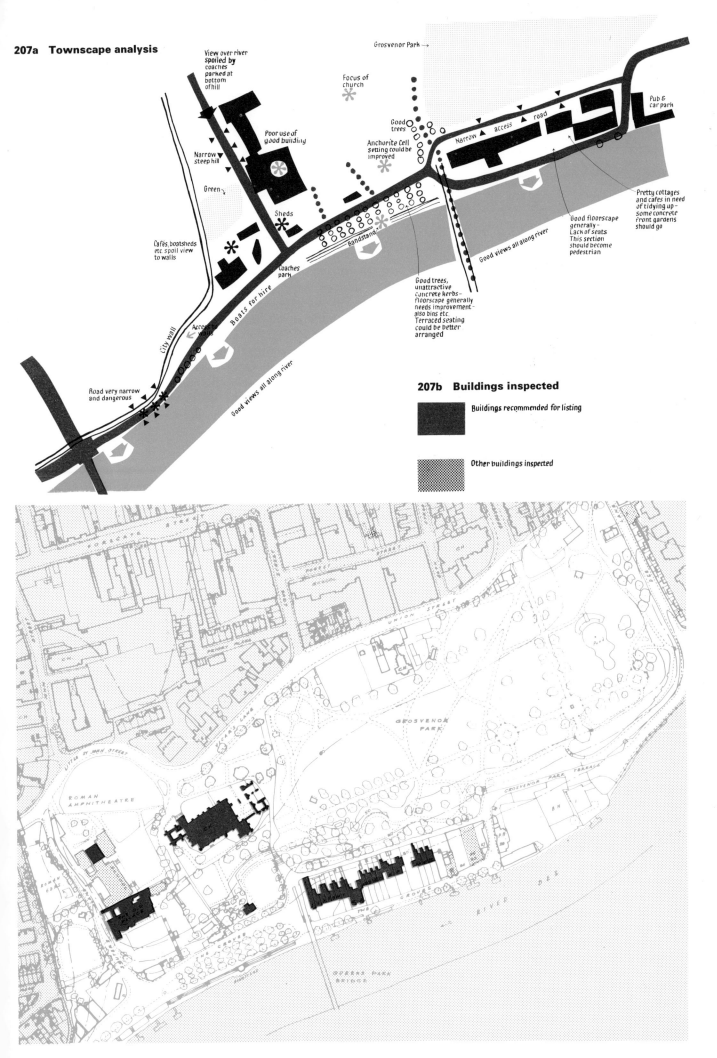

207a Townscape analysis

View over river **spoiled by** coaches parked at bottom of hill

Grosvenor Park →

Focus of church

Poor use of good building

Good trees

Narrow steep hill

Anchorite Cell setting could be improved

Narrow access road

Pub & car park

Green

Sheds

Bandstand

Pretty cottages and cafes in need of tidying up – some concrete front gardens should go

Cafés, boatsheds etc spoil view to walls

Coaches park

Good views all along river

Good floorscape generally – Lack of seats This section should become pedestrian

Boats for hire

City wall

Access to walls

Good trees, unattractive concrete kerbs – floorscape generally needs improvement – also bins etc. Terraced seating could be better arranged

Road very narrow and dangerous

Good views all along river

207b Buildings inspected

Buildings recommended for listing

Other buildings inspected

207

The Riverside's north-west approach is past a splendid architectural preamble—the buildings around the Roman amphitheatre. But, apart from the Anchorite Cell, dramatically set on its high rock outcrop, the buildings on the river bank itself contribute no great visual distinction to its attractions. They are pleasant and all-of-a-piece with the attractive suspension bridge, bandstand, kiosks (Fig. 208a), and early penny-in-the-slot machines.

Chester's riverside is extremely popular and well used, with pleasure boats and racing, plenty to look at, and good places to sit or to walk. The serried ranks of terraced seating which overlook the river are fully used and practical in summer, although exposed in winter. The many fine trees give shelter and character, and it is a pity to see so many in poor condition and set behind unattractive concrete kerbs (Fig. 208b).

The riverside is a wonderful amenity for pedestrian enjoyment and is at present somewhat spoiled by the poor traffic situation. Near the Old Dee Bridge, the road is extremely narrow, and the footpaths taper to nothing throwing pedestrians into the traffic. Beyond Queen's Park Bridge, fast traffic again spoils a delightful pedestrian area. Here the road and pavement textures are good, and the concreting of some gardens is a pity. Public seating is lacking at this end.

This whole area is a great asset to Chester, and its holiday atmosphere deserves enhancing by more landscaping, the improvement of details and surfaces, by better accommodation for its numerous cafés and amusements and by improved traffic control and parking facilities.

208a   Attractive kiosk in The Groves

208b   Concrete curbs are not part of the character of this area

208c   River Dee and The Groves

3.10.2 Architectural quality

The most important buildings are at the west. The Roman amphitheatre (currently being excavated) is Chester's most important relic of the period (Fig. 209a). The remains in the adjacent Roman garden, although interesting, have been brought from elsewhere. St. John's Church and its ruins have excellent twelfth-century work in a good setting. The nucleus of the Ursuline Convent is a typical Cestrian Georgian house with a good staircase, but it is now buried in later buildings. The thirteenth-century Anchorite Cell, a romantic survival, was much altered in the eighteenth century (Fig. 209c).

The most important building here is the former Bishop's Palace, now the YMCA. This is a Georgian red brick house set commandingly above the river. Its main quality is in its interiors: a good staircase and splendid rooms with finishes and decorations of very high quality.

209a   The Roman amphitheatre is still being excavated

209b   The Bishop's Old Palace is now a YMCA hostel

209c   The Anchorite Cell is partly medieval

Queen's Park Bridge is a graceful and attractive structure (Fig. 210a). The terrace to the east of it contains a pair of minor Georgian houses, with double bays and typical detailing, and a number of early Victorian brick villas—some plain and some fanciful. These are quietly attractive and the whole has a charming village character in its excellent river setting. To the east are the more ambitious Victorian buildings of the boathouse, club and pub (Fig. 210b).

Dee Lane, running straight downhill to the riverside, is bounded to the west by Grosvenor Park. Its east side consists mainly of a long thin terrace of mid-Victorian tenements which have strong architectural form but an impossibly restricted site. These are at present being cleared by the Corporation.

210a Queen's Park Bridge, 1923, is much used by pedestrians

210b Boathouse and pub are both part of the holiday atmosphere

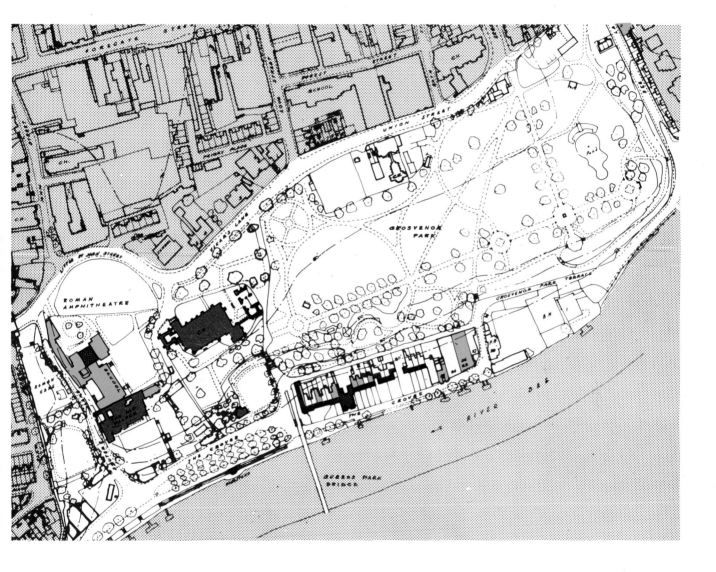

211 Architectural value

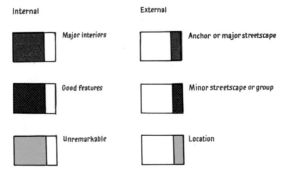

Internal

■ Major interiors

■ Good features

▨ Unremarkable

External

□■ Anchor or major streetscape

□■ Minor streetscape or group

□▨ Location

211

3.10.3 Ownership, use and condition

Most houses in this area are privately owned, but much land is in public ownership. This pattern expresses the dual function of the area. Whilst the Riverside and Grosvenor Park are two of the main recreational attractions of the City, the adjoining domestic terraces overlooking The Groves have a strong community spirit and a quiet residential atmosphere.

Use and suitability. Growing commercial pressures have not yet been sufficient to destroy the delicate balance between recreational and residential functions. Most of the buildings remain as attractive cottages. A few used as cafés cater for the seasonal demand.

The Bishop's Old Palace is almost the only property to suffer from inappropriate use. The requirements of a modern YMCA differ so much from the building's original function that the magnificent interiors have inevitably suffered (Fig. 209b). Apart from this, most of the riverside buildings are still convenient for their purpose, except that a few cottages still lack bathrooms which could readily be added.

Sandwiched between the river and Grosvenor Park, The Groves are not easy of access, and servicing is a problem. The rear service lane is too narrow for standing vehicles and too high for direct access.

Condition. Being well used, most buildings here are well kept. Many owners, proud of their splendid position overlooking the river, yet near to the heart of the City, keep their houses in immaculate order. The condition of the Bishop's Old Palace causes considerable anxiety, and the YMCA authorities are aware that the funds available are totally inadequate for the proper maintenance of this building.

212 Condition

  Satisfactory overall

  Deteriorating in whole or part

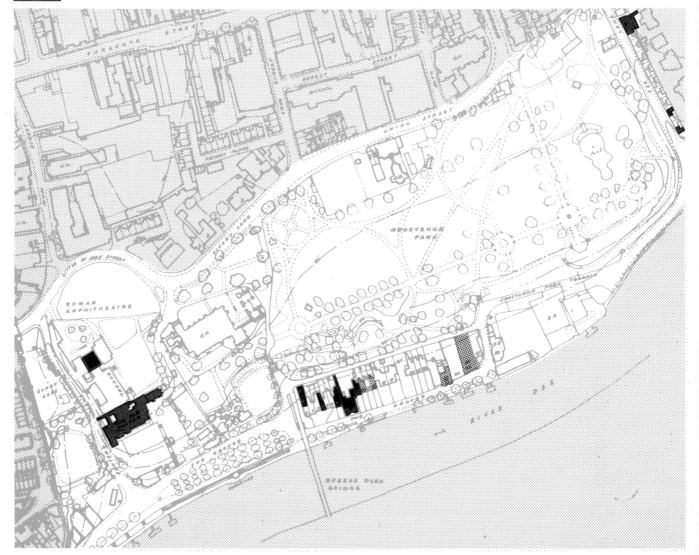 Individually serious defects

3.10.4 Conservation and action

Conservation in this area is more a matter of protection than action, except for the Old Palace. The Ursuline Convent, adjacent to the north, also suffers from an accommodation problem which is insoluble within its present confines, and the presence of this largely uninteresting building prevents full excavation and exposure of the Roman amphitheatre.

Considered as one group, with its splendid setting looking south over the river, there is an opportunity for remodelling this group of buildings as a hotel offering unique and no less than international attractions. The Palace could become the nucleus of splendid historical public rooms, with bedroom accommodation in a new rear block, extending to and set around the fully excavated amphitheatre. The result could be quite exceptional, both for its architecture and its facilities. This is a superb opportunity, and unquestionably the best position for a new hotel in Chester. An appraisal of hotel needs would be most timely.

Maintenance. Nine buildings call for improved maintenance (Fig. 213). In The Groves, this could be achieved by a combined maintenance scheme.

213 Recommendations

Inspected buildings recommended as worthy and capable of conservation

 For first aid action on serious defects

For urgent attention to adverse conditions

For protection and care

Inspected buildings incapable of, or not in need of, conservation

For renewal, clearance or otherwise admitting of replacement

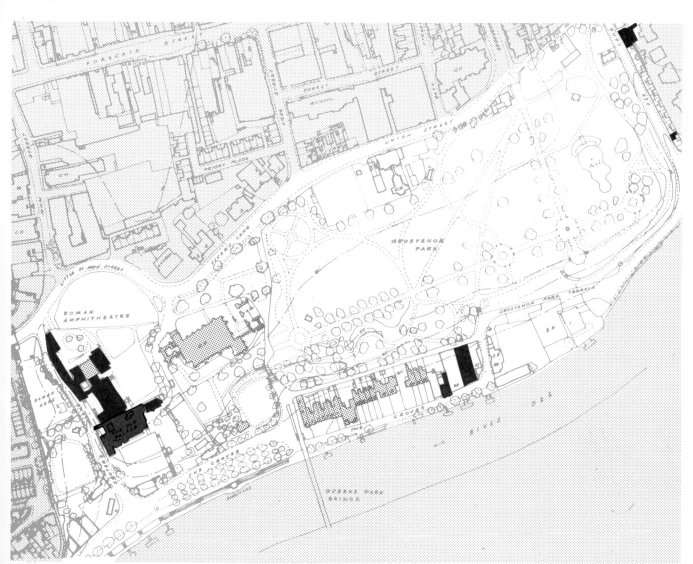

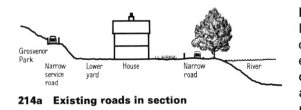

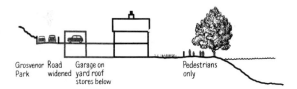

214a Existing roads in section

214b Proposals for closing The Groves to traffic, and provision of a rear access road

Environmental improvement

It is proposed to segregate traffic as far as possible by pedestrianising certain parts of *The Groves*. The narrow rear access lane at the eastern end could be widened to accommodate traffic. This will mean disturbing some trees, and will involve engineering works to the anchorages of the suspension bridge, but will be amply repaid by the real gain in terms of pedestrian safety along the entirely delightful strand between Queen's Park Bridge and the Boathouse Inn (Figs. 214 a/b). The dangerous narrow stretch of road in the lee of the City Walls (between Dee Bridge and Souters Lane) should become pedestrian.

214c Townscape recommendations

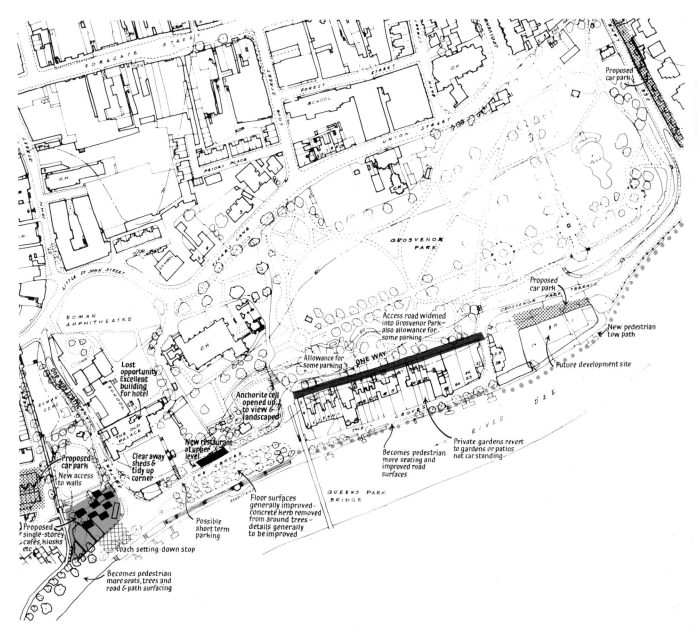

The section at the foot of the Walls should be cleared of its super-annuated boathouses and cafés, and an integrated development of single-storey buildings designed with a restaurant, kiosks, toilet facilities, amusements and so on, all set within a newly landscaped area. Direct access would be formed to the City Walls, beyond which the area would be served by additional car parking.

Along The Groves, a more interesting and less serried arrangement of seating would be an improvement. Beyond the suspension bridge, the charming small-scale village atmosphere can remain. But if in the long term the present cottages become uneconomic, a terraced development could take their place, with recreational facilities and cafés on the riverside level, and flats or maisonettes above, the latter having direct rear access from the widened road at this level. New buildings will need careful design to retain the informal, small-scale character that at present gives so much charm.

Beyond this section the Boathouse Inn has great potential as a much larger public-house and restaurant, with the addition of a riverside walk between the building and river, and a possible two-storeyed car park behind. Dee Lane could well provide more parking at this end of The Groves, when its east side has been cleared.

215a   Unsightly coach sheds and cafe by the Walls

215b   Plan of proposed development at the bottom of Souters Lane by the river

215c   A new riverside restaurant

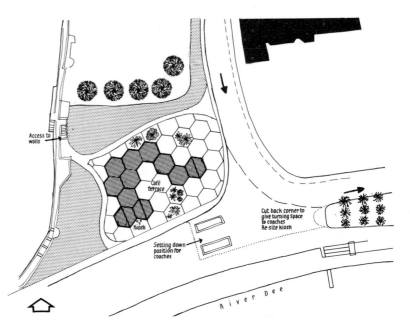

215

3.11 Outline Study Areas

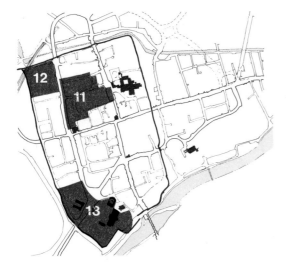

216a   Outline Study Areas

216b   New Market Hall, in Princess Street

216c   Proposals for arcades in front of existing shops in Northgate Street

Lastly, we summarise briefly the areas of less importance within our overall study area. These remaining areas have many different functions to perform in the development of Chester's future.

3.11.1   The Market area

This area lies between the Cathedral and Nicholas Street and between Hunter Street to the north, and Hamilton Place at the south. The only building of historic interest is the Town Hall, a typical example of Victorian civic architecture. The spire is visible from most parts of Chester.

This area is at present being developed. The recently completed new market is directly behind the Town Hall, and the new complex contains a theatre, an hotel and a supermarket on the site of the old market. Hunter Street is now a cul-de-sac off Northgate Street, giving access to a motley collection of fairly recent buildings, rather out of scale with the rest of the development, and to the recent tall office block overshadowing King Street.

Set between the Cross and the Cathedral, and with ready access from Nicholas Street, Northgate and Watergate, the area should become an increasingly successful and flourishing civic and market centre. The present somewhat formless perimeter needs carefully reintegrating with the established streets around.

In association with the new proposals for a Conference Centre, Market Square itself could be greatly improved. The excessive carriageway area could be reduced, and the square, relieved of standing buses, given back its pedestrian priority as the centre of the City.

The opportunity could be taken to introduce more sympathetic surfacing and planting. We also suggest that the miscellaneous shop fronts could be unified and pedestrian shelter provided in the Chester tradition, by a simple arcade treatment (Fig. 216c). The lack of definition between Market Square, as a place, and Northgate Street, as a street, would in this way be strengthened to the advantage of both.

3.11.2 The Infirmary area

The original Georgian building still remains as a nucleus for the south-western section of the Royal Infirmary (Fig. 217a). It has been much altered and modernised from time to time, but the demands of a modern hospital are inconsistent with the old structure, and new buildings are proposed. Recent additions to the north lack visual co-ordination, and any future rebuilding should be carefully considered as a whole.

The hospital car park, although necessary, is unsightly from the City Walls and Nicholas Street. But it could readily be screened by trees and planting.

217a Original Georgian building of the Infirmary

217b Thomas Harrison's portico to the Castle (1793)

3.11.3 Castle Precinct

This area within the City Walls includes the Castle (Fig. 217b), Grosvenor Street roundabout and the new Police building. This faces the main entry to the City over Grosvenor Bridge. The County Police offices are sited axially with the Castle across the diagonal line of Grosvenor Street, in contrast with the north-south grid pattern of Chester. The face of the Castle from the west is marred in the daytime by a sea of parked cars. But there are excellent views from the Walls back to the Castle and outwards across the Dee.

The approaching view from the bridge towards the Castle, set on its grassy mound, should be retained at all costs. Any new building proposed for Little Roodee (and especially its height), should be considered carefully with this in mind, although it could improve what is at present the prospect over an untidy car park. At least the riverside should be held for public access and recreation. A formal and civic character is lent by the siting and style of buildings, and by the width and boulevard quality of Grosvenor Street.

The police building is well related to Grosvenor Street and the Castle, and is 'in scale' with the road. The roundabout is well land-scaped and makes a good focus from the approach over the bridge, but the site of the proposed new Law Courts is a supremely important one. Being within the ring road, its new buildings should be related to the Chester grid rather than the diagonal approach.

218 **Swans on the Dee**

Conclusion:
striking a balance

Planning the resources of any city is an art of skilled management. This is the more so in historic towns, where development pressures can so easily damage an irreplaceable national asset.

Our study of Chester brings out not only a technique for surveying areas of historic importance, but a series of principles to guide their daily management. These can be set out as follows:

1 Each conservation area must be surveyed to define its assets, the intrinsic value of its buildings, its vitality and energies.

2 We must then plan to the full capacity of these assets to realise their full economic and aesthetic value.

3 A controlled balance can then be achieved between the resources and their potentialities, using every incentive to maximum effect.

The problem of our historic towns needs decisive action on a national scale. Following on the present pilot studies for Bath, Chester, Chichester and York, immediate pilot schemes of rehabilitation can next be carried through. We have suggested in outline the framework for such a scheme in Chester. We recognise that agonising questions on national priorities must be answered before the rescue and rehabilitation process can go forward at full pace. But once national and local energies have been mobilised, as in the present studies, this impetus must not be discarded or allowed to flag. Britain's historic towns are the nation's greatest legacy: they must not decay by default or by neglect.

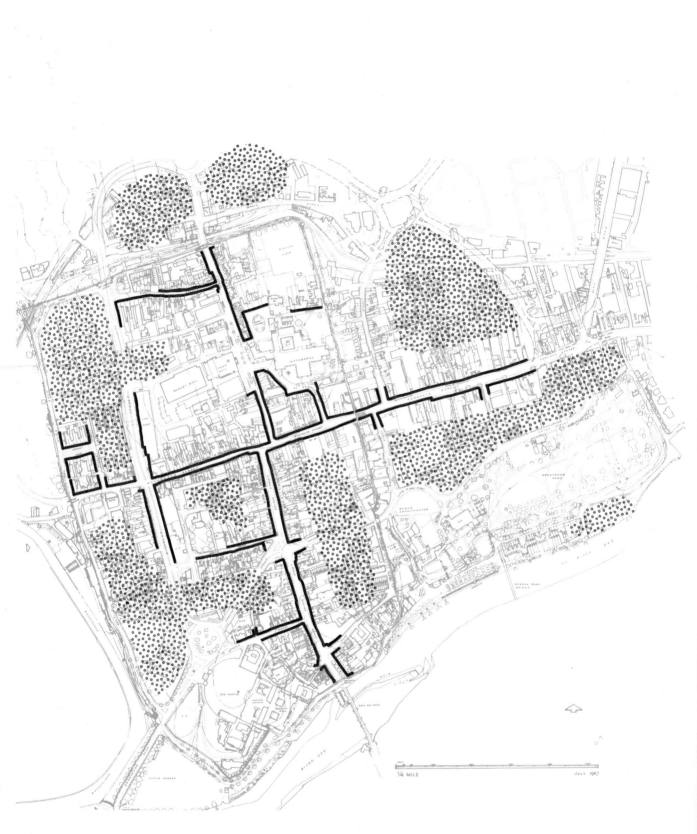

222 Conservation area: skyline control

Frontage lines of importance, for elevational survey
and special height control

Areas where taller buildings could be assimilated more readily,
subject to individual planning application and consent

4 Summary of recommendations: a conservation programme

4.1 Assumptions

Our recommendations for a conservation programme for Chester are based on the following main assumptions:

4.1.1 National and regional

That *population pressures* will continue to rise, encouraged especially by transport improvements, a possible Dee Crossing and by continued *industrial expansion* in the region.

That demands for *car ownership* will continue to rise at rates as forecast by the Road Research Laboratory.

That the County Development Plan should be implemented including the early completion of Chester's *outer ring road.*

4.1.2 City plan

That the City Development Plan should be implemented, as supplemented by the Chester Central Area Plan (1964), and except where amendments are recommended in this study.

4.1.3 City accommodation demands

That the pressures for *office and shop* use have been satisfied for the immediate future.

That requirements for *community, social and tourist* services must be provided for.

That remaining redevelopment capacity within the City centre can only be met by *renewed residential use.*

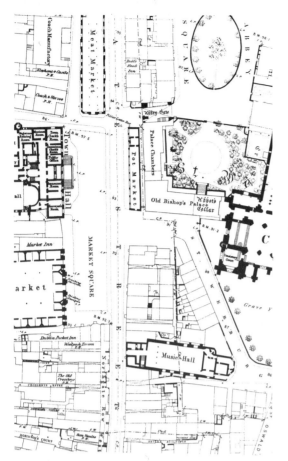

224a Extract from Ordnance Survey Map (1:500) of 1876

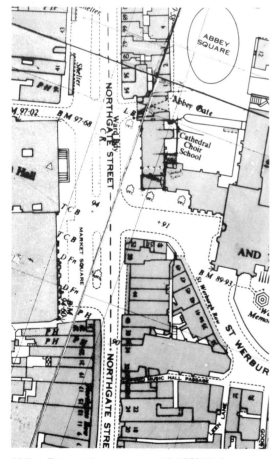

224b Extract from a recent 1:1250 Ordnance Survey Map

4.2 Chester Conservation Area

4.2.1 Designation

The City within the Walls, together with its immediate surroundings, the eastern approach along Foregate Street and the Riverside (Fold-out map 5) should immediately be designated as a Conservation Area under the provisions of the Civic Amenities Act 1967.

4.2.2 Maps and plans (see also Legal Section L.2.4)

Within the Conservation Area, the survey data of the present pilot study should be kept under continuous review. In particular we recommend, together with the maps and plans we have already presented, provision for:

1. Accurate air survey and levelling, together with a detailed air photographic record;

2. The preparation of up-to-date planning maps at 1/500th scale, giving full townscape and control data (for example, street surfacing and paving materials, heights of buildings and street furniture) (Fig. 225; see also Legal Section L.2.3.5);

3. The completion and publication of elevational surveys, as indicated in this study (Figs. 122a/b/c/d) for all principal streets defined in Fold-out map 5;

4. A full survey of the present condition of all trees and planting within the area, and a tree care and re-planting plan.

4.2.3 Control

Within the Conservation Area, we recommend:

1. A stricter development application and control procedure as outlined in the Legal Sections L.2.4 and L.1.7 of this study;

2. An Article 4 Direction, restoring planning control to 'permitted development' under the General Development Order, and especially foreground detail;

3. Skyline control to be applied as shown, within the zones defined in Fig. 222;

4. In considering development applications, every opportunity to be taken to complete and enhance the upper circulatory system at Rows and City Walls level;

5. Archaeological inspection to be a condition of planning consent, backed by guarantee funds or other approved insurances within each contract;

6. A Tree Preservation Order to be placed, as defined in the tree care and replanting plan.

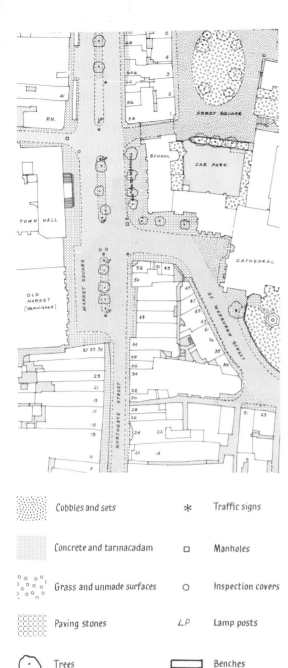

Cobbles and sets		*	Traffic signs
Concrete and tarmacadam		□	Manholes
Grass and unmade surfaces		○	Inspection covers
Paving stones		LP	Lamp posts
Trees			Benches

225 Suggested 1:500 map to be produced for conservation areas

4.3 Redevelopment of deteriorating areas

4.3.0 Pilot schemes

These schemes should be carried out at an early date, to encourage the redevelopment of previously deteriorating residential areas. These can be carried out through the following agencies:

4.3.1 City Corporation, as owner or in consortium with private developers

Example.   The Rows: Nos. 61 to 69 Watergate Street (page 128).

Ownership and implementation.   This land is at present owned by the City Corporation. We have therefore confined ourselves to actual building costs.

Costs*.   We estimate that a scheme as suggested could be built for approximately *£125,000* excluding land costs.

Return.   If shops were provided at both levels, and assuming 8 shops (at £900 inclusive per annum), 10 two-person flats (at £300 exclusive per annum) and 6 one-person flats (at £250 exclusive per annum), the income would be £11,700 per annum.

Incentive.   It will be seen that without land costs, the return is just under 10%. In this and similar cases, land and buildings owned by the Corporation are at present vacant and yielding no economic return. The City could here without other cost to itself promote immediate and effective redevelopment, by leasing the site to developers at a nominal ground rent for a defined period. Its value would thus revert to the Corporation; and especially if the policies recommended in this report are now implemented, land in central Chester cannot fail to remain a long-term investment.

4.3.2 Private owner as developer

Example.   Cathedral Precinct: Abbey Green (page 140).

Ownership and implementation.   We here limit our proposals to land within one ownership.

Costs*.   We estimate building costs at approximately *£270,000* excluding land acquisition costs.

Return.   At rentals of £400 per annum exclusive for maisonettes, and £500 per annum exclusive for houses and shops, the return would be approximately 10% on building costs.

Incentive.   In such cases, an owner will not be likely to invest in redevelopment until a return on the land value can also be obtained. We suggest in such cases the City might invest in the land, granting a lease-back arrangement at favourable terms on condition of early redevelopment to an approved scheme. In this way private capital could be released, and the value of the property regained on reversion to the City.

*See note 2 for definition, page xv.

4.3.3 Redevelopment by a housing society

Example. Northgate : King Street and Water Tower Street (page 186).

Ownership and implementation. The land is at present in varied ownership; but this illustrates one of several projects which could well be ideally tackled by a housing society.

Costs*. We estimate a necessary capital expenditure in the region of *£158,000.*

Return. Such an expenditure would be met by co-ownership rentals of approximately £600 per annum exclusive (five-person houses of three bedrooms). If this rental is felt to be above the market available, the cost of the public open space might reasonably be carried separately, as an amenity to the City. The rentals could then be reduced by approximately 17s. per week to approximately £555 per annum. But neighbourhood values and rentals will both be raised by the new development.

4.3.4 Local redevelopment by national resources

Example. Bridgegate : St. Mary's Hill (page 164).

Ownership and implementation. The land is again in varied ownership. This area is an example of those which would lend themselves to acquisition under the powers of the Land Commission, possibly by an Historic Towns Corporation (see Legal Section, L.3.0). It could be developed either as a whole, or as several parcels. To attract a suitably varied development, a combined project divided between a Housing Association (using a loan from local authority sources) and a Housing Society (using finance from the Housing Corporation and building societies) would appear very suitable. A Housing Association working to Ministry of Housing yardstick figures could be eligible for subsidies under the Housing Acts. A Housing Society, if it were to develop a co-ownership scheme, would be eligible for loans at lower rates of interest over a shorter period of 40 years, but would not necessarily be tied to yardstick figures.

Costs*. The necessary capital expenditure could be in the region of *£540,000.*

Return. Loan charges of 7% over 60 years could be met by rentals (exclusive) of £325 per annum (2-person flats), £375 per annum (three-person flats) and £400 per annum (four-person maisonettes) in these new dwellings, plus charges for garages where required, and comparable rents on converted older buildings.

*See note 2 for definition, page xv.

4.3.5 Local and national investment

It seems likely that if there is any means of balancing the site costs as suggested above (4.3.1-2) leaving building costs to pay for themselves, this will in many instances provide all the economic incentive necessary.

Failing Corporation ownership, is it possible that the powers of the Land Commission Act could be applied to this special situation of 'material development' in historic cities? To take a parallel, the funds already available at the discretion of the Historic Buildings Council have in the case of certain historic towns been allocated to block schemes of repair, assisted by annual contribution. In such schemes, not every building need be outstanding architecturally when, as here, the group value is undoubtedly so. In an area of mixed redevelopment for residential purposes, such at St. Mary's Hill, the powers of the Act could be eminently applicable. But in scattered sites, the conditions are perhaps less readily met.

For this reason, we recommend that the City should concentrate its own purchase and repairs programme upon isolated sites and buildings, in the knowledge that the larger schemes like the St. Mary's Hill redevelopment would then be in equally capable hands, possibly being carried out through the Corporation's own agency.

If a national body such as an Historic Towns Corporation can be established, this is the point from which its work will commence.

Schedule of buildings for 'First Aid' repair

Address	Condition*
4 Kings Buildings	E
5 Kings Buildings	E
2 King Street	E
16 King Street	E
22 King Street	E
24 King Street	E
26 King Street	E
ffolliot House, Northgate Street	E(p)
32 (Row) Bridge Street	E
11 Lower Bridge Street	E(p)
49 Lower Bridge Street	E
34-36 Lower Bridge Street	E(p)
38-42 Lower Bridge Street	E
44 Lower Bridge Street	E
46-48 Lower Bridge Street	O
76 Lower Bridge Street	E
78-80 Lower Bridge Street	E
90-92 Lower Bridge Street	E
Gamul House, Lower Bridge Street	E
25 Castle Street	E(p)
2 Shipgate Street	E
88 Watergate Street	E(p)
90 Watergate Street	E(p)
30 Queen Street	E
32 Queen Street	E
41 Queen Street	O
43 Queen Street	E
Former Congregational Church, Queen St.	E

*Key**

O = Occupied
E = Empty
E(p) = Part empty

4.4 Reconditioning historic buildings: A phased programme for Chester

4.4.0 Ways and means

In cases where repair and rehabilitation is otherwise uneconomic, special incentives are essential. These will need to be found by way of direct grant, by loan or by guarantee, but will be much reinforced by the effect on property values of clearly defined planning policies and public initiative.

Historic Buildings Grants. Local authorities and private owners are both eligible; and Chester should apply for aid under a 'town scheme' such as other historic towns already receive.

Improvement Grants. These should be widely advertised, and the Conservation Area should also become an Improvement Area under the Housing Act 1964, so as to attract the maximum private capital in basic property improvement.

Rate concessions. For buildings remaining in private hands, it may be possible to consider the advantages of encouraging private investment by a 'moratorium' on rate increases applied over a period of, say, ten years and applicable to all 'rescued' properties from a defined list.

Corporation purchase. For certain properties otherwise uneconomic to repair, the investment in building work is attractive (producing an average return of 10%); but when site acquisition costs are taken into account, the return is less so. Here again it would appear that the financial support required to secure implementation is in effect the present value of the site and existing buildings.

Example. Nos. 90-92 Lower Bridge Street (page 162).

Costs.* Conversions and repairs are estimated very approximately at £22,000, excluding site acquisition costs.

Return. At rentals of say £500 per annum for each shop and £300 per annum for each flat, this would show a return of approximately 10% on the cost of improvement works. The property being empty produces no rent, but there is little incentive to improve it.

Under these circumstances, the Corporation could consider purchase and lease-back arrangements under favourable terms and as a property investment, so as to fund the necessary repairs.

4.4.1 Year 1: A first-aid programme

Problem. Some 28 listed buildings are in immediate danger. First-aid protection is vital to arrest decay until they are permanently repaired.

Action. Six buildings are already in Corporation ownership. These and most others are meanwhile empty (see table). All are geographically scattered and call for individual rather than area action. The Corporation should (a) carry out emergency works to its own buildings; (b) approach owners for their co-operation, offering repair loans where necessary; failing which (c) carry out emergency repairs to empty properties under the Civic Amenities Act; or (d) if essential resort to compulsory purchase of the remainder, and carry out emergency works.

Costs * *and implementation*. We recommend a Corporation first-aid budget of £40,000 for first-year emergency works, and £10,000 for their continuation spread over the following four years and pending repairs. In view of the urgency, funds must first be found from local authority sources. This first stage of work would also qualify for aid as a 'Town Scheme' under the Historic Buildings and Ancient Monuments Act, 1953.

Publicity. Grant-aid and loans should be widely advertised in the press, with illustrations of repair techniques and full data on their materials and costs. A strong local press campaign would be invaluable in co-ordinating public effort and support.

Works programme. Each building must be surveyed for the exposure of urgent defects. First-aid works should be put in hand by a direct labour repairs squad, under a skilled Clerk of Works.

Urgent items are :

a wet penetration through defective roofs, windows and walls ;

b leaking gutters, downpipes and blocked drains ;

c dangerous structural weaknesses ;

d defective service pipes and electric wiring ;

e fire hazards ;

f defects allowing unauthorised entry ;

g sterilisation to prevent the spread of fungal attack.

First-aid works cannot be final but must be sufficient and secure. Leaks may be stopped by sheeting, weak structures propped and shored, and defective floors and windows boarded over. Subsequent regular inspection (at least quarterly) and continued maintenance will be essential pending permanent repairs.

4.4.2 Year 1: 'Early-warning care' for building groups

Problem. Nine main groups of buildings can be properly maintained only by communal action. These are the terraced buildings with inaccessible roofs and shared structural elements such as party walls.

Action. Once formed, associations of owners and residents could ensure regular and thorough contract inspection, based on payment of a fixed annual contribution, related to the 'share' of individual property-holders in the whole project.

The incentives would be :

a the assurance of regular care and of 'early warnings' of any increasing or fundamental defects ;

b the upkeep and increase of property values ;

c the financial convenience of small regular payments as against occasional and often unexpected major bills.

The local authority could provide a valuable extra incentive by organising group care schemes and by giving technical specialist advice.

*See note 2 for definition, page xv.

Scope. The main items of group care would be:

a. clearing concealed roof valley and parapet gutters;

b. replacing missing roof slates and tiles; and

c. cleaning rainwater pipes and gullies.

Items such as external painting and maintenance could also be included under individual arrangements if required.

Costs. The necessary annual contributions could best be based upon the rateable value of properties. The sums could be assessed realistically after a trial period of say three years. We suggest that an initial contribution of £25 per property would serve to establish the schemes, and this could then be re-assessed in the light of experience and of the scope of works included.

4.4.3   Years 1-5: an initial repair programme

Some 142 buildings urgently need permanent repair (including those already given first-aid); of these, 51 also need conversion. Only 6 of them are in Corporation ownership; the remainder are in private hands, and owners may be unable or unwilling to finance the work. These buildings are distributed throughout the City (see table) but tend to group in declining areas.

Surveys and plans. For each endangered property, whether publicly or privately owned, the Corporation should immediately prepare architectural survey drawings and detailed conversion proposals, with estimated costs. This would be cheaper than the potential costs of increasing decay, which will otherwise fall ultimately to the City.

Grants and loans to existing owners. These plans should be made available, and existing owners helped by all possible means. Grants and loans should be advertised, and owners circularised, to encourage their use.

Housing Association. The Corporation should take immediate steps to promote a strong local Housing Association, and to enlist every professional and civic support. The aims of the Association would be to purchase unwanted buildings by negotiation, and to convert and re-lease them at improved rents.

Corporation purchase. Where neither existing owners nor purchasers will invest unaided, the Corporation should purchase listed properties in decay, preferably by negotiation, or failing this by its compulsory powers under the Civic Amenities Act.

Corporation partnership. For buildings thus acquired, the Corporation may wish to encourage redevelopment by retaining freeholds, but leasing buildings at favourable terms either to their previous owners or to purchasers, offering repair loans secured against an early reversion. The right to approve all schemes and proposals would again be retained.

Corporation direct repairs. Where preferred, the Corporation should carry out the work on these buildings under direct labour, again selling a lease of the improved property on completion.

*See note 2 for definition, page xv.

Existing corporation property. Similarly here, surveys and re-construction projects should be put in hand, either by the City Engineer's Department (as at the Nine Houses) or by external consultants responsible to the Department.

Costs*. We estimate that the total expenditure needed on this initial repair programme and including both public and private outlay will be of the order of £1,000,000.

Return. Of this, some £626,000 will be spent on reconditioning buildings at present incapable of economic use and is therefore in part an investment against future rents.

4.4.4 Years 5-15: a continued repair programme

There are 229 buildings in this category. They are principally those needing the repair of comparatively slow-moving or minor defects. In others either a change of use is desirable or minor planning improvements are needed.

Ownership and means. Almost all these buildings are occupied and in private ownership. Owners will often be sympathetic to the needs of their buildings but will lack funds for proper care. This is especially so in the case of block property ownership. The main problems will occur where absentee landlords feel no incentive to keep their property in good repair.

Costs* and implementation. We estimate the total expenditure needed on repairs and improvements at approximately *£600,000*. Again, much of this figure is an investment, to be met by rents, but in many cases leaving a necessary 'incentive margin' to be found.

Some would qualify for grant aid from the Historic Buildings Council or the local authority, although present budget provisions are totally inadequate. But it is important to realise that by the time these works become more urgent, the effects of the initial five-year programme will have become apparent in a general rise in Chester's central property values, bringing, in turn, a greater incentive for private owners.

Review. Before this continued programme is implemented, a review of the current condition of all listed buildings should be carried out by the Corporation and the District Valuer in association with specialist advisers. The effect of this review would be to reassess the condition of buildings as then apparent, and to isolate those which still remain as or have become 'problem cases'. Means for dealing with them (for example by compulsory purchase) can then again be assessed and allocated as before, in a continuing programme of active conservation.

Approximate costs‡ of principal recommendations

Study area	Public facilities and environmental improvements		Pilot redevelopment schemes	
	Description	Approx. cost	Description	Approx. cost
City Walls	Improved maintenance	£20,000 p.a. (including current allocations)		
The Rows	Pedestrianisation of Watergate Street Bridging of Rows Streets Underpass at Nicholas Street Street improvement schemes Watergate Street library	* £35,000 * * *	Watergate Street 'gap site' (page 128)	£125,000 (excluding site value)
Cathedral Precinct	Repair of cobbled ways	£4,000 initial expenditure (£250 per annum on maintenance thereafter)	Abbey Green scheme (page 140)	£270,000 (excluding site value)
Whitefriars	Improvement of Grosvenor Street– Bridge Street junction	*		
Bridgegate			St. Mary's Hill scheme (page 165)	£540,000
Watergate	Pedestrianisation of Stanley Place	*		
Northgate			Water Tower Street and King Street schemes (page 186)	£158,000
Upper Northgate and Canalside				
Foregate	New Central Bus Station (Frodsham Street)	*		
Riverside	Riverside improvements and Restaurant	* or external caterers under licence		
All areas	Tree planting and landscaping Street lighting Surfacing and improvement of streets and pedestrian ways Tourist facilities	* * * *		
Phase totals				

*=classed as normal public expenditure

Approximate costs‡ of principal recommendations for listed† buildings reconditioning

| 'First aid' protection | | First phase: Reconditioning | | | | Second phase: Reconditioning | | | |
| | | Conversion & Repair | | Repair | | Conversion & Repair | | Repair | |
No. of Bldgs.	Approx. Cost	No. of Bldgs.	Approx. Cost	No. of Bldgs.	Approx. Cost	No. of Bldgs.	Approx. Cost	No. of Bldgs.	Approx. Cost
1	£1,800	9	£95,700	28	£73,100	5	£32,000	47	£115,000
				8	£34,200	1	£7,500	24	£58,400
		1	£14,000	9	£8,000	3	£21,000	20	£30,000
12	£21,500	20	£297,000	11	£65,000	4	£22,000	31	£39,300
2	£3,600	3	£58,300	21	£54,400			39	£69,000
8	£14,200	12	£121,000	6	£11,000	3	£8,500	20	£50,400
5	£8,900	6	£40,000	1	£15,000	1	£5,000	13	£28,200
				7	£11,300	4	£29,000	5	£13,700
						1	£55,000	8	£6,000
28	£50,000	51	£626,000	91	£272,000	22	£180,000	207	£410,000

† Including buildings herein recommended for listing

‡ see note 2 for definition, page xv.

CHESTER	Date 14/3/67.	Street WESTGATE.	Inspected by TF.
HISTORIC TOWN SURVEY ASSESSMENT OF PROPERTIES	Time(s) 4.30 p.m.	Number(s) 114.	Exterior ✓ / Interior ✓

OCCUPIED BY:	owner(s) / tenant(s) ✓ empty	BUILDING UNIT: extd ✓ subdvd frm / as orignl combd wth	CONSTRUCTION orignl 17th reblt DATES: addns 19th alterations 18th

BUILDING ELEMENT:	Check List:	Exterior: front; RHS; LHS; rear; roof; addns. Interior: cellar; bsmt; gd.fl; 1st.fl; 2nd.fl; 3rd.fl; attic; rf.spce	
	1 ARCHITECTURE: quality, structure	2 CONDITION: A=urgent repairs B=soon, C=long term	3 PLANNING: use and fitness

	1 ARCHITECTURE	2 CONDITION		3 PLANNING
EXT.				
Fr.	Plain 4s. 3b. Geo brick parapet, sashed. v.g. ped doorway.	'live' movement crack W.L.	A	
		o'jointed parapet	B	
LHS.	Orig. t.f exposed at I.F level – brick infill – long 'Gothick' stair window	w.r. in I.F. plate.	B	
Rr.	2s. Vict brick & slate addn.	bwk. o'jointed slating defective & tattered	B B	
INT				
Cellar	Rock cut	damp – fr. wall – d.r. in joist ends.	A	
G.F.	Good 17th C doors " early 18th C panelling.	p.r. from below in fr. wall panelling	A	1. fr L.R. } good size 1. rr. D.R. } & ht. well lit. K in addn – poor.
I.F.	Plain stop chamf scp. cg. beams. 17th C plaster o'mantel	finishes worn but currently O.K.	C	1 fr. B.R. } adequate 1 rr. B.R. } B in addn – O.K.
2.F.	do.	suspect f.b. in flr.	B	2 B.R.
3.F.	plain. min. finishes good turned to I.F. Chin Chipp to 3.F.	roof do. timbers & in c.p. O.K.	B	2 store only. easy & well lit.

SUMMARY					
1 ARCHITECTURE street value	Anchor bldg Major s/scape	Minor s/scape ✓ Group value Location value	Indispensable Keep if poss. ✓ Dispensable	MOHLG grade III Recommended listing: II	
2 MAINTENANCE	Good Average Poor ✓	Why absentee landlord	Grant H.B.C. aid County ✓ poss; Impmt.	Estimated cost of repairs:	A £ 1500 B £ 4000 C £ 500
3 INTERNAL PLANNING	Good Improvable ✓ Poor	Rec. changes (incl. use) refitted K in G.F. rr. & B in do I.F. – dem rr. addn.	Replan wthn bldg ✓ " wth other " " " new extn.	Estimated cost £ 1500.	

ADDITIONAL COMMENTS AND RECOMMENDATIONS	Goodish typical street front – v.g. int features. Detg. cond. Planning improveable by removal of poor rear addn.

Further visit? Yes/No. Made   Special photos? Yes/No. Made 20/3/67.

Donald W. Insall & Associates, Architects & Planning Consultants, 44 Queen Anne's Gate, London

236 A prototype building survey form

Legal powers and national action

Many of our recommendations for action in Chester apply in other historic towns and cities. We now widen the scope of our study by summarising the present administrative and legal procedures available in the conservation of historic areas and buildings and suggest improvements at national and local government levels.

The contents of this section were first submitted to the Minister of Housing and Local Government on request in February 1967. Many recommendations then dealt with points now found to be embodied in legislation and in Bills currently before Parliament. This is accordingly a condensed version, and has the following sections:

Section 1 deals with the listing of buildings and their development control;

Section 2 outlines a method of survey, and summarises available powers for control in conservation areas;

Section 3 recommends a new organisation—an Historic Towns Corporation—to tackle the active conservation of historic town centres; and

Section 4 considers grants, loans and other positive ways of encouraging owners to maintain old buildings, and recommends more efficiency in the use of national resources.

L.1 Listed buildings

1.0 The first step in conservation is always to select the buildings which merit special attention. The current listing procedure is summarised here with suggested improvements (1.1). The present criteria are outlined and improvements are recommended in them (1.2) and in the written description (1.3). Current procedure and the grading system are confusing; and a clarified system is recommended (1.4), together with improved notification (1.5) and recording (1.6) provisions.

1.1 Listing procedure

1.1.1 *Purpose*
Town and Country Planning Acts, 1947 to 1962, required the listing of buildings of special architectural or historic interest, for *the guidance of local planning authorities* (who remain the executive), and not automatically for the preservation only of those specific buildings.

1.1.2 *Stages*
Procedure and criteria for listing have evolved into three stages:

1 Provisional list (and short description).
2 Statutory list (confirmed by Minister).
3 Revision and amendment.

1.1.3 *Progress and budget*
In 20 years, the Historic Buildings Section of the Ministry of Housing and Local Government has issued provisional lists for 1,297 areas. 1,247 have been confirmed and 61 remain for completion*. The listing has been hindered by the small budget allocated.

1.1.4 *An example*
In Chester, a provisional list was issued in 1950 and confirmed in 1955. In 1963, amendments and additions were proposed; further additions were made to the provisional list in 1965 to cover nineteenth-century buildings, and all were confirmed in 1967.

1.1.5 *Case work*
Under the TCPA 1962 Section 33(3) applications affecting listed buildings are referred for advice to the same section of MoHLG.

Recommendations
1.1.6 *Completion*
The completion of the listing in conservation areas and in threatened town centres is urgent, and so is their immediate review. The Department should be allocated funds to finish the job by a defined date, (for instance, 1975).

1.1.7 *Assistance*
More staff is needed and a greater use of local expertise and interest, like that put to such good effect by authors and publishers, might help to achieve this programme.

1.1.8 *Delays*
A rapid and reliable phasing of submission, confirmation and revision is needed with a maximum of, say, 12 months for confirmation.

1.1.9 *Publications*
The lists are intended as tools of control, but they also contain valuable historical information, which could be widely useful. This should be published, with illustrations, maps and schedules.

1.1.10 *Distribution*
Copies should go to all local libraries and could be advertised for sale for example to local societies.

---

*Sept. '67.

1.1.11 *Analysis*

For historical purposes, lists could by analysed as a card index of data and photographs, for punch card and computer sorting. This would be a valuable research subject for a university or for a national, historical or amenity society.

1.2 Listing criteria

1.2.1 *Eligibility*

Buildings currently eligible for listing can be summarised as:

a The products of a distinct and outstanding creative mind.

b Examples of characteristic virtues of a particular school.

c Outstanding accidental or pictorial architectural groups.

d Important links in the chain of architectural development.

e Landmarks in engineering design and technique.

f Buildings of historic interest, either:

  i evidential (to the historian), or

  ii sentimental (to the tourist), or

  iii archaeological or sociological.

g Buildings as research material in unaltered condition.

h Planned architectural groups, and buildings whose alteration would mar an important group (planned or accidental).

i Buildings individually undistinguished but of group importance by their repetition or cumulative effect. This category was the origin of the 'Supplementary Lists'.

j Focal points in a designed or fortuitous landscape composition.

1.2.2 *Omissions*

Principal omissions are:

a Buildings after 1914.

b Street and pavement surfaces.

1.2.3 *Later criteria*

It is only in later lists that fuller attention is paid to:

c Examples of town planning history (for instance, Hampstead Garden Suburb).

d Architectural interiors, where known.

e Street furniture (for example, gaslamps in The Temple).

Recommendations

1.2.4 *No date restrictions*

There is little reason why a top-calibre modern building should not receive the same protection as an old one. A period of 5 to 10 years' grace would help to establish values. But, for example, buildings worthy of an RIBA Award or a Housing Medal might at least merit special care. Merit, not age alone, is a necessary criterion of conservation and date-limits detract from the value of listing.

1.2.5 *Essential local character*

Certain architectural forms are the essence of their locality (terraced Georgian houses in Bath, the Rows in Chester, Oast houses in Kent), where they rate a higher value than elsewhere. The lists, when reviewed, should give greater importance to local and regional architectural character.

1.2.6 *Architectural interiors*

Valuable interiors should be more systematically listed. Data is already available, for example, from the National Trust and from private owners given grants. *Listed interiors* should then qualify both for protection and for grant aid.

1.2.7 *Architectural features*

Occasionally only part of a building (for instance, the facade of a Georgian terrace) merits listing. The criteria should make this clear.

1.2.8 *Obscured features*

Where observable (for example, a timber-framed elevation inside later brickwork) these could usefully be specified as qualifying the building.

1.2.9 *Additions and detractions*

Where an original building is marred by additions, these should be clearly defined in listing. They could usefully be noted on photographs, which would especially help in managing the conservation areas.

1.2.10 *Missing units*

Urban fabric sometimes needs 'invisible mending', not patching in high colour. When a building has gone and special control is necessary in rebuilding (for example, one of a symmetrical terrace), the site should itself be listed for special notice.

1.2.11 *Street and pavement surfaces*

Paving and floor textures are at present excluded entirely from listing. But, being so near eye level, they can be a dominant element of townscape. They should be noted in listing, considered in planning, and conserved where of sufficient merit. Street surfaces should also qualify for grant aid—especially in conservation areas.

1.2.12 *Review of criteria*

Review at present varies with pressure of work and with changing standards of taste. Many Victorian buildings have already been added to the lists for London. The criteria adopted should be clearly defined in the preface to each list, as a guide in their future review.

1.3 Written descriptions

1.3.0 *Purpose*

The written descriptions may:

a Identify buildings.

b Give the reasons for listing.

c Assist in development control.

Recommendations

1.3.1 *Identification*

Identification would be simplified by map references.

1.3.2 *Justification*

The lists should give a clear *reason* why each building is listed.

1.3.3 *Control*

Development control would be aided by a photographic record.

1.3.4 *Omissions and references*

'Important and well-known mansions' are omitted from the written descriptions. Other well-documented buildings could equally be omitted and known sources of useful information quoted for reference.

1.3.5 *Numbering*

Street numbering may itself be confusing (for instance, Chester: the Rows), but the additional listing numbers bring more confusion and should be cross-indexed or else dropped.

1.3.6 *Identification map*

What are the physical limits of the building listed, for instance, of a railway station? It is inappropriate to list everything within an ownership curtilage. The item listed should be clearly defined on a plan and a copy attached to the notification.

1.3.7 *Location map*

The grouping of the buildings listed is of paramount importance. To help, for example, in considering road schemes, an identification map should accompany every list.

1.4 A clarified listing procedure

1.4.0 *The present lists*

The present lists are confusing. A building may today be on either an Interim or Provisional list (and 'graded' I, II*, II or III), on a Statutory list (in Grade I, II or II*, confirmed by the Minister) or on the Supplementary list. It may be in an area still unlisted. Or it can in emergency be 'spot-listed'. At any of these various stages, the lists may be under revision or of varying reliability. Certain buildings are also scheduled as Ancient Monuments.

The Historic Buildings Council once planned a further list of 'buildings of outstanding interest', although this was never completed.

The public, the planner and the owner are all in this way confused.

1.4.1 *Consultation with planners*

Importance of *location* in buildings (present and future surroundings) is not covered by the present lists.

Examples are a building essential to a certain skyline, a focal feature in townscape, or 'anchor' buildings in defined vistas like the view along a fine street as it exists or as planned. These are all correctly *elements of townscape and planning* and not necessarily covered by the investigators' lists.

1.4.2 *An example in Chester*

Figure 100a shows an undistinguished house of circa 1893 (replacing a Customs House of 1633) which now obscures a fine view of Holy Trinity Church, opened up by the new inner ring road. The church could have formed an admirable stop to the end of Watergate Street: but this building now obscuring it was listed in Grade III as one of 'group value' for special attention in planning. The group and value have both gone, but by its supplementary listing this building is protected to the architectural detriment of the City.

Recommendations

1.4.3 *Simpler lists*

All the data collected should be refined into a new and clearer system (see illustration).

The following stages are proposed to complete and rationalise the lists. Only two lists are suggested, representing, in effect, the 'nut' and its 'kernel'—those buildings we cannot afford to sacrifice.

1.4.4 *The planning list (all buildings of architectural and historic importance)*

This more comprehensive list would comprise all buildings noted by investigators and listed in all 'grades' for special planning consideration after:
a Completion and checking by the investigators;
b Review (to meet new criteria);
c Confirmation by the Minister.

1.4.5 *The conservation list (statutory)*

This successor to the present 'statutory lists' would then include *all* buildings selected from this expanded planning list, after:
a Consultation with planning authorities (to evaluate future significance of location);
b Reference to amenity and learned societies (for comment);
c Final evaluation by H.B. Section; and
d Confirmation by the Minister.

1.4.6 *Protection*

All buildings on this *conservation list* would receive the fullest statutory protection.

1.4.7 *Minor works*

To restore control over minor works and architectural defacement, the listing should override the block consents otherwise given by the General Development Order.

1.4.8 *Annual report*

It should become a statutory duty for local planning authorities to report each year to the Minister on the state of all listed buildings in their area, including those in both private and public ownership.

1.4.9 *Review*

Both lists would be subject to continuous review by the Historic Buildings Section on reference to local planning authorities or on representation to the Minister. The Section can, in this way, take into account likely future developments and can give the proper significance to future townscape values.

1.4.10 *Interim procedure*

The phrases 'provisional' and 'supplementary', and so on, would thus be dropped as confusing, there being in future only those two lists, each with a clearly defined purpose.

1.4.11 *Permanence*

Buildings from the present 'supplementary' lists would all be permanently transferred to the planning list. From this they would be deleted only on the initiative or advice of the H.B. Section and by confirmation of the Minister.

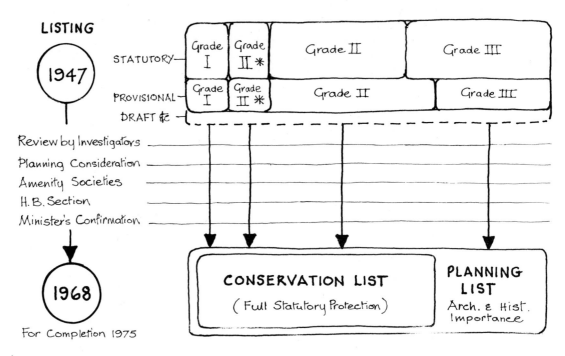

240 Analysis of present and proposed listing procedure

1.5 Notification

1.5.0 *Procedure*
Lists are deposited with each authority, the listing registered as a local land charge, and notice served on owners and occupiers.

Recommendations
1.5.1 *Form*
The system of notification to building owners has been threatening rather than encouraging. Much depends on an owner's pride in a building and willingness to care for it. The notification should say why a building is important, and what special grants and services are now available.

1.5.2 *Data*
Owners could also be sent the latest available photograph and could be invited to submit historical data of interest to the National Monuments Record.

1.5.3 *Reminders*
Tenants change frequently, especially in historic town centres. Local authorities should be asked to consider a system of periodical reminders (for example, every 10 years) to keep new occupiers informed of listing.

1.5.4 *Marking*
Listed buildings were marked in some areas during the 1939-45 War, though in some instances this defaced them. Signposting and marking features like earthworks and significant bumps in the ground, as the Ancient Monuments Board do, is often more to the point. But special interiors in an otherwise uninteresting building may justify a plaque, as do buildings listed purely for reasons of their history.

1.6 Recording

1.6.0 *Present procedure and progress*
Much progress has been made in historical recording. The National Monuments Record between 1941 and 1967 accumulated over 650,000 photographs and 15,000 drawings. It is now part of the Royal Commission on Historical Monuments.

1.6.1 *Inventories*
The RCHM has a programme of detailed research in successive counties, and occasionally in town centres. (Chester is not yet covered.) So far, this exacting and accurate survey has been published for seven counties. Photographs are now lodged with the National Monuments Record.

1.6.2 *Photography*
The Commission has seven photographers who in 1967 added 6,450 photographs to the Record, besides 28,337 received from other sources.

Recommendations: the future programme
1.6.3 *Emergency preliminary recording*
Investigators could carry cameras. Even a poor picture is useful in emergency. As an interim measure until an expert coverage is completed, investigators could easily take a preliminary photograph of each accessible elevation of every building they list.

1.6.4 *Priorities*
The main priorities in continuing the present programme of recording buildings are:
a to complete the photographic record of all listed buildings;
b to prepare surveys of buildings threatened with early destruction;
c in addition, we suggest a national appeal to correlate private collections which might otherwise be unknown (for instance, Chester Civic Trust has an excellent collection, but this is not widely known);

d the cross-referencing of public and private slide collections (Victoria and Albert Museum, Architectural Association, National Trust, and so on) as already in the U.S.A. A national initiative is needed if this is to be achieved;

e the local planning authority could prepare continuous strip-elevations of architecturally important streets, especially in conservation areas. These are valuable in considering applications and should be made publicly available.

1.6.5 *Long-term applications: photogrammetry*

Further study is needed, with a more realistic everyday approach, into this useful method. Simple photogrammetry is especially valuable in recording elevations. Stereophotogrammetry is more specialised but valuable and can be time-saving. In all photographic recording detailed camera and viewpoint data should be noted, to facilitate photogrammetric plotting in any emergency.

1.6.6 *Measured drawings*

More financial assistance is needed to attract schools of architecture and photographic societies, in contributing to the record of listed buildings.

1.6.7 *Application drawings*

Survey drawings 'as existing', submitted with planning applications could readily be microfilmed and stored at the NMR for better reference.

1.7 Planning control for listed buildings:

Recommendations

1.7.0 *Survey drawings*

Adequate survey drawings 'as existing', scaled at least $\frac{1}{8}$ in. to 1 ft., should be submitted as a condition of application. They should show structural form, with details such as structural framing where these are a reason for listing (for example, a medieval oak Hall-house).

1.7.1 *Neighbouring buildings*

The relationship with neighbouring buildings should be shown in detail.

1.7.2 *Proposal drawings*

Proposals should be drawn to the same scale to show clearly all changes, with details of fenestration, flank walls and projections (including any which may not appear on elevation).

1.7.3 *An application form for listed buildings*

A new and clearly designed *application form* is needed. Existing and proposed materials could be shown in parallel columns.

1.7.4 *A specimen application form for development consent affecting a listed building. This would require the following information:*

i *Estimated date of building* ('age' is too vague)

ii *Materials*

a *Roofing*
  Materials, coursing and fixing
  (e.g. Tiles: clay or concrete, hand or machine made, slates and stone tiles, and whether in diminishing courses. Sheet lead, copper or other metal: type and spacing of fixings).

b *Walls* (including front, both flanks and rear)
  Materials, coursing, bonding, jointing, pointing, surface, texture
  (e.g. Brick: hand-made or machine-made, height of courses, bond employed. Mortar: lime or cement, struck or tuck-pointed, etc. Stone: quarry and bed, how dressed, range of sizes, coursing and surface finish).

c *Windows* (each wall)
  Type, materials and glazing
  (e.g. Sashes: vertical or horizontal, whether boxings concealed or exposed, number of panes, size of glazing bars and whether painted. Type of glass: e.g. clear, obscured 'crown').

d *Doors* (in each wall)
  Type of materials
  (e.g. 'front central: 6-panel, polished hardwood. Rear: 4-panel, painted deal').

e *Plumbing* (rainwater, soil and waste)
  Whether internal or external, materials and fixing.

iii *Architectural relationship with neighbouring buildings, building groups and spaces*
  State how considered and how the new will be integrated with the old.

1.7.5 *Samples*

Submission of samples, where required, should be a condition of application. (For example, hand-made bricks and facing tiles.)

1.7.6 *External surfacing material*

Any change in external surfacing material (for instance, stuccoing or painting previously unpainted brickwork, stripping plaster from timber framing or the substitution of concrete for clay tiles) should be clearly defined as an alteration affecting the character of the building.

L.2 Conservation Areas

2.0 Under the Civic Amenities Act, local planning authorities will 'determine' areas for 'conservation and enhancement'.

The following section recommends statutory provision for the survey of each area (2.2) and sets out a survey method (2.3) * based on practical experience. Methods of management are suggested, based on existing procedure for development plans and control (2.4).

2.1 Determination

Authorities are likely to vary widely in response. In some cases, direction by the Minister may become necessary. In others, further guidance may be needed in co-ordinating standards and in defining boundaries.

---

* This method was outlined for the Civic Trust and first published in 'Conservation Areas' (special number, *The Architects' Journal:* Jan. 1967), of which this is a condensed account.

2.2 Survey

Recommendations: statutory provision

An inherent danger (as in listing buildings) is that 'determination' of conservation areas may become an end in itself, and a substitute for action. The LPA should be given a statutory duty to initiate an immediate survey of each conservation area, so as to produce a coherent policy for its improvement and enhancement.

2.2.1 *Co-ordination*

Many LPAs lack the special skills and time to tackle conservation areas within their department. Many have called in specialist help from consultants. Special care is then needed to co-ordinate the plans with future development control and to keep them under running review.

2.2.2 *Budget*

A budget provision is needed for survey, analysis and planning of conservation areas. Their value after improvement and rehabilitation may well exceed the original sum of property values plus repair costs, but only when an imaginative assessment and policy exist.

2.2.3 *Training*

The need for special training for architects and planners in conservation work is now internationally recognised. Provision for these skills should be a basic element of professional training.

2.3 A method of survey

Preparatory research

2.3.1 *History*

To understand the character of a town, we must first know its past. The identity of a place is as precious to a town as to a person. *Antiquities* are increasingly rare as cities grow: for example, many City Walls, at first obstacles, have now become treasured relics. *Evidence of historical events* has strong local significance. In analysing neighbourhood identity, *'areas of like development'* can also usefully be plotted.

2.3.2 *Regional plans*

Regional policies on the distribution of population, employment and trade will fundamentally affect the local property market and the uses to which older buildings can be put. Questions to consider are: Will a town expand? What will be the main future demands? Where will the supermarkets be, and the top land values? Where will new trade go? What are the regional transport plans? Will central areas be by-passed? What type and volume of traffic will remain?

The survey must look to the future, to new vehicle types, new life and leisure patterns. It should consider the likely effect of taller buildings, increased mobility and every foreseeable trend.

2.3.3 *Assumptions*

Every survey is prepared from current knowledge. An area plan is not a blueprint, but a living and developing policy. It will one day be reassessed. On what assumptions was it based? To take an example, will national and local land pressures continue to increase: and will they still be governed by present trends and policies, population drifts and patterns of industrial development? Will the increasing specialisation and wider spacing of shopping centres continue? May new transport methods vary the acceptable journey to work, and will standards of pedestrian accessibility change? Later review is easier where a note of current standards and principles was noted in the plan. A record is needed of the wider framework of regional surveys or the context of other recent studies within which it was prepared.

2.3.4 *Previous surveys*

Valuable data is often already to hand. A local Chamber of Commerce may have surveyed trade. A civic or archaeological society may have recorded the history and growth of the town. The Ministry's 'lists' give valuable information on buildings. Earlier traffic counts provide useful facts about the growth and distribution of traffic and parking. It is important to make allowances for trends since earlier data was collected. There may be variations in scope and emphasis, for example in boundaries, or in any bias on the part of investigators. Other useful data is in municipal records; and informed local people (librarian, archivist, secretary of a civic society or parson) may have long memories in locating earlier facts and surveys.

2.3.5 *Base maps*

The first requirement is a revised base map. In Chester it was possible, through MoHLG, to obtain copies of the current draft Ordnance Survey revision sheets. Sites with planning consent can also be added.

Air survey can give accurately plotted levels, and air photographs give much information on the structural identity of buildings.

Contours at 5-ft. intervals help in planning for pedestrians.

Street surfacing, trees, walls and townscape features are usefully added.

Augmented maps must be dated and carry their sources of information.

2.3.6 *Areas for survey*

Areas for different degrees of study must be defined and kept under review, for example:

At town scale, major townscape elements and architectural types.

At area or neighbourhood scale, other patterns to be isolated for study, for example, pedestrian movement and the distribution of shopping frontage.

2.3.7 *Architectural groups*

Groups of buildings may justify closer examination. (Circulation and interior planning, detailed history and structural condition.) Groups at first defined may need revision during survey.

2.3.8 *Area survey*

The first duty of a survey is to distinguish the essence of a place, what makes it 'special' or unique and gives it character and distinction.

2.3.9 *Procedure*

Notification. Property owners should be notified well in advance. Appointments can take much time to arrange, for instance where multi-tenancy is involved.

Forms. In Chester, as elsewhere, 'building analysis forms' have been used for survey—one for each building (irrespective of postal numbering). These are completed by ticks, crosses or well-known abbreviations.

Mapping. Other methods include the mapping of single qualities of a block of property (for instance, condition, use or viability).

Management. Town survey cannot be delegated to inexperienced staff and demands a balanced approach. But time can be saved by good management.

2.3.10 *Aspects for study*
Subjects may include the following:

Architectural character. Architectural groups and their special individuality need to be defined. The soft red brick and the tile-hanging of Kent, and the oak framing and pargetting of East Anglia are obvious examples. The quintessence of Bath is the Royal Crescent. Of Lavenham it is the Market Place; and of Tunbridge Wells, the Pantiles.

Often a primary area of architectural interest will have within it lesser groups, strongly contrasting with one another, for example, the Nash terraces of Regent's Park, contrasted with the independent villas of Park Village.

Townscape. A building may form an important focus to a long vista, or it may close a street picture. Its silhouette may dominate the skyline from a significant viewpoint, or even if itself uninteresting, it may be one of a layout of buildings whose importance lies in their collective symmetry.

Planned improvements. The planning authority will be able to consider planned improvements (for example, by which a building will be revealed to view by street widening, when its face and alignment may be of new importance). The building's merit in terms of town planning, in fact, may be purely that it is just where it is.

Individual buildings
2.3.11 *Present structural condition*
Maps and forms provide for detailed analysis of buildings both externally and internally and at each floor. Items will include construction, materials, finishes and typical defects (rising damp, dry rot, defective rainwater gutters, and so on). Prevention of incipient defects can well be noted, as well as their cure, and urgent repairs must be distinguished from those that can wait. Any danger to public safety must, of course, immediately be notified to the building inspector.

2.3.12 *Architectural care and condition*
Is the building all of one date? Have original sash windows lost their glazing bars, or been replaced by metal casements? Or blocked, because of a later window tax? Is the roofing material as original, and if not, is it appropriate? Are later shopfronts well designed?

Has a house been subdivided to the best advantage? Do two houses interlock with one another? And could this easily be rectified?

2.3.13 *Potential uses and suitability*
Maps or forms can record present facilities (ceiling heights, daylighting, rear access, storage, garaging and mains services) and current uses, noting special requirements and facilities, nuisance, traffic generation and required improvements such as better display or access. The survey can usefully note potential future user-classes where consent for change would be appropriate (for example, domestic to office, or office to shop).

2.3.14 *Economic viability*
Would better pedestrian access help trade? Is the present rear access adequate or might it be improved?

Are valuable architectural features unrealised? Do additions conceal the original exterior, and make the building dark or damp? They often need more maintenance than they are worth and are better removed.

Does the circulation pattern work well? Could future plumbing or service units be better grouped? Are there good fire-escape routes? Lastly, what might be the approximate cost of conversion? And would this be met in the increased property value?

Analysis and presentation
2.3.15 *Plotting data*
Much information shows up clearly during site survey, but analysis in the office yields new conclusions. The simplest way of collating information is by transparent overlays, on which the main problems and opportunities of the area are mapped for comparison. Illustrations are an essential element in the collected data. Photographs can pinpoint architectural and townscape features which many citizens may never have noticed, although they pass them daily.

2.3.16 *Assets and debits*
A convenient way of analysis is by the 'plus and minus' method. Overall and in detail, this encourages balanced and thorough survey and presents the facts clearly. The 'assets' map summarises the main buildings, features and frontages of importance. Examples from other recent reports include sketches of 'stopped vistas' and enclosure (at Newark and at Blanchland) a survey of valuable trees (in Lavenham) and paving textures (at Thaxted).

The 'debits' map can note eyesores, untidy sites, spoil heaps, overhead wires, exposed junk yards and so on. Traffic noise and fumes are a frequent and localised debit. So are air and water pollution, especially in densely populated areas. Another is lack of access (usually behind a barrier such as a railway line, but sometimes in areas themselves marooned by traffic, like Eros, in Piccadilly). Not least in its impact is the rising tide of street furniture, signs and general flotsam whose appraisal is a vital element in town survey.

Pictorial survey is a good way to draw attention to the problems often caused merely by lack of co-ordination (for example, lamps, traffic and council notices, each on their own poles).

2.3.17 *Opportunities*
The opportunities map can be employed to show opportunities, present or future. Examples from other recent surveys include the following:

a Valuable empty sites (New York is carrying out a special survey of these) and car parking sites;

b An opportunity for a new building on a run-down 'island' site in a market place and for a better 'focus' at the end of an otherwise undistinguished street;

c The most limited of land purchases can help to give better pedestrian access;

d New planting can screen traffic noise, and new rear access may be had simply by joining existing rear lanes;

e A reclaimed village green has been suggested as the revived focus of a village. Elsewhere a large private garden has been purchased as a future open space in a rapidly expanding town;

f Even good street furniture, special lighting, town maps, seats for the elderly and acceptable advertising sites, have benefited from positive thinking with an eye for opportunity.

2.3.18 *Future development*

Assess the effect of proposals already known; and define sites which offer special opportunity for new building (for instance, half-used back land in old urban areas). Consider their relation to present access and frontage. Might consent be given for extension by existing users? Could properties be opened up by better pedestrian access at ground level? A cinema in Newark has brilliantly used the inside of a shopping island without disturbing the run of shopfronts. In the event of increased redevelopment pressures, what historic buildings might need special care or consideration, or be at risk? Are there useful remedies or opportunities?

The shopping precinct in Chester successfully relates new and old. Surveys may recommend what broad form of new building might be appropriate. The important architectural considerations are in such terms as scale, especially in length of shopping frontage and in materials, rather than in detail.

Publication, implementation and review
2.3.19 *Publicity*

Experience underlines the importance of widespread publicity. The survey should always if possible be published, with every conclusion clearly made and graphically illustrated. Photographs and perspectives are clearer to the reader than plans.

2.3.20 *Exhibitions*

Exhibitions are of great value. In this country we have nothing to compare with presentations like the Philadelphia Panorama, with its models of whole areas of the city, showing new projects in three dimensions and easily recognisable form. Such a centre makes a wonderful focus for lectures to schoolchildren. Films and television are powerful visual media of incalculable effect.

2.3.21 *Action programme*

A conservation area survey will succeed only when it formulates a definite programme for positive action. Policy proposals take shape only when they are laid at someone's door as a duty.

2.3.22 *Review*

Development control is a sensitive, organic process. No area can be held in indecision against all change. The survey should lastly make specific provisions for its future review.

2.4 Conservation areas: recommendations on planning control

2.4.0 Within the conservation areas, and once a survey and plan have been prepared, a special and detailed degree of development control will be needed. The following are preliminary suggestions based on the legal powers available at the time of survey (1967).

Maps
2.4.1 *Special planning maps*

Current surveys show how special planning maps would aid urban development planning and the management of conservation areas. These should be produced by the Ordnance Survey as an expansion of the excellent series of new 50 in. maps.

2.4.2 *Air cover*

Some counties already maintain annual air cover. This idea is worth adopting in all conservation areas. Air photographs are extremely valuable in elucidating building forms, and should be available to all planning authorities.

2.4.3 *Planning guides*

Planning authorities should give guidance by publishing booklets, like those already produced in some counties on the special character of each conservation area.

Development plans
2.4.4 *Review and inquiry*

When a city development plan is submitted or reviewed, the citizen may lodge objections and give evidence at inquiry. But at the scale of city plans, it is impossible outside a planning department to finance and test out alternative proposals. New procedures should promote a constant process of informed public participation long before formal inquiry.

2.4.5 *Examples*

a The reviewed Plan for Bristol (published July, 1966 with an inquiry eight months later) proposed road layouts estimated alone to cost £90,000,000. The report at 7gns. was beyond the pocket of the interested public. Formal objections were registered by the local Chapter of Architects and the Civic Society. But at this stage and scale, no citizen body can afford the specialist effort needed to assess and counter-plan.

b In Salisbury the plan was referred back to the planning department after a national alarm. Here, it was said, pressures of political discussion hindered the proper consideration of all possible planning alternatives.

2.4.6 *Advice*

An inspector can evaluate individual objections at an inquiry. But he has neither time nor facilities to prepare alternative plans. An extended service of advice is needed to guide LPAs in schemes of massive public expenditure affecting historic neighbourhoods and cities.

2.4.7 *Inquiry*

To forestall uncertainty and planning blight, a quoted period of less than 12 months should be given for a decision.

Special provisions
2.4.8 *Highway works*

The Minister's first circular under the Act calls for closer consultation between planning and traffic authorities to co-ordinate signposting, anti-parking notices, and so on in conservation areas. LPAs should consider an Article 4 Direction, restoring planning control over all highway works.

2.4.9 *Traffic splays*

Much architectural harm is caused by over-zealous vehicle sight-lines and vision splays. Some towns have a corner sliced diagonally off every corner site. In townscape, a corner is a corner; a splay is indeterminate. Cut-off corners are not always appropriate even for traffic, which may turn faster into side routes.

2.4.10 *Building lines*

An out-of-date concept which many authorities still follow is to impose "building lines". The most attractive streets in historic towns have a broken frontage line, with recessed and projecting buildings. There is no merit in development being "pushed flat" as by a straight-edge. Seen in perspective, the street must have interest of itself as a place in which to be. Flat streets seem anxious to have you hurry through: the difference is like that between a home and a railway station. "Building lines" should not be used in conservation areas.

2.4.11 *Parking sites*

Present highway subsidies give no encouragement to authorities to buy urban land for car-parks, whose value to a developing community increases rapidly. A subsidy to help buy suitable sites would bring long-term economies.

2.4.12 *Trees*

Local planning authorities should be asked to consider an immediate Tree Preservation Order on all trees in conservation areas, pending their detailed survey.

2.4.13 *Street lighting*

Technical regulations should be revised to permit proper flexibility in design, taking into account illuminated vertical as well as horizontal surfaces.

2.4.14 *Advertisements*

Special care is needed over outdoor advertisements in conservation areas. Where necessary, LPAs. should consider the necessity of defining areas of Special Advertisement Control.

In Chester, a high degree of control is exercised. Nameboards and notices are restricted as far as possible to information, not advertisement. But on appeal, the City's unusually high standard has not always been supported by the central authorities. A local standard higher than the average should be encouraged wherever it is appropriate.

2.4.15 *Location value*

There is a whole category of buildings which although unworthy of individual listing, have a key townscape function (enclosure and screening, for example), and would be irreplaceable once demolished, due to modern building-lines or Building Regulation requirements. Defects like limited space at rear, or obscured traffic sight-angles, may be less important than the townscape function of the building.

A new category of control is required for buildings whose sole justification is their precise location, alignment or height. Architectural "listing" would be inappropriate, and a new category of *Location value* needs to be defined (see page 99).

Demolition of buildings so listed would then be permitted only for redevelopment within individually stated limits (for example, of use, height, materials and frontage line).

2.4.16 *Slum clearance*

Where old houses are compulsorily purchased under the Housing Acts, as "unfit and incapable of conversion at reasonable cost", an authority may be chary of rehabilitating them, whatever their architectural importance.

The word has never been tested in the Courts: but it seems there may be a statutory *obligation* to "demolish" preventing even the reincorporation of an old facade. This is illogical and should be clarified.

2.4.17 *Rebuilding in replica*

The requirement to restore an illegally demolished building "to its former state" can be a nonsense. History cannot be rebuilt, even had we the skills to tackle the job. Preservation must be by protection. A decaying building, however good, should be repaired wherever possible.

2.4.18 *Gap sites*

There is an exception: a Georgian Square or a Nash Terrace is an entity. So sometimes is a whole neighbourhood like Edinburgh New Town. A breach in the ranks here does call for replacement—at least in spirit and in outline—or the unity of the group may be damaged. Gap sites may justify rebuilding as a copy.

2.4.19 *Areas of special uniformity*

The Minister's guidance is needed in distinguishing between areas whose character is one of diversity, and those whose uniformity is their essence. Some areas of special architectural unity, like parts of Belgravia, are unthreatened because they are young or are in well-run estates. Here a firm line is needed before change brings precedent for more. Conservation areas will need strong Ministerial guidance on this point; and it may be necessary to define some as of special uniformity. Elsewhere area conservation (as distinct from listing buildings) cannot preclude appropriate and well-designed buildings in the spirit of their own time.

2.4.20 *Dangerous structures*

No listed building should be demolished without being inspected by a suitably qualified person, who should be able to get there as quickly as any demolition contractor.

2.4.21 *Street clutter*

For conservation areas there is a case for a "small works department" within the planning office. This may be easier in larger authorities set up after the Royal Commission on Local Government. After a drastic initial campaign, a simple procedure could bring day-to-day control of clutter within the capacity of one qualified assistant.

Development applications in conservation areas
2.4.22 *Planning applications*

As with listed buildings elsewhere, a special degree of attention is required to all applications in conservation areas.

2.4.23 *Full information*

Development control can be more rapid and efficient when proper information is supplied. To unscramble an application which shows no levels or natural site features causes delay and misunderstanding.

2.4.24 *Existing and proposed*

For vacant sites, full information should be supplied. This can be given quickly and clearly in separate *survey* and *proposal* drawings.

2.4.25 *Site survey*

The plan *as existing* should show contouring at close intervals (maximum 5 ft.), and all major site characteristics (access points, inward and outward viewpoints, trees and features).

2.4.26 *Site analysis*

An *analysis* overlay, showing diagrammatically the principles followed, can be quickly grasped and will often enable an application to be passed immediately for planning committee approval.

2.4.27 *Adjoining buildings*

In applications for "infilling" between existing buildings, their main form and features should be shown so as to demonstrate the effect of new proposals.

L.3   An Historic Towns Corporation

3.0   The scale of investment available (3.1) compared with what is needed to redeem historic towns, is beyond local authorities (3.2) and calls for a new national agency, perhaps an Historic Towns Corporation (3.3). This could use existing powers under the Land Commission Act (3.4) and should promote urgent pilot schemes (3.5) in selected conservation areas.

3.1   Financial aid for historic buildings

3.1.1   *Budgetary limitations*

The Gowers Report (1950) *Houses of Outstanding Historic or Architectural Interest* led to the formation of the Historic Buildings Council.

Historic Buildings grants have been disbursed with wonderful skill and economy. But they are now inadequate even for the repair of country houses. Decaying historic city centres can hardly be touched.

The present budget for historic buildings (1967) is under £500,000. The following figures give some impression of comparative expenditure:

Housing Corporation: working capital	£100,000,000
Williamsburg (USA): outlay to 1965 (approx.)	£6,000,000
"Concorde" airliner (latest forecast)	£500,000,000
New Towns programme (to March 1966)	£430,260,000
Road Improvements:	
Hyde Park Corner, London	£5,000,000
Euston Road, London	£4,500,000
Historic Buildings Council for England:	
annual budget	£450,000

3.1.2   *Town grants*

The £33,000 per annum so far allocated to a few historic towns (Bath, Bradford-on-Avon, Brighton, Cheltenham, Harwich, King's Lynn, Winchester and York) futher reduces the minimal budget available.

The H.B.C. might be unable to undertake wider powers, but this heavy burden of historic towns remains untackled. If a new agency were set up to cope with this, at least the original budget would be freed for its own work.

3.2   Conservation:

A national or local responsibility?

3.2.1   *Inadequacy of grants*

Much is to be achieved, and historic towns change fast. Limited energy and finance must be effectively managed. Grants often bear no more relation to costs than school prizes to the cost of education. Would the conservation of old buildings be better achieved by setting up a new central authority, with really adequate powers?

3.2.2   *Local resources*

No local authority has unlimited capacities or resources. Many historic areas have been lost because of local party-political inertia. It is difficult for local authorities to initiate successful projects of long-term benefit whose advantage may not be attractive to the present councillor and to the electorate.

3.2.3   *Wider benefits*

The benefits of an historic town or conservation area may serve a neighbourhood much larger than the place within whose boundary it falls. Yet the cost must be met from local rates and the next election is never far ahead. Only massive financial aid could make a local authority undertake restoration work of the scale needed in a deteriorating national asset like Poole Old Town.

3.3   A new national agency: recommendations

3.3.1   *Financial support*

This is a problem of a national order. It seems certain that a new national agency is needed to deal with it.

Only a new, strong body with powerful financial support can cope adequately with the problems of historic town centres. These might best be tackled by a new corporation, perhaps called the Historic Towns Corporation.

3.3.2   *Staff and offices*

The order of funds and expenditure needed would require an able professional staff with offices in each region. These could well be related to the regional economic planning councils.

3.3.3   *Powers*

The new Corporation would need wide powers to acquire property, and to repair, manage and dispose of it efficiently.

3.4   The Land Commission Act and its powers

3.4.1   *Acquisition and development powers*

The Land Commission was given power to acquire areas that need redevelopment, conversion and repair. The land must, however, be "suitable for material development" within the meaning of the Land Commission Act, 1967, and its regulations. Leading experts on legal matters confirm that residential redevelopment such as that suggested on pages 164 and 226 of this report for Chester would be within the Act's scope.

3.4.2   *Procedure*

Planning permission is first required, and when this has been obtained, the Commission can step in under Section 6. After confirmation of a Compulsory Purchase Order, the Commission may carry out development itself, or do so in association with a local authority, or dispose of the land to a developer. Disposal can be by means of sale or the grant of a tenancy.

3.4.3 *"Best consideration"*
The Act only permits the Land Commission to dispose of land for the "best consideration in money or moneys worth which can reasonably be obtained". Land cannot, therefore, be sold for less than the acquisition costs.

3.4.4 *Exceptions*
Two exceptions to this are mentioned in the Act: where the Minister of Housing and Local Government so directs; and where disposal is by way of a Concessionary Crownhold.

3.4.5 *Concessionary Crownhold*
This tenure can only be granted for housing but would be eminently suitable for example in the St. Mary's Hill development suggested in this report. Further, covenants under the Concessionary Crownhold could ensure that the value of the environmental improvement gained by the redevelopment would eventually return to the community.

3.4.6 *Scale of resources*
Although it is anticipated that Land Commission betterment levies will produce £80,000,000 per annum eventually, only limited funds are so far available from land-dealing. A separate body like the suggested new Corporation could be set up under the auspices of the Land Commission and affiliated to it, specifically to deal with schemes in historic town centres. This can be achieved under existing legal powers.

3.5 Pilot schemes for conservation areas

3.5.1 *Selection*
The first duty of the Corporation would be to select a short-list of conservation areas for immediate survey and for "conservation and enhancement" as laid down in the Civic Amenities Act. The current pilot surveys commissioned by the Minister may afford a valuable immediate start.

3.5.2 *First duties*
A national assessment and grading of towns is virtually impossible. Limited available energies and resources are best concentrated at the most productive points.

3.5.3 *Reconstruction projects*
After completing the surveys, specific pilot reconstruction and rehabilitation schemes could be begun, in close association with each local authority. These should be widely publicised and accurate progress data kept.

3.5.4 *Re-investment*
In association with the Land Commission, the Corporation could manage each project in turn with the aim of re-sale on completion, thereby realising capital for each new scheme.

3.5.5 *Land economics research data*
Adequate data on the changing property values in conservation areas would help local authorities to analyse and manage them. A detailed study should be undertaken within the areas of the present pilot surveys

to plot values estimated biennially by the District Valuer over a 20-year period. This would provide invaluable information on urban economics that is not at present available.

3.5.6 *Maximum use of funds*
The Corporation would only be allowed to own property that was essential for its purposes. Where only a facade is valuable ownership can be limited to this, or, if planning control is insufficient, to covenants over it. The occupant would, in effect, merely transfer the value of the covenant. In this way, available capital could be used to maximum effect.

3.5.7 *Management*
There is no reason why the State should not manage these schemes as efficiently as the private London Estates or the Church Commissioners do.

Conservation locally: recommendations
3.5.8 *Local organisation*
The new Corporation could also promote the establishment of local conservation areas, run by local associations. The pattern would follow that of the present Housing Corporation and its local housing associations.

3.5.9 *Management*
Management would remain in the hands of the local authority, but the Corporation would promote local plans by grant or loan and in any situation of deadlock could assist by using its own special powers.

L.4 Positive planning: grants, encouragement and efficiency

4.0 Conservation can be encouraged by grants, loans and other positive incentives. The Historic Buildings Council (4.1) and the Historic Buildings Bureau (4.2), local authorities (4.3), private trusts (4.4) and purchasers (4.5) have each their part to play. National efficiency could at least be improved by a concerted effort to help planning authorities and private bodies to use skilled time to the maximum advantage (4.6).

4.1 The Historic Buildings Council: Recommendations

4.1.1 *Future budget*
The fund for country houses remains itself grossly inadequate, and unless the HBC's activities are to be still further restricted, the figure calls for urgent review.

4.1.2 *Conditions*
Grant conditions already require an assurance that the owner is unable without assistance to maintain the fabric, an undertaking on public access and approval of specifications and of the work by the Ministry's architects.

4.1.3 *Maintenance undertakings*
A prudent extra condition would be an undertaking on regular future repair and maintenance. This could include a triennial inspection, or a report from the architect.

4.1.4 *Emergency loans*

Both local authorities and the Historic Building Council can now assist by repair loans. An immediate loan can enable an owner to arrest galloping decay, such as dry rot. An emergency fund, at the disposal of the Council, could bring some economies in repair costs.

4.1.5 *Capital gains tax*

Estates mostly pay for repairs from capital, rather than from income. When capital assets are realised, capital gains tax is now incurred. This brings a disincentive to bear on grant-aided repairs, by increasing their cost. Either the tax provisions must be amended, or more grant money allocated.

4.1.6 *Chattels*

A grant may be made for repairing chattels; but it seems wrong that furnishings and art works designed for a house, or essentially part of its history, can be divorced from it in the name of estate duties, for instance, the Adam desk from Harewood. Furnishings essentially part of an historic house should remain in place, even if nationally owned.

4.1.7 *Dedicated covenants*

One way of bringing listed buildings under extra care would be by help in maintenance, in return for dedicated covenants. This might be given either by cash grant or, as in the case of Ancient Monuments under guardianship, by direct labour under qualified regional direction. Covenants would include the right to carry out regular structural surveys on behalf of the H.B.C. The possibilities are worth investigating.

4.2   The historic buildings bureau:

Recommendations
4.2.1   *Programme*

The Bureau has in the past been limited in its powers (e.g. to properties currently under consideration for a grant). An imaginative new programme is called for to co-ordinate all public and private efforts.

4.2.2   *Beneficial use*

By no means all historic buildings owned by local authorities are well looked after or in beneficial use. Some fine houses have been publicly purchased for the sake of their grounds. Many have thereafter been neglected or disused.

4.2.3   *Minister's powers*

In such cases, the Historic Buildings Bureau should have the duty of pressing the point. Where it seems a user can be found, the Minister should be ready to use his powers of compulsory purchase.

Funds for compulsory purchase and repair
4.2.4   *A holding fund*

When a building is threatened with sale for demolition, an authority can step in, but may be obliged to play down its value for fear of aiding the opposition. But a stranded building needs time and publicity to find its purchaser.

4.2.5   *A bank for buildings*

A means of breaking this deadlock would be a National Holding Fund for threatened property in effect a bank for buildings which could then be purchased at their open market value, improved and re-sold.

4.2.6   *Acquisition by the local authority*

The Minister may assist by grant an authority which compulsorily acquires an outstanding historic building under the Local Authorities (Historic Buildings) Act, 1962. But applications are rare and the power little used, because the acquiring authority must still find the whole cost of repairs.

Meanwhile, neglected buildings need not reach the market, and an owner may hold on to them, allowing decay to increase, so as to force the authority's hand. Under the Civic Amenities Act, an authority can purchase and re-sell an endangered building, but has still no incentive to take the risk.

4.2.7   *Offers to tender*

Powers might be given to local authorities to advertise such a property, inviting "offers to tender" before acquiring it. It could then be re-offered with the backing of grant aid and a local authority mortgage, on condition of repair to a specified standard.

4.3   Assistance by local authorities

Local Historic Buildings Grants:
Recommendations
4.3.1   *Progress*

Little opportunity has yet been taken by some councils of the grant and loan powers available to them under the Local Authorities (Historic Buildings) Act, 1962.

4.3.2   *Publicity*

Counties have differed widely in their liveliness. The Civic Trust quotes contrasting annual averages of £7 18s. and 2s. 0d. per 1,000 population. The grant system should be widely publicised.

4.3.3   *An annual return*

No central record is yet kept of the grants made. An annual return should be required to remind authorities of their powers and responsibilities.

4.3.4   *Subsidy*

The reluctance of authorities might be overcome by a regular annual subsidy, withheld in any year when no grant had been made. A "pound-for-pound" agreement can often help.

4.3.5   *Token grants*

The time-cost to the local authority of assessing an application is high. It may involve a structural survey, an architectural assessment, financial enquiries and the inspection of the work. Grants of less than, say, £250 might well be restricted at the discretion of planning committees to "policy" items like re-thatching. Public effort could thus be spent on the building rather than in administration.

Application procedure
4.3.6   *Report*

Local authorities would find it helpful to have stronger central guidance on the conditions and administration of these grants. Reports and quotations by commercial specialists can frighten tenants into collecting death-watch beetles as "evidence" or abandoning the property. A proper architectural report, required as a condition of application, would safeguard the spending of public money.

4.3.7 *Specification*
A priced specification should be required, showing the cost of all items for assessment.

4.3.8 *Contract*
Formal conditions of contract should be submitted (for instance, rates for overheads, profit and transport).

4.3.9 *Drawings*
To facilitate consideration, a photograph and a drawing of the existing state of the property should be required with every grant application. Afterwards, these might go to the National Monuments Record.

Recommendations on improvement grants
4.3.10 *Standards*
Most are sensible, but it is illogical to require larders as a condition of grant, in days of refrigerators. It is understood that this requirement is under review.

4.3.11 *Procedure*
A standard procedure would help, for instance, clear guidance on what rate of fees and expenses is eligible and whether competitive tenders are required.

4.3.12 *Time limit*
A time limit for dealing with grant applications would help to reduce indecision and planning blight.

4.3.13 *Cost increases*
To bring home the realities, the approved cost of the works should be defined as including basic cost-increases incurred during the time an application is under consideration.

4.3.14 *Subdivided houses*
Listed buildings are often subdivided, so that a new bathroom for each part would call for external additions, now or in future. An incentive would be increased grants for recombining these divided units.

4.3.15 *Improvement areas*
The Housing Act 1964. In these obligations can be placed upon owners of houses which lack basic amenities. Councils using the procedure could usefully thereby advertise improvement grants and their scope (for instance, partitioning-off 'corridor' bedrooms and damp-proofing).

4.3.16 *Advice*
In visiting improvement areas and houses applying for grant aid, council officers could give much help by advising on simple structural maintenance.

Removing disincentives
4.3.17 *Rate increases*
An illogical situation arises when a building has been expensively repaired and reduced in size. By becoming more manageable, it incurs higher rates. Even new central heating can bring a back-hander for owners.

A small and virtually notional way of encouraging owners to improve listed properties would be to grant a period of grace of say 10 years without rate increase. The cost would be nominal, while removing a deterrent to good management.

4.3.18 *Closing and demolition orders*
Public health departments have sometimes to look for trouble and defects, with less opportunity of making positive repair recommendations.

Certain situations are 'crossroads', after which no return is possible. For a listed domestic building, a Closing Order can be fatal. An authority serving an Order should be required to notify the Minister.
Closer definition. An order at present covers an entire property, both its good and bad parts. It can thus be served even on a listed building whose unfitness is caused by worthless later rear additions. Closer definition is needed.

4.3.19 *A maintenance advisory service for listed buildings*
Little provision is yet made for ready public advice on the structural condition of a listed building (except technically for Ancient Monuments in 'guardianship'). Small timely improvements can often save deterioration and loss. Many people have no idea of the needs of a building. Architects and surveyors will know the almost dread reflection when first introduced to a building, of 'if only I had been asked before'. Neglect accumulates at compound interest.

4.3.20 *Property inspections*
We suggest a service of property inspections, designed to help owners of older property. This could readily be given by the building inspector; but it needs to be more positive than any system yet known to us.

4.3.21 *Local authority initiative*
Building inspectors could also draw to the attention of their authority any building known to be in need of urgent grant assistance. Often an indigent owner has no knowledge of these grants.

4.3.22 *Repair loans*
Loans for conversion, repair and improvement (Housing [Financial Provisions] Act 1958) are available, although few are aware of the loans available, which should be more widely publicised.

4.4. Private trust funds

4.4.1 *County trusts*
Several counties have set up Historic Buildings Trusts. But their funds are limited and rarely stretch to town-centre property.

4.4.2 *Charitable trusts*
Of our 100,000 private charitable trusts in Britain, many give grants for old buildings. The Pilgrim Trust (£150,000 per year) and the Historic Churches Preservation Trust (£300,000) alone almost equal the budget of the Historic Buildings Council. The National Trust spends £1,500,000 annually on maintenance.

Recommendations

4.4.3 *Tax remission*
Trustees are selected for ability and rarely live on the premises. Trust beneficiaries receive the income but may have no other interest. Taxation is a disincentive to good management and needs recasting to allow tax remissions for repair work.

4.4.4 *Group ownership*
Property value is often collective rather than individual. Voluntary pooling of ownership on a shareholder basis can give stronger bargaining power and economy in costs. Resale can include covenants in the common interest.

4.4.5 *Church property*
Church of England. Churches as well as parsonage houses are now inspected quinquennially. The reports often go astray, and a copy should be collated (if possible, at the Council for the Care of Churches) as a valuable source of reference.

Other denominations. No system exists. Regular qualified inspection is a necessity to guard against damage and loss.

4.5 Private purchase and mortgage

4.5.1 *Mortgages*
Much property is owned by building societies, who are strongly placed to encourage good management. Yet the difficulty of obtaining mortgages on older property is well known. Almost £1,000,000,000 annually is advanced by building societies, the loans being based upon valuation.

4.5.2 *Under-valuation*
Since only for a new house is any exact cost known, valuations may cover against error by quoting lower figures for older houses. There are thus two values: the actual market figure at which older properties change hands; and the notional one at which valuations are covered. The colossal value of older property held by building societies means that the difference between these two represents many millions of pounds.

Recommendations

4.5.3 *Underwriting valuations*
We suggest therefore either: (*a*) a system of encouraging a less pessimistic valuation (for example, by underwriting open market prices for building societies); or (*b*) setting against the rare losses through forced sale, the true value of undervalued property already in building society ownership. This would release a great fund of actual but unrecognised values; and we recommend research into how it could be done.

4.5.4 *Guarantee scheme*
An extension of the insurance company guarantee scheme, which societies already themselves apply to high-percentage mortgages, might enable this false ceiling to be most usefully raised.

4.6 Efficiency and national resources

4.6.1 *Simplified application forms*
A *Standard Application Form for planning con* should be designed with extreme clarity to remove confusion between:
a identifying particulars;
b statements for signature;
c questions for answer;
d requests for descriptions;
e alternatives for deletion;
f references to enclosures;
g supplementary sections for special cases;
h the relevant definitions, notes, instructions exhortations which usually follow.

Careful layout, numbering, tabulation and printing give a document clarity, and save time and confu Application forms, not only for planning consent, for grants (Improvement Grants and Historic Build Grants), Forms of Notification (of listing), Orders as Tree Preservation Orders, and the rest, are in fusion. Yet they could so easily be clearly designed time is ripe for a massive recasting of documentatie

4.6.2 *Publicity*
Explanatory circulars or posters like those issued b General Post Office would encourage clear applica and better public relations.

4.6.3 *Time-cost of planning*
It is the lack of appreciation of the value of time v in this country bedevils progress and development. may be divided into 'time taken' and 'time wasted' many delays fall into the latter category.

4.6.4 *An American example*
An application to demolish or alter a 'landmar New York is considered within 30 days. If the appl claims that a 'reasonable return' (defined as 6 per on the valuation of the property) is impossible, are 90 days for consultation. Tax exemption or remi is considered and may be recommended on any re of consent. Failing this a sale or lease must be arra within 180 days. After this the Landmarks Commi must acquire a protective interest, or the owner is to proceed.

4.6.5 *Avoiding delay*
Delay in considering planning applications is costly owner. Procedures in any new legislation shoul designed to encourage good development by approval.

4.6.6 *Time limits*
More time may be given to local planning autho to consider applications for listed buildings; and period of notice is now extended to a maximu 6 months: but this must not make for automatic d

4.6.7 *Inadequate applications*
Planning officers are kept from 'opportunity' plar and from public initiative projects by the time energy taken in redesigning ineptly prepared app tions. Ministers' circulars should support plar authorities in rejecting these, making clear that they not redesign all material thoughtlessly or impro submitted. Good material should be quickly pa other applications suffering the consequences of own inadequacy.

4.6.8 *A management study*
The future of planning will be clearer after the Royal Commission on Local Government has reported. Accurate data is needed on the staffing and skills of the planning offices. A management survey into the cost of time and the best skills for the job would help to recast for maximum efficiency.

4.6.9 *More time or more efficiency*
It is unnecessary to increase the time for a procedure when simpler methods might bring greater economy. The efficiency of individual departments should be tested by periodic review. Would for example a single conservation department be more efficient for the work now divided between the Historic Buildings Council, the Royal Commission on Historical Monuments, the Royal Fine Art Commission, the Ancient Monuments Board of the Ministry of Works, the Historic Buildings Section of the Ministry of Housing, and so on?

4.6.10 *Departmental mergers*
The Departments of State appear to some to overlap, and the Minister may wish to consider the opportunity of further mergers like that between his Advisory Committee and the Historic Buildings Council, in rationalising their work.

4.6.11 *Private societies*
Similarly in the private field, many say amenity societies should combine. But here the mainspring which makes these societies so productive is the opportunity they bring for devoted, if often underpaid service. It is likely that a forced marriage would be less productive than the present friendly rivalry. The Civic Trust, formed to focus the work and objectives of local societies, is now dividing into regional Trusts. Overlapping should be reduced by joint consultation and with a minimum loss of identity.

Terms of reference

Ministry of Housing and Local Government,
Whitehall
August 1966

1   The Consultant is asked to study and report on the implications of a conservation policy for the historic centre of Chester.

2   The broad object of the policy will be to preserve and, where possible, promote and enhance the architectural and historic character of the area, in order to maintain its life and economic buoyancy.

3   The conservation area which is to be the subject of the study will be that within and including the immediate exterior of the City Walls with an addition bounded by the planned line of the inner ring road to its junction with Foregate Street and thence along Dee Lane and the right bank of the River Dee to the south-east angle of the City Walls.
The Consultant will within that area:
categorise the condition and quality of buildings in relation to their value to the Chester scene under the headings of:
a must be preserved;
b should, if possible, be preserved; and
c buildings not within (a) or (b) which are unlikely to remain economically viable and are expendable; and define any areas which are worthy of conservation as a group even if they contain few or no listed buildings.

4   The study should identify in detail the particular features—buildings, groups of buildings, street patterns, street scenes, spaces and other aspects of the selected area—which it is thought desirable to preserve, and should explain the reasons for the choice. It will also be necessary in some cases to consider the suitability of these buildings or groups of buildings to fulfil their present function or their adaptability where necessary to some other function.

5   The study should:
i *take account* of the various practical problems, among others—
a motor traffic and car parking, covering both long-term solutions and interim remedial measures; for this purpose the Consultant may assume the completion within a reasonable period of years of the inner ring road and outer ring road as planned and the provision of central and peripheral car parks as shown in the Grenfell Baines central area plan which has been adopted in principle by the Council;
b commercial pressures on the area, and how they can be met without damaging its character, or alternatively how they can be accommodated elsewhere; for this purpose the Consultant will be supplied with statistics relating to recent large-scale shopping and office development and similar development for which planning approval has been given, and in considering this aspect the Consultant may wish to give special consideration to the Queen Street and Lower Bridge Street areas as potential growth points in relation to conservation needs in those areas; and
ii *deal with*
a the preservation of listed buildings in the area, including the economics of restoration and maintenance, or where necessary conversion to new uses. This may involve some consideration of the existing or proposed land uses within the area and of the amounts of accommodation likely to be required for different purposes in future;
b the measures to be taken for environmental improvement in the area;
c the control and guidance of any necessary new development, to ensure that it is sympathetic to the environment both in design and quality;
d generally, the total cost of conservation, including the public expenditure required (other than public works which the local authority would normally undertake apart from the direct needs of a conservation policy) and the programming of this expenditure;
e any possible new sources of revenue which may occur to the Consultant or which may be drawn to his attention.

6   It will not be possible to consider the problems of the conservation area in isolation from the rest of the town, and the Consultant will need to relate his proposals to the current planning proposals for the town as a whole. But if he finds it impossible he should say so and why.

7   Similarly, while the study will necessarily be carried out within the framework of existing legislation, the Consultant will be free to suggest any changes in the law which seem to him to be necessary.

8   The Council will make available to the Consultant any existing survey information or other relevant material in their possession including up to date Ordnance Survey maps. He should also take into account any conservation measures already being prepared or carried out by the local authority or other bodies, for example, the Civic Trust or preservation society.

9   The results of the study and recommendations should be presented in the form of a report with supplementary maps and diagrams not later than 31st October 1967, the report to become the property of the Ministry and the Council, to whom all publication rights will be surrendered.

10   The Clients will be jointly the Ministry of Housing and Local Government and the Chester County Borough Council. For the purposes of co-ordination any further instructions shall be conveyed to the Consultant by or through the Town Clerk of Chester, but this should not exclude inter-consultant co-ordination arranged by the Ministry.

Acknowledgements

This survey has been prepared throughout in close co-operation with the officers of the Chester City Corporation and the Ministry of Housing and Local Government. Of the former we especially acknowledge with gratitude the patience and assistance of the Town Clerk, Gerald Burkinshaw, OBE, and the City Engineer and Surveyor, A. H. F. Jiggens, MIMunE, AMICE, FRICS, AMTPI, and their respective staffs. At the Ministry we have received special co-operation from the Preservation Policy Group, the Historic Buildings Section and the Map Library.

Our gratitude is due to G. Grenfell Baines, OBE, DipTP, FRIBA, MTPI, of Building Design Partnership, whose report *Chester: A Plan for the Central Area* (October 1964) has been a valuable basis for our continued studies of the City's conservation problems. Whilst the conclusions of our report differ in detail, this is the inevitable result of alternative approaches to the developing problems of a living city.

In Chester, we have received the utmost help and co-operation from all sides. We particularly wish to thank the Very Revd G. W. O. Addleshaw, MA, BD, Dean of Chester; Quentin Hughes, MC, B Arch, PhD, DipCD, FRIBA; James Chandler, MBE, and Dr John Tomlinson, MB, BS, Chester Civic Trust; Peter Shobbrook, ARIBA; P. D. Pocklington, FLA, and his staff at the library; D. F. Petch, BA, FSA, AMA, of the Grosvenor Museum; Mrs Berry, City Archivist; F. H. Thompson, MC, MA, FSA, AMA, the former Curator; and Captain Quellyn Roberts, DSO.

We would also thank the Clerk, the Planning Officer and the County Architect of the Cheshire County Council, and Tom Hancock, FRIBA, for valuable help and advice.

Much specialist information has been freely provided by the public service undertakings, notably the Cheshire Constabulary, the Chester Fire Brigade, the Post Office, the Gas Board, the Electricity Board, the Water Board, Chester Telephone Area, British Rail, and the Corporation and Crosville Bus Companies.

Many professional firms, estate agents, manufacturers, store and shopkeepers, local newspaper offices and hoteliers spared us much of their time and gave us valuable information. For their kindness, interest and forbearance our most grateful thanks go to the Cestrians who invited us freely and generously into their buildings. Without them, this survey would not have been possible, and would lack any real understanding of the City's fundamental nature and problems.

Our thanks are also due to David Challis and John Saville, who designed this Report in conjunction with our editorial advisor, Michael Wright.

Photography and illustrations

Permission to reproduce photographs and illustrations is gratefully acknowledged as follows:

Walter Scott, Bradford (by courtesy of Leslie Burnett): 22a, 27, 119b;

Will R. Rose Ltd (by courtesy of Chester City Library): 23, 26 (by courtesy of Peter Shobbrook) 30, 155c;

Aerofilms Ltd: 112b, 130b, 142b, 150b, 168b, 176b, 188b, 189a, 198b, 206b;

Chester City Library Photographic Collection: 29a, 50a, 101b;

Chester Archaeological Society Journal, Vol. 45: 22b;

The Times: 61c;

Chester Chronicle: 36c, 79a, 82a, 95, 97, 98;

Chester Observer: 46a;

Cheshire County Planning Department: 155a and c, 156a, 158b, 160;

The late P. H. Lawson: 91b;

K. H. Williams: 67;

The map on page 21 is adapted from one by F. H. Thompson, who also allowed us to use photograph 20a.

All the remaining photographs were taken by Christopher Dalton and by members of the survey team.

Survey team

Donald W. Insall, ARIBA, ÁMTPI, SPDip
Peter E. Locke, ARIBA
Iona M. Reid, Dipl Arch, ARIBA
Alan J. Frost, AA Dipl, ARIBA, DCHM
Allan G. Tapley, ARICS, AIQS
Janet E. Smith
Margaret Tallet, ARIBA
Peter Britton, ARICS
Marjorie Law
Geoffrey Lawson, AMIMunE, AMInstHE
Roger France, AADipl, ARIBA
G. Scott Calder, ARIBA
Michael Burrell, ARIBA
John Sanday, B Arch, Dipl Arch, RWA

Specialist advice
Legal: Desmond Heap, LLM, PPTPI
Rosalind J. Mackworth
A. Elizabeth Insall, BA
Land Economics: Messrs Gerald Eve & Co.
Traffic: Professor Alan Proudlove MEng, MIMunE, AMIHE
Regional Economics Board and the Council for the North West

Editorial
Michael Wright, MA

Artwork and illustration
Catherine Conder, DipAD
Angela Symes, DipAD
Caroline Bullock, DipAD
Carol Shillito
Noel Quesada
Barbara Oxley, DipAD
Audrey Frew, ARCA
Jennifer Granville-Dixon
Michael Ritter

Secretarial, research and co-ordination
Margaret Sharp
Caroline Scott
Alice White
Nora Rackstraw
Josie Cunningham

Fold-out map 1
Pedestrians in Chester
This map shows the existing
network and hazards

Green spaces open to the public

Pedestrian routes

∗ Serious accidents

★ Slight accidents

Pedestrian routes crossing roads
and shared roads

Areas of dual use
pedestrian and vehicles

● Access points between
different pedestrian levels

▼ Barriers to
through-pedestrian passage

·········· Narrow

Fold-out map 2
Historic buildings
This map shows those at
present listed by the Ministry
of Housing and Local
Government, 1955

Grade I

Grade II*

Grade II

Grade III

¼ MILE

Fold-out map 3
Historic buildings
This map shows the proposed
revision of the Ministry's lists

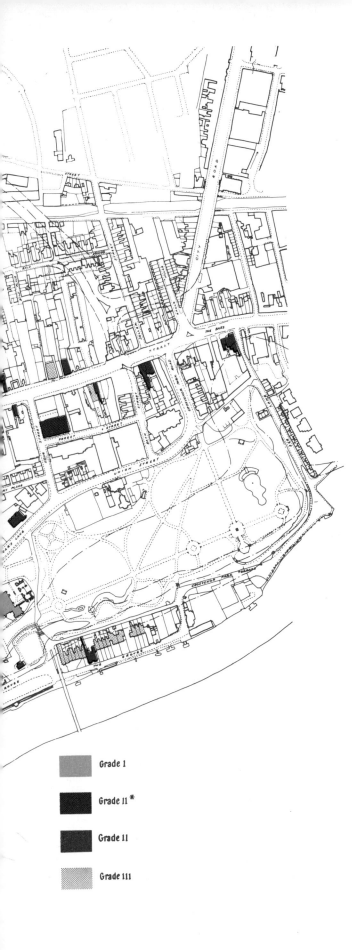

Grade 1

Grade 11 *

Grade 11

Grade 111

¼ MILE

Fold-out map 4
Financial distribution
This map indicates the expenditure now required to secure the future of Chester's historic buildings

Inspected and listed buildings
needing more than £1,000 spent on them

■ £10,000 and over

■ £5,000 — 10,000

▨ £1,000 — 5,000

JULY 1967

**Fold-out map 5
Summary of the report's
recommendations**

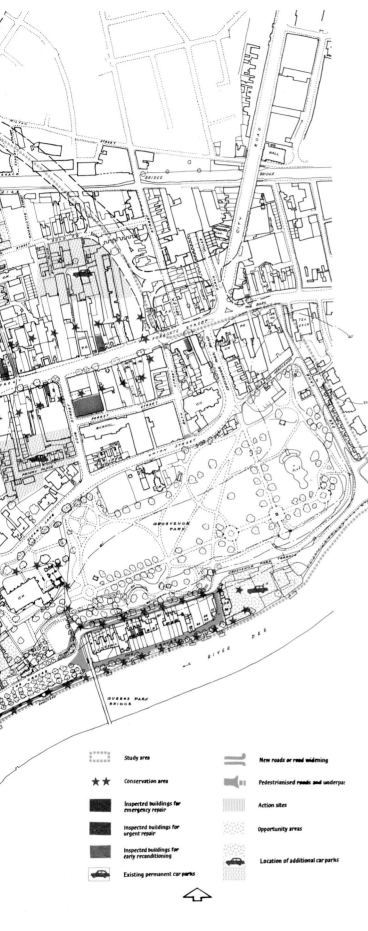

Study area		New roads or road widening	
★ ★ Conservation area		Pedestrianised roads and underpa:	
Inspected buildings for emergency repair		Action sites	
Inspected buildings for urgent repair		Opportunity areas	
Inspected buildings for early reconditioning		Location of additional car parks	
Existing permanent car parks			

Studies in conservation

Classified guide to selected topics

	Bath	Chester	Chichester	York
Advertisement control				
Areas of special control		L.2.4.14	4.48ff	
			7.64	
			10.03	
Window stickers			7.115	
Agencies for Conservation				
(See also Civic Societies				
Economics & Finance, Ownership)				
Role of the local authority	112	4.3	8.31	6.3
	123	L.3.5.8	8.49	10.3ff
	136		Chapter 9	
	238			
	247			
Historic Buildings Council	112ff	L.4.1	7.139	6.4
Housing Societies		4.3.3		7.37
Land Commission		L.4	8.34	8.13
			Chapter 8	Appendix G
A National Agency?	124-5	4.3.4		10.3
		4.3.5		
		L.3		
University Grants Committee	142			9.20–21
	Appendix B 1a			
Churches				
Condition & Use	62		2.09	6.6
			2.17	8.105
			4.43	8.123
			6.26	
			7.81	
Cathedral cities		3.3	3.03ff	
			3.27	
Civic Societies				
As agents in rehabilitation schemes	100	L.4.6.11	4.44	6.5
			7.138	
			9.08-09	
			9.12	
Conservation Areas				
Conservation section proposed				10.3
Criteria and check list for			Appendix II	
Designation of		4.2	5.01	6.18
Differing views about their proper size and function	35	L.2	5.01-02	10.5
			Chapter 9	10.9
				10.10
Development control in		L.2.4	7.102	10.7
			10.13	
Cost-Benefit Analysis		2.6	8.05-10	Appendix G 4.0
Densities				
Residential		2.7.1	4.02	7.18
			6.76	7.27
			7.33ff	8.12

	Bath	Chester	Chichester	York
Design of buildings				
Control by planning authorities	92ff	2.3		
New design in relation to old buildings	94-100	2.3.9	5.09ff	8.144
	243-5		6.40ff	10.17
			7.66	
			7.99-124	
			9.45ff	
			10.10	
			10.13	
Height of new buildings				8.138
Materials			5.11-12	
			6.40-43	
			7.94ff	
			9.40	
			10.03	
			10.11	
Economics and Finance				
Costs of conversion and renovation	143-4	2.6	Chapter 8	9.15ff
	149-152	4.3	9.49	Appendix G
	156-7	4.4		
	160			
	Appendix B			
Grants				
(a) By local authority	112ff	4.4	4.40	6.15ff
	133	L.4.3	7.139	
	136		Chapter 8	
	161		10.17	
(b) By Exchequer	121ff	4.3	Chapter 8	6.15ff
	239	L.3	10.17	
	241	L.4.1		
Historic Buildings Council and Town Schemes	112ff	L.4.1	7.139	6.4
Housing improvement grants	117ff	L.4.3		
Recoupment			Chapter 8	9.19ff
				Appendix G 5.0
Employment		1.4	3.29-31	3.6
			6.78	3.8
Industry				
Compatibility with historic area	70	2.7.1		3.7
Relocation of		2.7.1	4.02	4.7ff
			4.47	
Legal Aspects				
Present legislation considered adequate	101ff			
	246			
Changes in compulsory purchase and			Chapter 8	
compensation provisions suggested			10.18-19	
Possible conflicts with particular enactments	103ff	2.8.4	7.99	10.7
(e.g. Building Regulations, Housing Acts)	142ff			
General review of legislation		L.1-L.4		
Use Classes Order				8.144
Lists of buildings of special architectural or historic interest				
Assessment of the lists and	18ff	2.8.6	7.130-141	6.11-13
suggestions for revision		L.1	10.12	
Offices	68-69	2.7.4	6.49	3.8
		4.1.3	6.52-54	4.15
			7.65ff	
			7.85	
			10.06	

	Bath	Chester	Chichester	York
Townscape appraisal		2.3	4.44-45	Appendix B
		Chapter 3	6.04ff	
			7.03ff	
Traffic				
Effect on environment	44	2.4.1	3.38ff	5.23
	72	2.4.8	5.06ff	
	240	2.4.9	6.95ff	
	Chapter 5			
Industrial				5.44ff
Local, analysis of		2.4.2	6.100ff	5.12
Pedestrians and traffic	Chapter 5	2.4.9	4.12ff	5.52
		2.4.10	5.06ff	
			6.95ff	
			7.145ff	
			9.33ff	
			10.04	
Public transport		2.4.6	4.30-32	5.14ff
		2.4.7	7.28	
		2.4.10		
Management schemes and parking	Chapter 5	2.4.3	4.17-18	5.13
	242	2.4.7	6.79-83	5.20
		2.4.10	Chapter 7	5.29ff
			10.14	
Noise, reduction of		2.4.8		5.47
Servicing	41	2.4.5	4.15-16	5.39ff
	Chapter 5	3.2.3	6.84-87	
			7.07ff	
			9.35	
Through traffic			4.08	5.6
			7.07	
Turntables			7.18	
			7.25	
New types of vehicle			4.30-32	5.32
			7.28	
Trees and open spaces	29ff	2.7.1	2.06	8.139ff
		2.7.6	3.11-13	
		2.8.3	4.45	
		Chapter 3	6.19-20	
		4.2.2	6.56-58	
			7.29-63	
			9.42ff	
Use of land and buildings				
Condition and maintenance	38	2.7	6.61ff	Chapter 7
		2.8.2	7.94ff	
		2.8.4		
		Chapter 3		
Unused upper floors	37	2.7.3	6.47ff	7.8
	51	2.8.1	7.65ff	7.21
	168	3.2.3	8.25-6	7.29ff
	235	3.5.3	10.03	
			10.07	
			10.09	

Cost of conversion — see under Economics
Student accommodation — see under Residence

St. Clements Fosh & Cross Limited, 80/92 Mansell Street, London E1